Praise for THE GREEN NEW DEAL

"Jeremy Rifkin's *The Green New Deal* presents the most comprehensive and compelling narrative to transition the U.S. energy, telecommunications, and transportation sectors into a smart Third Industrial Revolution. While our national leaders have been unable to find common ground, Rifkin provides a bipartisan means to accelerate our nation's path toward decarbonization."
—Robert Wilhite, Managing Director, Navigant Consulting (Navigant Global Energy is the largest energy and sustainability consulting team in the industry)

"The United States is falling behind the European Union and now China in the race to prepare our economies for the low-carbon future. Rifkin's new book gives the US the crucial narrative it needs to confront the 'carbon bubble' of stranded assets increasingly threatening the stability of the global financial system. And his advice is not just for the US. The 9,200 cities that are part of the Global Covenant of Mayors for Climate & Energy have a lot to learn from Rifkin's work with pioneer smart cities and regions in Europe." **—Maroš Šefčovič, Vice President of the European Commission and Co-Chair of the Global Covenant of Mayors for Climate & Energy**

"Rifkin is bold, prescient, and revolutionary. The urgent global public health and humanitarian impacts of Climate Change are well upon us and accelerating. Rifkin charts a tough and achievable path forward—distributed, open source, glocal and green—and brings us to the threshold of a New Beginning."
—James Orbinski, MD, former International President of Doctors Without Borders

"*The Green New Deal* is impressive in its ability to connect the dots of environmental, political, social, and geographical issues that define our sustainable future. Rifkin has laid out a vast Green New Deal plan that is radical and defensible for a historic twenty-year retrofit of the nation's millions of buildings to reduce global warming emissions, taking us into a green century."
—Gordon Gill, Principal, Adrian Smith + Gordon Gill Architecture (ranked the number one architecture firm in the United States of America by *Architect* magazine)

"In *The Green New Deal*, Jeremy Rifkin presents a survival imperative for the millions without work and for a planet that needs healing. In this timely book, he defines the urgent steps that will need to be taken to transition from fossil fuels to renewable energy and reclaim public infrastructure."

—**Dr. Vandana Shiva, feminist, ecologist,**
and recipient of the Right Livelihood Award

"Energy is the economic, social, and existential issue of our time. Jeremy Rifkin's command of the issue in all its shades and shapes is unsurpassed. His narrative deftly deconstructs the future energy problem set, soberly chronicles the zeitgeist, and offers a bold snapshot of the future with an accompanying roadmap. *The Green New Deal* is singular in its holistic perspective on the necessary energy revolution—from addressing the clean resource mix to identifying financing alternatives to emphasizing the importance of reinventing the oft-forgotten grid infrastructure to the overarching demand for social equity. It's all here—a must read."

—**Anne Pramaggiore, CEO of Exelon Utilities**

"Jeremy Rifkin's groundbreaking ideas have long been the staple diet of enlightened political leaders across the world. *The Green New Deal* shows why his work remains more important than ever. In charting the natural decline of fossil fuel industrialization, Rifkin offers a compelling prescription for how the green economy has the potential to unlock the sustainable growth of the future."

—**Paul Polman, former CEO of Unilever and**
Vice-Chair of the United Nations Global Compact,
the world's largest corporate sustainability initiative

THE
GREEN
NEW DEAL

THE GREEN NEW DEAL

WHY THE FOSSIL FUEL CIVILIZATION WILL COLLAPSE BY 2028, and THE BOLD ECONOMIC PLAN TO SAVE LIFE ON EARTH

JEREMY RIFKIN

ST. MARTIN'S GRIFFIN

NEW YORK

Published in the United States by St. Martin's Griffin, an imprint of St. Martin's Publishing Group

THE GREEN NEW DEAL. Copyright © 2019 by Jeremy Rifkin. All rights reserved. Printed in the United States of America. For information, address St. Martin's Press, 120 Broadway, New York, NY 10271.

www.stmartins.com

Design by Meryl Sussman Levavi

The Library of Congress has cataloged the hardcover edition as follows:

Names: Rifkin, Jeremy, author.
Title: The green New Deal : why the fossil fuel civilization will collapse by
    2028, and the bold economic plan to save life on earth / Jeremy Rifkin.
Description: First edition. | New York : St. Martin's Press, 2019. | Includes
    bibliographical references and index.
Identifiers: LCCN 2019021341 | ISBN 9781250253200 (hardcover) |
    ISBN 9781250253217 (ebook)
Subjects: LCSH: Energy policy—Environmental aspects. | Clean energy—
    Government policy. | Sustainable development—Government policy.
Classification: LCC HD9502.A2 R537 2019 | DDC 333.79—dc23
LC record available at https://lccn.loc.gov/2019021341

ISBN 978-1-250-76611-3 (trade paperback)

Our books may be purchased in bulk for promotional, educational, or business use. Please contact your local bookseller or the Macmillan Corporate and Premium Sales Department at 1-800-221-7945, extension 5442, or by email at MacmillanSpecialMarkets@macmillan.com.

First St. Martin's Griffin Edition: 2020

10 9 8 7 6 5 4 3 2 1

To Carol, for suggesting that I write this book.
As usual, you were ahead of me.

CONTENTS

THE
GREEN
NEW DEAL

INTRODUCTION

We are facing a global emergency. Our scientists tell us that human-induced climate change brought on by the burning of fossil fuels has taken the human race and our fellow species into the sixth mass extinction event of life on Earth. Yet few people alive today are even aware of this emerging reality. The Intergovernmental Panel on Climate Change (IPCC), a scientific body of the United Nations, issued a dire warning in October 2018 that global warming emissions are accelerating and that we are on the verge of a series of escalating climatic events, imperiling life on the planet. The IPCC estimated that human activity has caused the temperature to rise 1°C (Celsius) above preindustrial levels and predicted that if it crosses a threshold beyond 1.5°C, it will unleash runaway feedback loops and a cascade of climate-change events that would decimate the Earth's ecosystems.[1] There would be no return to the kind of life we know today.

According to the famed Harvard biologist Edward O. Wilson, "the extinction of species by human activity continues to accelerate, fast enough to eliminate more than half of all species by the end of this century"—by the time today's toddlers are senior citizens.[2] The last time the Earth experienced an extinction event of this magnitude was 65 million years ago.[3] The IPCC concluded that to avoid the environmental abyss we would have to cut the emission of global warming gases 45 percent from 2010 levels—and we only have twelve years left to make this happen.[4] This will require a transformation of our global economy, our society, and our very way of life without precedent in human history. In other words, the human race faces a razor-thin timeline for a radical reorientation of civilization.

The wakeup call came in the November 2018 national elections in the United States. A younger generation of congresspersons came to Washington and the House of Representatives passionately committed to a radical redirection of the American economy to address climate change while simultaneously creating new green businesses and employment that will ensure a more equitable distribution of the fruits of life. In November, young protesters from the Sunrise Movement stormed the halls of Congress and staged sit-ins in the offices of Nancy Pelosi, soon to become Speaker of the House of Representatives, and Steny Hoyer, the incoming majority leader of the House. The protesters were joined by Congresswoman-elect Alexandria Ocasio-Cortez.

Ocasio-Cortez called for the creation of a select committee in the incoming House tasked with the mission of creating a "Green New Deal" for America. The committee would set a one-year deadline to create an industrial plan to address climate change, decarbonize the economic infrastructure within ten years, create new business opportunities, and employ millions of disadvantaged workers in an emerging green economy—a bold "aspirational" proposal far beyond anything yet put forward by America's cities, counties, and states.[5] In the new term, congressional leadership equivocated on the proposal and ultimately established a Select Committee on the Climate Crisis with little power to act.

Meanwhile, on February 7, 2019, Ocasio-Cortez in the House and Ed Markey in the Senate introduced a Green New Deal resolution. One hundred and three members of Congress have already cosponsored it, including several of the major presidential contenders within the Democratic Party: Bernie Sanders, Kamala Harris, Cory Booker, Elizabeth Warren, and Kirsten Gillibrand.[6] Democratic presidential hopefuls Julián Castro and Beto O'Rourke have also lent their support to a Green New Deal. So have former vice president Al Gore and three hundred state and local government officials from across the country, including South Bend mayor Pete Buttigieg, another Democratic presidential aspirant. There is no doubt that the Green New Deal has energized both progressive politicians and a younger generation of voters and will be a central theme of the 2020 national electoral campaigns.

Elected officials are sensing a sea change in public opinion that is quickly moving the issue of climate change from near obscurity to make it the central issue facing the American people. In blue and red states across America, individuals, families, workers, and businesses are becoming frightened about the violent changes in the weather and the deteriorating impact that climate change is having on ecosystems, causing widespread property damage, disruption of the business cycle, and loss of human life.

A December 2018 public opinion poll conducted by the Yale Program on Climate Change Communication and the George Mason University Center for Climate Change Communication found that 73 percent of respondents think global warming is happening—an increase of 10 percentage points since 2015—and nearly half (46 percent) say they have experienced the effects of global warming—an increase of 15 percentage points since 2015. Moreover, 48 percent of Americans agree that people across the United States "are being harmed by global warming 'right now,'" an increase of 16 percentage points since 2015. Most disquieting of all, an overwhelming majority of Americans believe that global warming is harming the world's poor (67 percent), plant and animal species (74 percent), and future generations (75 percent).[7]

The turnaround in the national mood comes in the aftermath of an escalating number of catastrophic climate events over the past decade. What makes climate change so terrifying is that it disrupts the Earth's hydrosphere, which is essential to maintaining life. Earth is the watery planet. Our ecosystems have evolved over eons in consort with the water cycles that traverse the planet via the clouds. Here's the rub. For each one-degree rise in the temperature on Earth attributed to the increase of global warming emissions, the water-holding capacity of air increases by approximately 7 percent, leading to more concentrated precipitation in the clouds and the generation of more extreme water events: frigid winter temperatures and blockbuster snows; devastating spring floods; prolonged summer droughts and horrifying wildfires; and deadly category 3, 4, and 5 hurricanes, with untold loss of life and property and destruction of ecosystems.[8] The Earth's biomes, which developed in tandem with a fairly predictable hydrological cycle over the 11,700 years since the end of the last ice age, cannot catch up with the runaway exponential curve currently driving the Earth's hydrological cycle, and they are collapsing in real time.[9]

It's no wonder, then, that a survey of American voters conducted just after the 2018 national elections asking their opinion on launching a Green New Deal plan for addressing climate change, akin to the New Deal mobilization in the 1930s that helped lift America out of the Great Depression, found widespread support across all political affiliations. The Green New Deal "would generate 100% of the nation's electricity from clean, renewable sources within the next 10 years; upgrade the nation's energy grid, buildings, and transportation infrastructure; increase energy efficiency; invest in green technology research and development; and provide training for jobs in the new green economy." Ninety-two percent of Democrats supported the idea, including 93 percent of liberal Democrats and 90 percent of moderate-to-conservative Democrats. But 64 percent of Republicans—including 75 percent of moderate-to-liberal Republicans and 57 percent of conservative Republicans—also backed the policy goals outlined in the Green New Deal. Eighty-eight percent of independents endorsed the policies as well.[10]

The widespread support for a Green New Deal among Democrats, Republicans, and independent voters suggests a potential watershed in American politics with far-reaching implications for the 2020 presidential elections and beyond. Climate change is no longer only an academic issue and long-term policy concern but, rather, a frightening reality for millions of Americans who sense that the country and the world are facing a new and harrowing future unlike any previous period in human history.

The American public is not the only constituency that is running scared and motivated to act. The global elite of heads of state, CEOs of Fortune 500 companies, and billionaires meeting in Davos, Switzerland, at the annual get-together of the World Economic Forum in January 2019 were abuzz about the dire warnings from scientists. Conversation about the impacts that climate change is having on economies, businesses, and the financial community dominated the public sessions and private huddles. In a survey of attendees, climate issues accounted for four of the top five risks that could cause the most damage to the economy.[11] Gillian Tett of the *Financial Times* reported that even though "Davosians apparently fear that extreme weather events are becoming more common," they agreed that "the world has no effective mechanism to respond."[12]

At the same time that the World Economic Forum was meeting in Davos, a group of twenty-seven Nobel laureates, fifteen former chairs of the Council of Economic Advisers to the President, four former chairpersons of the Federal Reserve, and two former US secretaries of the treasury joined together in an urgent appeal to the US government to enact a carbon emission tax as the best and quickest means to help cut carbon dioxide emissions and encourage businesses to transition into the new green energies, technologies, and infrastructure of a zero-carbon era. Larry Summers, a former treasury secretary and president emeritus of Harvard University, spoke for the group, saying, "The gravity of the climate change problem concentrates minds and leads people to put aside differences. People who agree on little seem to agree on this. And that's striking."[13]

The signers said that the proposed carbon tax would send "a powerful price signal that harnesses the invisible hand of the marketplace to steer economic actors towards a low-carbon future" and "promote economic growth." They recommended that the tax "should increase every year until emissions reductions goals are met and be revenue neutral to avoid debates over the size of the government," because "a consistently rising carbon price will encourage technological innovation and large-scale infrastructure development and accelerate the shift to low and zero carbon goods and services." The proposal includes an additional feature designed "to maximize the fairness and political viability of a rising carbon tax." All of the revenue generated from the tax will be "returned directly to US citizens through equal lump-sum rebates" so that "the majority of American families, including the most vulnerable, will benefit financially by receiving more in 'carbon dividends' than they pay in increased energy prices."[14]

Americans are not alone in clamoring for a Green New Deal. More than a decade ago, a comparable movement to address climate change swept across the European Union. It, too, was called the "Green New Deal," and it inspired a growing legion of activists. The name stuck and remains a powerful rallying cry among political parties across the member states of the EU to this day, providing a central theme in the 2019 elections to select the new president of the European Commission and the members of the European Parliament.

On March 15, 2019, more than a million students of the Gen Z cohort joined ranks with their millennial elders and walked out of their classrooms and onto the streets in an unprecedented one-day strike, taking part in over two thousand demonstrations across 128 countries protesting their governments' inaction on climate change and demanding a global transformation into a postcarbon green era.[15]

Although there's widespread agreement across the political spectrum that transitioning to a zero-carbon society is daunting, a path does exist that might stave off the additional half-a-degree rise in temperature that would doom life on Earth and give us a chance to reorder our relationship to the planet. Here is the possibility: Solar, wind, and other renewable energies are quickly coming online. According to a November 2018 study by Lazard—one of the world's largest independent investment banks—the levelized cost of energy (LCOE) of large solar installations has plummeted to 36 dollars/megawatt hour, while wind has fallen to 29 dollars/megawatt hour, making them "cheaper than the most efficient gas plants, coal plants, and nuclear reactors."[16] "LCOE is an economic assessment of the average total cost to build and operate a power-generating asset over its lifetime divided by the total energy output of the asset over that lifetime."[17] Within the next eight years, solar and wind will be far cheaper than fossil fuel energies, forcing a showdown with the fossil fuel industry.[18]

The Carbon Tracker Initiative, a London-based think tank

serving the energy industry, reports that the steep decline in the price of generating solar and wind energy "will inevitably lead to trillions of dollars of stranded assets across the corporate sector and hit petro-states that fail to reinvent themselves," while "putting trillions at risk for unsavvy investors oblivious to the speed of the unfolding energy transition."[19] "Stranded assets" are all the fossil fuels that will remain in the ground because of falling demand as well as the abandonment of pipelines, ocean platforms, storage facilities, energy generation plants, backup power plants, petrochemical processing facilities, and industries tightly coupled to the fossil fuel culture.

Behind the scenes, a seismic struggle is taking place as four of the principal sectors responsible for global warming—the Information and Communications Technology (ICT)/telecommunications sector, the power and electric utility sector, the mobility and logistics sector, and the buildings sector—are beginning to decouple from the fossil fuel industry in favor of adopting the cheaper new green energies. The result is that within the fossil fuel industry, "around $100 trillion of assets could be 'carbon stranded.'"[20]

The carbon bubble is the largest economic bubble in history. And studies and reports over the past twenty-four months—from within the global financial community, the insurance sector, global trade organizations, national governments, and many of the leading consulting agencies in the energy industry, the transportation sector, and the real estate sector—suggest that the imminent collapse of the fossil fuel industrial civilization could occur sometime between 2023 and 2030, as key sectors decouple from fossil fuels and rely on ever-cheaper solar, wind, and other renewable energies and accompanying zero-carbon technologies.[21] The United States, currently the leading oil-producing nation, will be caught in the crosshairs between the plummeting price of solar and wind and the fallout from peak oil demand and accumulating stranded assets in the oil industry.[22]

Let's be clear that this Great Disruption is occurring, in large part, because the marketplace is speaking. Every government will have to follow the market or face the consequences. Governments that lead in the scale-up of a new zero-carbon Third Industrial Revolution will stay ahead of the curve. Governments that fail to move with market forces and instead remain in a collapsing twentieth-century fossil fuel culture will falter.

Not surprisingly, a worldwide movement to divest from the oil industry and invest in renewable energies is rapidly gaining strength. The wild card is likely to be the over $40 trillion in global pension funds, of which $25.4 trillion is in the hands of the American workforce.[23] Pension funds were the largest pool of capital in the world by 2017. If pension funds were to remain invested in the fossil fuel industry, the financial losses to millions of American workers would be incalculable at the juncture where the carbon bubble bursts.

A deep conversation has just begun within the financial community around whether to stay the course and continue to support the fossil fuel industry with trillions of dollars of investment or abandon ship and invest in the new green energies and the new business and employment opportunities that would come with the build-out and scale-up of the new green infrastructure in America and around the world. Many institutional investors, led by global pension funds, have begun cashing out of fossil fuels and investing in renewable energies in what is becoming the biggest divest/invest campaign in capitalist history. More than a thousand institutional investors in thirty-seven nations, including some of the biggest cities and labor unions, have thus far committed to divesting

$8 trillion in funds from the fossil fuel industry and reinvesting in the green energies, clean technologies, and business models that will take us to a zero-carbon future.[24]

The emergence of the carbon bubble and stranded fossil fuel assets concurrent with a popular movement for a global Green New Deal opens a window to the possibility of an infrastructure shift into a near-zero-carbon ecological era over the coming twenty years.

While the call for a Green New Deal is quickly gathering momentum, there is a realization among its proponents and supporters that there is as yet no clear path to an "Industrial Revolution" that could accomplish the mission. This book will share my experience over the past two decades in the European Union and, more recently, in the People's Republic of China, helping both governments prepare their Green New Deal–style transitions into a zero-carbon Third Industrial Revolution (TIR). I hope and expect that the grassroots movement for a Green New Deal now spreading across America will find it useful as the United States crafts its green, post-carbon Third Industrial Revolution infrastructure to mitigate climate change and create a more just and humane economy and society.

On a more personal note, I'd like to address those who have voiced their skepticism about a Green New Deal and the likelihood of making an economic transition of this magnitude in the short span of twenty years. The global companies and industries that I work with—the telecoms, electric utilities, transportation and logistics, construction and real estate, advanced manufacturing, smart agriculture and life sciences, and the financial community—know this can be accomplished. We're already on the ground doing it in regions around the world.

And to those elected officials across the United States who argue that a Green New Deal is impractical, I would like to say that the governments of the European Union and the People's Republic of China know that a transformation on this scale can be accomplished in a generation. They are both doing it in real time. Here in the United States we are late and past due. It's time to take off the blinders and show the world what we can do when we set our mind to a new vision—this time a Green New Deal for America, humanity, our fellow creatures, and our shared planet. It is my hope that the United States will join with the European Union and China and lead the world into a zero-carbon ecological age.

America's signature, from its earliest beginnings, has been its can-do, roll-up-the sleeves optimism that has seen it through more than two hundred years of trials, tribulations, challenges, and opportunities. This is in our cultural DNA. Now, a new generation of Americans is stepping onto the national and global stage to take up a mission that is without parallel in human history. It is very likely that the Green New Deal will have long legs and continue to pick up widespread popular support, especially among the under-forty generation, the cohort of digital natives who are ready and eager to imprint their stamp on the body politic in the coming decades.

PART I

THE GREAT DISRUPTION

The Decoupling Stampede
and Stranded Fossil Fuel Assets

1

IT'S THE INFRASTRUCTURE, STUPID!

We need a Green New Deal economic vision for America and the world. It must be compelling and executable in big cities, small towns, and rural communities. And it will have to be deployed quickly and scaled within twenty years or so if we are to meet the deadline of decarbonizing the global economy and reenergizing it with green electricity and accompanying sustainable services. We should step back, then, and ask the question, "How do the great economic paradigm shifts in history emerge?" If we know how they occur, governments everywhere can draw up roadmaps to deliver the Green New Deal.

The Third Industrial Revolution Paradigm

The major economic transformations in history share a common denominator. They all require three elements, each of which interacts with the others to enable the system to operate as a whole: a communication medium, a power source, and a transportation mechanism. Without communication, we can't manage economic activity and social life. Without energy, we can't power economic activity and social life.

Without transport and logistics, we can't move economic activity and social life. Together, these three operating systems make up what economists call a general-purpose technology platform (a society-wide infrastructure). New communication, energy, and mobility infrastructures also change society's temporal/spatial orientation, business models, governing patterns, built environments, habitats, and narrative identity.

■ ■ ■

In the nineteenth century, steam-powered printing and the telegraph, abundant coal, and locomotives on national rail systems meshed in a common general-purpose technology platform to manage, power, and move society, giving rise to the First Industrial Revolution. In the twentieth century, centralized electricity, the telephone, radio and television, cheap oil, and internal combustion vehicles on national road systems converged to create an infrastructure for the Second Industrial Revolution.

Now, we are in the midst of a Third Industrial Revolution. The digitalized Communication Internet is converging with a digitized Renewable Energy Internet, powered by solar and wind electricity, and a digitized Mobility and Logistics Internet of autonomous electric and fuel-cell vehicles, powered by green energy, atop an Internet of Things (IoT) platform, embedded in the commercial, residential, and industrial building stock, that will transform society and the economy in the twenty-first century.

Sensors are being attached to every device, appliance, machine, and contrivance, connecting every "thing" with every human being in a digital neural network that extends across the entire global economy. Already, billions of sensors are attached to resource flows, warehouses, road systems, factory production lines, the electricity transmission grid, offices, homes, stores, and vehicles, continually monitoring their status and performance and feeding Big Data back to the emerging Communication Internet, Renewable Energy Internet, and Mobility and Logistics Internet. By 2030, there could be trillions of sensors connecting the human and natural environment in a global distributed intelligent network.[1]

Connecting everything and everyone via the Internet of Things offers enormous economic benefits. In this expanded digital economy, individuals, families, and enterprises will be able to connect in their homes and workplaces to the IoT and access Big Data flowing across the World Wide Web that affects their supply chains, production and services, and every aspect of their social lives. They can then mine that Big Data with their own analytics and create their own algorithms and apps to increase their aggregate efficiency and productivity, reduce their carbon footprint, and lower the marginal cost of producing, distributing, and consuming goods and services and recycling waste, making their businesses and homes greener and more efficient in an emerging postcarbon global economy. (Marginal cost is the cost of producing an additional unit of a good or service after fixed costs have been absorbed.)

The marginal cost of some goods and services in this green digital economy will even approach zero, forcing a fundamental change in the capitalist system. In economic theory, we are taught that the optimum market is one in which businesses sell at marginal cost. Businesses are encouraged to introduce new technologies and other efficiencies that can reduce the marginal cost of producing and distributing their goods and services, enabling them to sell at a cheaper price, win over market share, and bring back sufficient profit to their investors.

However, it never occurred to economists that one day there might exist a general-purpose technology platform so hyperefficient in the production and delivery of goods and services that it plunges the marginal cost of economic activity so low that profit margins shrink dramatically, undermining the capitalist business model. At extremely low marginal costs, markets become too slow and eventually irrelevant as business mechanisms. This is what the green digital Third Industrial Revolution does.

Markets are transactional and start/stop mechanisms. Sellers and buyers come together at a moment in time and fix on a transaction price, the good is delivered or the service rendered, and the two parties walk away. The downtime between transactions is lost time against fixed overhead and other expenses, where the seller is in limbo. Aside from lost production costs, consider the time and expense in bringing the seller and buyer together again—think advertising costs, marketing, the cost of storing goods, downtime across the logistics and supply chain, and other overhead expenses that still have to be paid out. This phenomenon of shrinking marginal cost and shrinking profits playing out against the slow transaction of one-off sales of goods and services between sellers and buyers makes traditional markets all but useless in a digitally enhanced high-speed infrastructure. In the Third Industrial Revolution, the "transaction" of goods gives way to a continuous "flow" of 24/7 services.

In the new economic system now emerging, ownership gives way to access, and sellers and buyers in markets are replaced, in part, by providers and users in networks.

In provider/user networks, industries and sectors are replaced by "specialized competencies" that come together on platforms to manage the uninterrupted flow of goods and services in smart networks, returning sufficient profit, even at low margins, by the 24/7 continuous traffic across the system.

Margins for some goods and services, however, shrink so low "toward zero" that profits are no longer viable even in capitalist networks because the goods and services produced and distributed are nearly free. This is already occurring and giving rise to a new phenomenon—the Sharing Economy. At any given time of the day, hundreds of millions of people around the world are producing and sharing their own music, YouTube videos, social media, and research. Some are taking massive open online courses (MOOCs), taught by professors at the best universities, and often receiving college credit, for free. All one needs is a smartphone, a service provider, and an electrical outlet to power up.

More and more people around the world are also generating their own solar and wind electricity for use off-grid and/or for sale back to the grid, again at near-zero marginal cost. The sun and wind have yet to send a bill. Increasing numbers of millennials are sharing homes, rides, clothes, tools, sporting equipment, and an array of other goods and services. Some of the sharing networks like Uber are capitalist provider/user networks where the marginal cost of connecting riders and drivers is nearly zero, but the providers command a price for temporary access to the service. Other sharing networks are nonprofits or cooperatives where members freely share knowledge, goods, and services with one another. Millions of individuals are constructing the knowledge of the world and sharing it on Wikipedia, a nonprofit website that is the fifth-most-trafficked website, all for free.[2]

The sharing of a range of virtual and physical goods is the cornerstone of an emerging circular economy, allowing the human race to use far less of the resources of the Earth while passing on what they no longer use to others and, by doing so, dramatically reducing carbon emissions. The Sharing Economy is a core feature of the Green New Deal era.

The Sharing Economy is now in its infancy and is going to evolve in many directions. But this much is assured: The Sharing Economy is a new economic phenomenon made possible by the digital infrastructure of communication, energy, and mobility that is changing economic life. To this extent, the Sharing Economy is the first new economic system to enter onto the world stage since capitalism and socialism in the eighteenth and nineteenth centuries.

Already, a younger generation of digital natives—under the age of forty—are ensconced in this new hybrid economic system. Part of the day, they are sharing all sorts of goods and services for nearly free in open-source commons around the world, much of which is not measured in the GDP or standard economic accounting. The rest of the day, they are increasingly intertwined in capitalist provider/user networks, paying for access to goods and services. This hybrid economic system is the playing field on which a Green New Deal will emerge in the years ahead.

The build-out of the Green New Deal smart infrastructure will involve every competency: the ICT sector, including telecommunication, cable companies, internet companies, and the electronics industry; power and electric utilities; transportation and logistics; the construction and real estate industries; the manufacturing sector; retail trade; the food, agriculture, and life sciences sectors; and the travel and tourism industry. The new smart sustainable infrastructure, in turn, makes possible the new business models and new kinds of mass employment that characterize the shift to a green economy.

The transition from a Second Industrial Revolution to a Third Industrial Revolution will be formidable—comparable to the shift from agriculture to an industrial society—and will require the collective talents and skills of two generations of Americans. To make this happen, we will need to train millions of people and put them to work, or back to work.

We will have to decommission and disassemble the entire stranded fossil fuel and nuclear energy infrastructure—the pipelines, power plants, storage facilities, etc. Robots and AI won't do that. It will necessitate a far more agile semiskilled, skilled, and professional workforce.

The communication network will have to be upgraded, with the inclusion of universal broadband. Human beings will have to lay the cable and make the connections.

The energy infrastructure will need to be transformed to accommodate solar, wind, and other renewable energies. Robots and AI will not install solar panels and assemble wind turbines. The dumb centralized electricity grid will have to be reconfigured into a smart distributed digital Renewable Energy Internet to accommodate the flow of renewable electricity produced by countless green micro power plants. Again, this is complex work that can only be done by semiskilled and skilled professionals.

The antiquated twentieth-century nationwide electricity transmission grid will need to be replaced by a twenty-first-century high-voltage smart national power grid. This will marshal the employment of a huge workforce over a twenty-year transformation.

The transportation and logistics sector will have to be digitized and transformed into a GPS-guided and autonomous Mobility Internet made up of smart electric and fuel-cell vehicles powered by renewable energy and running on intelligent road, rail, and water systems. Here, too, low-tech and high-tech skilled employees will be put to the task. The introduction of electric and fuel-cell transportation will require millions of charging stations and thousands of hydrogen fueling stations. Smart roads, equipped with ubiquitous sensors, feeding real-time information on traffic flows and the movement of freight, will also have to be installed. Again, more jobs.

Buildings will need to be retrofitted to increase their energy efficiency and be equipped with renewable-energy-harvesting installations and converted into micro power-generating plants. Skilled laborers will have to install insulation and new windows and doors. Energy-storage technologies will have to be built into every layer of the infrastructure to secure intermittent renewable energy. Again, this is going to provide ample employment.

The digital economy also raises risks and challenges, not the least of which is guaranteeing network neutrality to ensure everyone has equal access to the networks, protecting privacy, ensuring data security, and thwarting cybercrime and cyberterrorism. How do we prevent nation-states from hacking into other countries' social media and spreading misinformation to influence the outcome of their elections? How do we push back against giant internet companies becoming monopolies and commodifying our personal online data for sale to third parties for commercial uses?

The dark side of the internet will require vigilant regulatory oversight at the local, state, and national levels, backed up by layers of redundancy built into the system to ensure that any disruption on the smart digital Internet of Things infrastructure can be counteracted by disaggregating, decentralizing, and reorganizing into new networks at the neighborhood or community level at a moment's notice to absorb the shocks.

The transition to a fully digital economy and the Third Industrial Revolution results in a leap in aggregate efficiency far beyond the gains achieved by the Second Industrial Revolution in the twentieth century. During the period from 1900 to 1980 in the United States, aggregate energy efficiency—the ratio of useful to potential physical work that can be extracted from energy and materials—steadily rose, along with the development of the nation's infrastructure, from 2.48 percent to 12.3 percent. Aggregate energy efficiency began to level off in the late 1990s at around 13 percent and then peaked at 14 percent in 2010 with the completion of the Second Industrial Revolution infrastructure. Despite a sizable increase in aggregate efficiency, which gave the United States unparalleled productivity and growth, 86 percent of the energy the country used in the Second Industrial Revolution was wasted during transmission.[3] Other industrializing nations experienced similar aggregate efficiency curves.

Even if we were to upgrade the carbon-based Second Industrial Revolution infrastructure, it would be unlikely to have any measurable effect on aggregate efficiency and productivity. Fossil fuel energies have matured. And the technologies designed and engineered to run on these energies, like the internal combustion engine and centralized electricity grids, have exhausted their productivity, with little potential left to exploit.

New studies, however, show that with the shift to an Internet of Things platform and a Third Industrial Revolution, it is conceivable to increase aggregate energy efficiency to as high as 60 percent over the next twenty years, amounting to a dramatic increase in productivity while transitioning into a nearly 100 percent postcarbon renewable energy society and a highly resilient circular economy.[4]

I regularly meet with heads of state, provincial governors, and mayors around the world; during our discussions I describe the smart green infrastructure shift into a zero-carbon Third Industrial Revolution economy that is the very centerpiece of a Green New Deal, then ask them if they have a better plan for mitigating climate change and creating the new businesses and employment opportunities that come with it. The response I often get is silence, because the only other alternative is to remain trapped in a dying, carbon-based Second Industrial Revolution economy, whose aggregate efficiencies and productivity peaked decades ago and which is now taking the world into the sixth extinction event. What, then, is holding us up?

Connecting the Dots

Over 9,000 cities and local governments have come together in the Global Covenant of Mayors for Climate & Energy to create sustainable communities and address climate change.[5] These cities can boast of introducing scores of high-visibility green "pilot projects," including solar and wind installations, electric vehicles and hydrogen fuel-cell buses, LEED-certified buildings, recycling programs, etc. But what communities often end up with is disconnected siloed initiatives and little else.

Missing is the green Third Industrial Revolution infrastructure, which is the "nervous system" that would connect all these isolated projects. Infrastructure, at the deepest level, is not just an incidental appendage to commerce and social life, as popular lore would have it. It is always new infrastructure that is the indispensable "extended body" of a new body politic.

Infrastructure, at the deepest level, is a techno-socio bond that brings together new communications technologies, new energy sources, new modes of mobility and logistics, and new built environments, enabling communities to more efficiently manage, power, and move their economic activity, social life, and governance. Communication technology is the brain that oversees, coordinates, and manages the economic organism. Energy is the blood that circulates through the body politic, providing the nourishment to convert nature's endowment into goods and services to keep the economy alive and growing. Mobility and logistics are extensions of our limbs, allowing communities to interact physically across temporal and spatial domains to facilitate the movement of goods, services, and people. Buildings are the skin—the semipermeable membranes that allow our species to survive the elements, store the energies and other resources we need to maintain our physical well-being, provide secure and safe places to produce and consume the goods and services we require to enhance our existence, and serve as a congregating place to raise our families and conduct social life. Infrastructure is akin to an immense technological organism that brings large numbers of people together as an extended figurative family collectively engaging in more complex economic, social, and political relationships.

For example, think of the Second Industrial Revolution of the twentieth century as a technological nervous system to manage the affairs of a new economic paradigm. Urban America was electrified between 1900 and the onset of the Great Depression in 1929, and rural America followed suit between 1936 and 1949.[6] The electrification of factories made way for the era of mass-produced goods, with the automobile as the kingpin. Without electricity, Henry Ford would not have had available electric power tools to bring the work to the workers and manufacture an affordable automobile for millions of Americans. The mass production of the gasoline-powered Model T car altered the temporal and spatial orientation of society. Millions of people began to trade in their horses and buggies for automobiles. To meet the increased demand for fuel, the nascent oil industry revved up exploration and drilling, built oil pipelines across the country, and set up thousands of gasoline stations to power the millions of automobiles coming off the assembly lines. Concrete highways were laid out over vast stretches of America, culminating in the US Interstate Highway System—the largest public works project in world history—creating a seamless coast-to-coast road system. The interstate highways were the impetus for a mass exodus of millions of families from urban areas to the newly emerging suburbs popping up off the highway exits. Thousands of miles of telephone lines were installed, and later radio and television were introduced, recasting social life and creating a communication grid to manage and market the far-flung activities of the oil economy and auto age.

That was then, this is now. The United States is the clear outlier today among the highly developed industrial nations and even among many developing countries. In the World Economic Forum's 2017 report ranking the quality of nations' infrastructures, the United States ranked a dismal ninth, behind countries like the Netherlands, Japan, France, Switzerland, and Korea.[7] A report by McKinsey Consulting projected that the United States will have to increase its current overall infrastructure investment by 0.5 percent of GDP between 2017 and 2035 just to keep pace with the conventional infrastructure needs of the country.[8]

Unfortunately, in relation to a key measure of the new digital infrastructure of the emerging Third Industrial Revolution, the United States ranks even worse, an abysmal nineteenth among the nations of the world in fixed-broadband internet subscriptions, with slower internet speeds.[9] When it comes to the formation of a digital Renewable Energy Internet and an autonomous Mobility Internet, the United States is not even at the table.

It's sad when we reflect that in the First and Second Industrial Revolutions, the United States was unmatched by any other country in the world in its commitment to bring the full force of the national government, states, localities, and economy to bear on building world-class infrastructure. It is becoming self-evident that the United States is long past due for a blunt reassessment of its economic priorities in a world that is fast leaving it behind in the twenty-first century.

The Third Industrial Revolution is already scaling up in both the European Union and the People's Republic of China. My offices in Brussels and Washington, DC, have worked closely with the EU over the past twenty years on the conception and deployment of a Third Industrial Revolution infrastructure. Since 2013, our office in Beijing has also worked alongside the leadership of the People's Republic of China on a similar Third Industrial Revolution roadmap and deployment currently operationalizing in the thirteenth Five-Year Plan.

I'm often asked the question, "Why has the US lagged so far behind the European Union and China?" To answer, I would like to take you back to President Barack Obama's reelection campaign in 2012, and an incident that captures America's recalcitrance on the question of infrastructure. President Obama, speaking to supporters in Roanoke, Virginia, on July 13 of that year, strayed from conventional campaign rhetoric to reflect on what policies in the course of American history made the United States a beacon for the rest of the world. The president mused on how the success of private enterprises in the nineteenth and twentieth centuries depended, to a great extent, on government involvement in "big-picture infrastructure shifts." He told the crowd:

> If you were successful, somebody along the line gave you some help. There was a great teacher somewhere in your life. Somebody helped to create this unbelievable American system that we have that allowed you to thrive. Somebody invested in roads and bridges. If you've got a business—*you didn't build that.* Somebody else made that happen. The Internet didn't get invented on its own. Government research created the Internet so that all the companies could make money off the Internet.[10]

President Obama went on to cite the federal government's funding of various infrastructure projects and government research that allowed businesses to function and flourish. His Republican opponent, Mitt Romney, pounced on the phrase "you didn't build that," claiming that President Obama was undermining the role that small businesses play in making a strong American economy. But the president was merely trying to explain the contribution that federal, state, and local governments make in providing the infrastructure and public services that every citizen relies on and that are indispensable to both the success of the business community and the general well-being of the public.

Obama's "you didn't build that" moment instantly went viral on social media, creating a national controversy over the role small businesses play in America's economic success story. Within days, Republican talking heads spread a counternarrative with the phrase "we built it," suggesting that small businesses, not government, are primarily responsible for America's preeminence. "We built it" became so popular with the Republican base that the Republican National Convention in Tampa incorporated the theme into the proceedings.[11]

The "you didn't build that" remark struck a nerve in a country where small business owners feel overtaxed, over-regulated, underrepresented, and underappreciated for their contribution to the building of the American economy on Main Streets across the country. All justified! Still, "you didn't build that" speaks to a more unsettling reality—that is, a feeling on the part of many Americans that Big Government is constantly encroaching on their lives in ways that undermine their personal freedoms and the workings of the free market. President Ronald Reagan had popularized this theme in his 1980 run for the presidency with the one-liner "Get the government off the backs of the people."[12]

To be fair, most Americans know that many of the things they depend on day to day come from taxpayer dollars and local, state, and federal government programs: the public schools our children attend, the roads we drive on, the air traffic controllers that guide our flights, the National Weather Service that keeps us abreast of local conditions, the public hospitals that minister to the sick, the motor vehicle departments that register our cars, the US Postal Service that delivers our packages and mail, the fire departments and police departments that protect our safety, the prisons that guard convicted felons, the systems that flow water into our businesses and homes, the sanitation departments that recycle our waste, etc.

Public opinion polls show that, in theory at least, Americans support spending more federal, state, and local funds to improve infrastructure.[13] As to the particulars of how much, on what, and whether the deployment of that infrastructure should remain the responsibility of the government or be put in the hands of the marketplace, the reaction is far more divided and acrimonious.

In the European Union, EU citizens recognize the importance of maintaining a balanced partnership between government and commerce, and there is a deep appreciation for the role that the government plays in providing public infrastructure and services from which both the business community and the public benefit in their day-to-day lives. For this reason, taxpayers in Europe are willing to shoulder higher taxes in return for the advantages they secure with public services, from universal healthcare to high-speed rail systems.

By contrast, everywhere we look across America today, the public infrastructure is in dire straits and disrepair: roads, bridges, dams, public schools, hospitals, public transit, etc. Every four years, the American Society of Civil Engineers (ASCE) issues a report card on the condition of the country's infrastructure, including its rail transit, inland waterways, levees, ports, schools, wastewater and solid waste treatment, hazardous waste disposal, parks, aviation, and energy. In its 2017 report card, the ASCE gave the nation's public infrastructure an embarrassingly low score of D+. Noting that the deteriorating public infrastructure is becoming a drag on the American economy and a growing threat to the health, well-being, and security of the nation, the ASCE report warns that the country is only paying half of America's infrastructure bill, leaving an investment funding gap that hurts businesses, workers, and families.[14]

This means poor roads and more travel time, collapsed bridges, airport delays, aging electricity grids and power shortages, unreliable water distribution systems, the breakdown of sewer systems and a host of other public services, all of which "translate into higher costs for businesses to manufacture and distribute goods and services." According to the ASCE, "these higher costs, in turn, get passed along to workers and families." The ASCE estimates that the continued deterioration of the nation's infrastructure will cost the US GDP $3.9 trillion and result in $7 trillion in lost sales and a loss of 2.5 million jobs by 2025. Lest there be any doubt about the magnitude of the losses and the impact they are already having on American families, the ASCE estimates that because "the cost of deteriorating infrastructure takes a toll on families' disposable household income and impacts the quality and quantity of jobs in the U.S. economy . . . from 2016 to 2025, each household will lose $3,400 each year in disposable income."[15]

The ASCE concludes that the United States will need to invest an additional $206 billion annually over ten years (2016–2025) on infrastructure just to achieve a B grade—and overall will need to come up with $4.59 trillion by 2025. This is $2 trillion more than the United States currently invests in infrastructure.[16]

History tells us that the vitality of a nation is measured by the willingness of its citizens to sacrifice a portion of their income and wealth to secure the public infrastructure and services that advance the productivity, health, and general well-being of its people. When that commitment wanes, it's a clear signal of the nation's decline and fall. To a large extent, the rhetorical phrase "Make America Great Again" rings hollow at a time when a sizable segment of the population is no longer willing to commit to America's future by supporting a rebuilding and transformation of the nation's infrastructure in anticipation of the needs of not only the present generation but also generations yet to come.

If there was ever a case to be made for America being "penny-wise and pound-foolish," it's our general disregard for the importance of infrastructure. And while in the short run this just means bad roads, rickety bridges, unreliable public transportation, and slow mobile phones, in the long run, if we fail to make the investment in Third Industrial Revolution infrastructure, it could pose a more existential threat for us and the planet. Perhaps if we better understood the payoff of such investments, it would become easier to commit tax revenue to infrastructure. A comprehensive 2014 study by the University of Maryland for the National Association of Manufacturers says it all. The study found that infrastructure improvements add $3 to the country's GDP for every dollar invested.[17] To add icing on the cake, McKinsey estimates that increasing infrastructure spending by just 1 percent of GDP would add 1.5 million jobs to the US economy.[18] What more is there to say except "woe is us"?

Who Should Own the Infrastructure?

The Green New Deal is a powerful plea by the younger generations—the millennials and Gen Z, now the dominant cohorts in the United States—to turn America around and move forward, this time with a far more important agenda: not just to improve the social prospects and economic well-being of every American but also to position America and its people at the forefront in mitigating climate change and saving life on Earth. The transformation from a dying fossil-fuel-weighted Second Industrial Revolution infrastructure to a smart green zero-emission Third Industrial Revolution infrastructure is the very nucleus of the Green New Deal.

Infrastructure revolutions require a healthy social-market economy that brings together government, industry, and civil society at every level with the appropriate mix of public capital, private capital, and social capital. In the United States, both the First Industrial Revolution of the nineteenth century and the Second Industrial Revolution of the twentieth century relied on a strong and robust public-private partnership in the build-out and scale-up of the new infrastructures that transformed American life.

The American public may be aware of the New Deal that accompanied the Second Industrial Revolution. They may not know that a New Deal accompanied the First Industrial Revolution as well, although it wasn't called that. The federal government's Morrill Land-Grant Acts of 1862 and 1890 established land-grant public colleges and universities across the country, providing the education and skills necessary to transform American agriculture and industry. Millions of Americans have attended these schools over the past 150 years. If you went to Penn State, Ohio State, the University of Georgia, Texas A&M, the University of Arizona, the University of California, or any of the other land-grant institutions in every state of the country, you have the federal government's Morrill Land-Grant Acts to thank. The federal government financed the first telegraph installation, which stretched from the Capitol Building to Baltimore.[19] The federal government's Homestead Acts ceded over 270 million acres of federal public lands—10 percent of the total US land area—for free to 1.6 million homesteaders.[20] The federal government's Pacific

Railroad Acts authorized the issuance of government bonds and land grants to railroad companies, hastening the build-out of a transcontinental rail infrastructure.

President Franklin Delano Roosevelt's New Deal in the 1930s included not only new financial reforms but also large-scale federal programs, including the Public Works Administration (PWA), to promote the infrastructure transition to a Second Industrial Revolution.[21] The Work Projects Administration (WPA) hired millions of unemployed people to carry out public works projects, including the construction of buildings and roads and the stewardship of public lands.[22] The Roosevelt administration also introduced a mammoth electricity-generation project—the Tennessee Valley Authority—that built giant dams to produce cheap subsidized hydroelectricity for rural communities that had not yet become electrified.[23] The government then assisted the rural regions in establishing electric cooperatives to bring that electricity to millions of Americans living in remote areas of the country. As mentioned, the federal government's National Interstate and Defense Highways Act of 1956 connected the country with a single road system, spawning the development of suburban America.[24] The federal government's GI Bill offered free higher education for nearly 8 million veterans after World War II and the Korean War, providing the knowledge needed to promote a high-quality workforce to both complete the build-out of the Second Industrial Revolution infrastructure and manage the new business opportunities that plugged into it.[25] The Federal Housing Administration (FHA)—created in 1934—helped millions of Americans afford home ownership after the war in the burgeoning suburbs just off the interstate highway exits (although it should be noted that minorities were often discriminated against by the FHA in securing mortgages). The Green New Deal, in turn, will require a similar effort if it is to succeed.

The First and Second Industrial Revolution infrastructures were engineered to be centralized, top-down, and proprietary, and they needed to be vertically integrated to create economies of scale and return profits to investors. The result is that at the end of the Second Industrial Revolution, the global Fortune 500 companies, most of them US-based, account for $30 trillion in revenue, or around 37 percent of global GDP, with only 67.7 million employees out of a global workforce of nearly 3.5 billion people.[26] This statistic tells us everything we need to know about how the benefits of the industrial era have been shared.

That is not to say that the fruits of the first two industrial revolutions in the nineteenth and twentieth centuries weren't a boon for large numbers of people, especially in the Western world. Arguably, most of us in the highly developed nations are far better off than our ancestors were before we began the industrial age. However, it's also fair to say that nearly half of the population of the world (46 percent), living on less than $5.50 per day, the dividing line that defines poverty, is at best only marginally better off than their ancestors, and perhaps no better off.[27] Meanwhile, the wealthiest human beings have triumphed. Currently, the accumulated wealth of the eight richest individuals in the world equals the total wealth of half of the human beings living on the planet—3.5 billion people.[28]

Conversely, the Third Industrial Revolution infrastructure is engineered to be distributed, open, and transparent, to achieve network effects, and it scales laterally, allowing billions of people to engage directly with each other both virtually and physically at very low fixed costs and near-zero marginal cost in localities and regions that stretch around the world. All they need is a smartphone and an internet connection to give them instant access to Big Data and a global network of millions of other businesses and their websites.

This more intimate and inclusive engagement in commerce, trade, and social life, made possible by a distributed and smart postcarbon Third Industrial Revolution platform, is being accompanied by a shift from globalization to "glocalization" as individuals, businesses, and communities engage each other directly, bypassing many of the global companies that mediated commerce and trade in the twentieth century. Glocalization makes possible a vast expansion in social entrepreneurship with the proliferation of smart high-tech small and medium-sized enterprises (SMEs) blockchained into laterally extended cooperatives operating in networks circling the world. In short, the Third Industrial Revolution brings with it the prospect of a democratization of commerce and trade on a scale unprecedented in history.

The shift from globalization to glocalization is transforming the relationship between national governments and local communities, in a sense, reversing the locus of responsibility for the workings of the economy and the affairs of governance from the nation-state to the regions. This change in governance presages a revolution in the way humanity organizes its economic and social life.

So what role does this leave for the federal government? While the federal government will be a key player in some of the infrastructure build-out in the country, its primary responsibility will be to establish the new codes, regulations, standards, tax incentives, and other financial incentives for the transition into a Third Industrial Revolution infrastructure and zero-carbon economy. Cities, counties, and states, in turn, will be tasked with developing their own customized goals and deliverables, Green New Deal roadmaps, construction sites, and deployment initiatives for transitioning into a Third Industrial Revolution paradigm. They will then cross-border and create an integrated national infrastructure network composed of the Communication Internet, the

Renewable Energy Internet, and the Mobility Internet atop the Internet of Things platform, stretching across the building stock and built environment. The new Third Industrial Revolution infrastructure will be accompanied by new business models that plug into the platforms and take advantage of the new potential aggregate efficiencies across their value chains and supply chains.

The partial shift in political power from nations to local regions will change the nature of governance. Although all politics is local, in the glocal era economic development will also be increasingly distributed between localities connected all over the world. "Regional empowerment" will be the battle cry of the coming glocal era.

Some market proponents acknowledge that the rotting infrastructure across the United States needs to be addressed, and they even support the build-out of parts of the smart digital Third Industrial Revolution infrastructure, but they are opposed to a Green New Deal, which they say would mean more Big Government encroachment in the day-to-day affairs of the American public and American businesses. They prefer that the federal, state, and local governments incentivize the private sector with generous tax credits and subsidies. With these incentives in hand, private developers will come forward and finance the shoring up of the existing Second Industrial Revolution infrastructure and the build-out of the Third.

The privatization of the nation's infrastructure has been picking up speed for several decades but is now on the verge of exploding as America transitions from a Second to a Third Industrial Revolution. Many businesses are hoping to use the current debate over America's disintegrating infrastructure to make the case for privatizing much of it in one fell swoop over the course of the next several decades.

The specter of the privatization of all the public infra-

structure that every American relies on to survive and flourish seems misguided and politically unwise. Putting every
citizen's daily life in the hands of a disparate array of unac-
countable commercial interests over whom the public has
little or no control, and even less ability to access and sway re-
garding the services that maintain everyone's daily existence,
is little more than a capitulation of democratic governance
and oversight. Yet that is already happening—unfortunately,
not only in the United States but, to a lesser extent, in other
countries as well.

More ominous still, consider the prospect of privatizing
the entire smart digital infrastructure that makes up the
Third Industrial Revolution. On the one hand, the opportunity to connect the human race in a global nervous system,
enabling every person, if they so choose, to access every other
as part of a diverse and globally connected figurative family—
and at near-zero marginal cost—is appealing, especially to a
younger generation who think of the planet as their extended
home and playing field. On the other hand, what if the smart
digital Third Industrial Revolution infrastructure were to be
exclusively in the private hands of global companies with
little or no accountability to the communities they serve, giving them free license to surveil the lives of every citizen and
sell the data they collect to third parties for marketing and
advertising, or to political parties and lobbyists to advance
their agendas?

I love Google. It's the magic box. Whenever I have a
query to search, I ask Google. But what if Google were the
only search engine and everyone in the world had to turn to
it for their inquiries? Facebook is a tremendous service. It
has brought together 2.32 billion human beings in a global
embrace, creating the largest extended virtual cohort in history.[29] But if Facebook were the only forum where we could
"meet up" on a global scale, we would each be subject to its

access criteria, 24/7 surveillance, and algorithm governance. The same with Amazon. The company's global logistics network is impressive. But if Amazon were to become the only carrier through which we could send items to one another, we would all be subject to its dictates and the continued surveillance of our comings and goings in our daily lives. How likely is this grand new scenario? Look no further.

Google Governance and the Antidote

In October 2017, Prime Minister Justin Trudeau of Canada held a high-profile press conference in Toronto. Appearing alongside him were Eric Schmidt, then the executive chairman of Alphabet Inc., the parent company of Google; Kathleen Wynne, premier of the Province of Ontario; and John Tory, the mayor of Toronto. Together they announced a public-private partnership between Sidewalk Labs, an urban design and development company owned by Alphabet, and the city of Toronto to develop a mixed-use neighborhood on the Toronto waterfront.[30]

The plan is to build out Canada's first smart, digitally connected urban neighborhood, replete with state-of-the-art sensors across a seamless Internet of Things neural system. Ubiquitous sensors will provide surveillance, collecting data on activity taking place in the homes, the shops, and the streets, with the goal of helping speed efficiencies and conveniences in commerce, social life, and governance. If the prototype neighborhood is successful, the next step might be to expand outward, eventually transforming the entire infrastructure of the metropolitan region of Toronto into a showcase smart city. The catch is that Google's smart city experiment gives the internet giant its first foray into algorithmic governance over entire cities.

In 2007, humanity reached a milestone, with a majority of human beings living in urban areas, many in megacities and suburban extensions with populations of 10 million or more.[31] This was the year we became *"Homo urbanus."* Jump a decade to today. Billions of human beings use Google's search engine, Google Maps and Waze for location identification and navigation, YouTube videos, and countless other Google data-driven services, primarily in dense metropolitan regions. For Google, the next frontier is the privatization of entire cities under the watchful eyes of the company's sensor networks.

At the press conference announcing the new partnership between Sidewalk Labs and Toronto, Schmidt thanked Canada for allowing Google in, saying that his company's long-held dream had come true: for "someone to give us a city and put us in charge."[32]

Writing in the *Globe and Mail* a year later, Jim Balsillie, the former chairman and co-CEO of Research In Motion, a company that commercializes intellectual property in more than 150 countries, summed up the significance of this first trial run in creating a privatized smart city that so excited Schmidt. Balsillie pointed out that "'smart cities' are the new battlefront for big tech because they serve as the most promising hotbed for additional intangible assets that hold the next trillion dollars to add to their market capitalizations." The real commercial value, according to Balsillie, is that "'smart cities' rely on IP and data to make the vast array of city sensors more functionally valuable, and when under the control of private interests, an enormous new profit pool."[33]

In the year since the official announcement, it has become even clearer that Sidewalk Labs wants Toronto's blessing, but it does not relish the city's active involvement and oversight in the build-out and management of the smart neighborhood on the waterfront.

Meanwhile, the ongoing negotiations between Sidewalk Labs and Waterfront Toronto, the development body for the site, have been steeped in secrecy. As Balsillie points out, Waterfront Toronto is an "unelected, publicly funded corporation with no expertise in IP, data or even basic digital rights . . . in charge of navigating forces of urban privatization, algorithmic control and rule by corporate contract."[34] By the closing days of 2018, the outlook for Sidewalk Labs' smart city project seemed bleak, at least in its present articulation. The great fanfare that surrounded the initial announcement a year earlier had faded as doubts began to pile up among government officials and the general public.

What had begun as a public relations coup for Prime Minister Trudeau, Canada, and Toronto had devolved into a public nightmare, exposing Waterfront Toronto to ridicule. The vision of a Google-inspired smart futuristic city had become lost amid the growing fear of "Big Brother"—Alphabet—taking over a small segment of Toronto's waterfront and transforming it with smart technology into a 24/7 surveillance cloud for the purpose of collecting data on the daily activity of its citizens, which Sidewalk Labs could exploit by selling it to third parties for commercial use.

In July 2018, Will Fleissig, the chief executive of Waterfront Toronto and an early supporter of Sidewalk Labs, resigned abruptly. Shortly thereafter, Julie Di Lorenzo, a prominent local real estate developer, departed the board of directors of Waterfront Toronto, saying she was uncomfortable with Alphabet as a partner. She questioned what might happen if future residents of the smart development didn't agree to sharing their data, asking, "Would you segregate them and tell them 'you can't live here'?"[35]

Bianca Wylie, a technology policy advisor and cofounder of Tech Reset Canada, expressed the sentiment of many fellow Torontonians when she said that "we need to have these issues decided by organizations that are accountable to the people, not by private vendors." Wylie made clear that she was not opposed to a smart infrastructure incorporating "plausible surveillance" of use to residents, businesses, and the community, but, she added, "we need to state clearly and unambiguously that this infrastructure is public."[36] In October, Ann Cavoukian, the former information and privacy commissioner of Ontario, resigned from the venture. What made her resignation particularly meaningful is that she was commissioned by Sidewalk Labs to help establish a "privacy by design" protocol for the development, only to find out later that third parties might enjoy access to "identifiable data." In her resignation letter, Cavoukian said, "I imagined us creating a smart city of privacy as opposed to a smart city of surveillance."[37]

The problem does not lie with Sidewalk Labs' expertise. The company boasts some of the best talent available for establishing digitally connected, efficient, and environmentally sustainable smart cities. All to the good. Rather, it is the business model that is at fault, as is the case with any public-private partnership in which the commercial interest of the developer is primarily in securing lucrative revenue streams and profit over time; more often than not, this compromises the notion that infrastructure should be treated as a public good and a service everyone relies on and therefore best belongs in the hands of local governments that represent the will of all the citizenry. (In chapter 6, we will describe a public-private business model— energy service companies—that enables private businesses to finance, build out, and manage infrastructure for governments and secure appropriate revenue streams, while local governments maintain control over the nature of the deployment and management, with the citizenry benefiting from the public services rendered.)

Shortly after the Trudeau/Sidewalk Labs press conference,

I was in Ottawa meeting with federal ministers on the prospect of transforming the federal government building stock into a smart digital, zero-carbon Internet of Things built environment. In one of the meetings, a deputy minister asked my opinion of the Toronto announcement. I said that I was not surprised: In all of the seven regions our global team has worked with to scale smart Third Industrial Revolution infrastructure, the public voice of the people has been clear. While the citizenry would welcome the help of businesses in laying out smart neighborhoods, and even their involvement in helping to scale and manage the platforms, the oversight and decision-making power had to remain with the governing authorities and the public. And even then, there was a consensus that the Third Industrial Revolution digital infrastructure needed to be governed and accessed as public open-source commons. Further, that oversight and regulation, in every instance, would need to ensure that every citizen enjoys the unequivocal right to participate in or opt out from any of the smart services at any time.

The way to ensure public engagement at every step along the way to transitioning into a green smart city or region is to embed "deep public participation" and involvement at every stage of development, from conception to ongoing deployment. This is the takeaway issue in the Google-Toronto smart city debacle.

Our team's experience in the European Union might be helpful here. We have three current green test regions in Europe that have developed comprehensive Third Industrial Revolution roadmaps and transformed their jurisdictions into twenty-year construction sites where they are deploying infrastructure projects. Our prior work in four other regions convinced us that the traditional model that we were using to engage these governments was inadequate to the task. We came to the realization that the decision-making process and governance needed to be compatible with the distributed, open, and laterally scaled infrastructure being deployed.

When Hauts-de-France (formerly Nord-Pas-de-Calais), the first of these lighthouse regions, asked our consulting consortium, TIR Consulting Group LLC, to develop a green zero-emission Third Industrial Revolution deployment plan, we initially declined. Hauts-de-France is the industrial rust belt of France and a former coal-mining region, holding more than 9 percent of the mainland's population. I suggested to the president of the region that the government abandon its traditional role of "decider-in-chief" and instead become a "facilitator" of a more laterally distributed and shared governance made up of hundreds of individuals in primary committees and several thousand individuals in secondary informal networks from the public sector, the business sector, civil society, and academia working together in a "peer assembly," reflecting the more distributed, laterally scaled infrastructure they were being asked to envision and deploy.

We wanted to be unequivocal that we were not simply talking about soliciting ideas, suggestions, and approvals from focus groups and stakeholder groups. Rather, we were talking about ongoing peer assemblies crossing all the generational cohorts that would continue the work on the construction site over twenty years, irrespective of which political party might be governing at any moment, in order to maintain both continuity and solidarity to ensure the long-term success of the infrastructure transition. Hauts-de-France agreed to this radically new governing arrangement, and we began the collaboration.

The region, which subsequently received the coveted European Entrepreneurial Region Award from the EU Committee of the Regions, representing all 350 regions across the twenty-eight member states, is in its sixth year of TIR deployment and is currently involved in over 1,000 projects employing several thousands of its citizens.[38] It has become the poster child of the new peer-assembly approach to economic and political empowerment.

Similar peer assemblies were established in our other two test regions: the twenty-three cities in the Metropolitan Region of Rotterdam and the Hague, which is the petrochemical complex of Europe, and Luxembourg, a key financial and political capital of the European Union.

These peer-assembly governing models allow regions to move more quickly to deploy infrastructure rollouts while maintaining a cohesive approach to developing their construction sites over time, with little citizen backlash. Although other localities and regions around the world have experimented with small-scale peer assemblies that are narrowly circumscribed by very specific projects with limited time spans, the three lighthouse test regions mentioned above are, to our knowledge, the only large-scale peer assemblies currently in deployment.

When Angela Merkel became chancellor of Germany, she invited me to Berlin in the opening weeks of her administration to address the question of how to incentivize new business opportunities and create new employment in Germany. I described the distributed, open, and laterally scaled architecture of the Third Industrial Revolution infrastructure and how its design features are best taken up and deployed by localities and regions who then customize it to their own unique circumstances, after which they digitally connect up with other regions. The chancellor commented that she liked this distributed, laterally scaled Third Industrial Revolution infrastructure for Germany. I asked the chancellor why, and she said, "Jeremy, you need to know a little more about the history of Germany. Our country is a federation of states, and these states exercise a great deal of independence in managing their economic affairs and governance. The Third Industrial Revolution governance model fits Germany, assuring that the economic decision-making process and government oversight is lodged at the local and regional level."

Similarly, municipalities, counties, and states across the United States are also uniquely suited to adopt the peer-assembly model in the scale-up of customized Third Industrial Revolution infrastructures. Like Germany, the United States is conceived as a federal republic in which political power and economic development traditionally rest largely in the hands of governing jurisdictions at the state, municipal, and county levels. The federal government, for its part, is expected to represent and uphold shared national narratives, provide a sense of national identity, ensure the nation's security, and create the laws, statutes, regulations, codes, and incentives that allow localities and states to be in alignment across the country.

While the federal government will be important in framing the Green New Deal transformation, much of the heavy lifting in the deployment of the green infrastructure revolution will fall to the states, municipalities, and counties, as it should in an emerging laterally distributed glocal era.

2

POWER TO THE PEOPLE

The Sun and Wind Are Free

Where do we stand at this inflection point in history? There is a growing sense that we are paying a terrible price for the fossil fuel civilization that we built and exulted in for more than two centuries and that is now taking us into a series of climate-changing events and a new reality that we can barely fathom.

Humanity is experiencing a great awakening of a different kind. We are beginning to see ourselves as a species and just beginning to ponder our common fate on a planet where nature's rhythms and patterns are becoming alien.

A younger generation is coming forward with an intimate sense of the darkness that is unfolding around them and a steely determination to break through the lethargy that has allowed us to slip to the very edge of a planetary crisis. They are angry, determined, and motivated, and unwilling to listen to why we can't do this and can't do that, mulling over what's realistic and what's not, at a moment when realism itself seems so unrealistic and inadequate to the mission ahead of us.

However, we are not totally in the dark and without possibilities. There is a way forward. A path has been laid across the European Union and the People's Republic of China, and even here at home in California, New York, Texas, Washington State, New Mexico, Hawaii, and other scattered parts of America, that can take us on a new journey away from a death-driven Second Industrial Revolution and into a life-affirming Third Industrial Revolution.

How EU Political Activists Launched the Green New Deal

The enthusiasm around a Green New Deal that is echoing across America is music to my ears—a sweet refrain that takes me back to 2007. Just as Alexandria Ocasio-Cortez and the Sunrise Movement have captured the attention of the country with an urgent "slap in the face" reality check, that feeling and sense of urgency surfaced across the European Union more than a decade ago.

The EU was on the move. By 2007, Europe had surpassed the United States and become the "idea factory" and deployment engine for decarbonizing society. That year, the EU was finalizing the 20-20-20 formula, binding the EU member states to the Great Disruption that would bring on an ecological age. These new protocols required all EU member states to increase their energy efficiency by 20 percent, reduce their global warming emissions by 20 percent (based on 1990 levels), and increase their generation of renewable energies by 20 percent by the year 2020, making the EU the first major political power to establish a formal, legally binding commitment to address climate change and transform the economy of hundreds of millions of citizens.[1] I'll come back to the history of this path-changing event and what has happened since in the coming pages.

The 20-20-20 mandate was a powerful tonic, providing Europe with the framework it needed to transform the continent into a zero-carbon society. While the ink was still drying on the new global warming mandates, the first buds of a Green New Deal movement appeared.

Nine people, all of whom had been longtime climate campaigners, came together in the UK to create the Green New Deal Group.[2] The group was eclectic, made up of individuals from a wide range of fields, including experts in energy, finance, journalism, and environmental science—just the kind of interdisciplinary collective needed to rethink the economic paradigm in a world facing climate change.

In 2008, the Green New Deal Group issued a 48-page declaration titled *A Green New Deal: Joined-Up Policies to Solve the Triple Crunch of the Credit Crisis, Climate Change and High Oil Prices.*[3] This plan encapsulated the central themes adopted that year around the newly mandated 20-20-20 formula and outlined the key building blocks and components of what would become a zero-carbon Third Industrial Revolution paradigm shift.

Admittedly, it's a bit ironic that a European-based group latched on to America's greatest public works project—President Roosevelt's New Deal—to find inspiration for envisioning a transformation of the European economy into a green era. But that's exactly where the Green New Deal got its legs.

Just a year later, in 2009, the Heinrich Böll Foundation—the official foundation of the German Green Party—issued a manifesto titled *Toward a Transatlantic Green New Deal: Tackling the Climate and Economic Crises.* Heartened by the election of Barack Obama to the US presidency and recognizing that the US and the EU account for "a large share of the world economy," our EU friends hoped that a Green New Deal might be the right narrative at the right time to bring the US and the EU together in a powerful transatlantic partnership to advance a postcarbon transition.[4] In November of that year, the Heinrich Böll Foundation held a conference in Berlin where we discussed the potential of the Green New Deal as an overarching narrative and game plan for the upcoming Copenhagen Climate Summit several weeks later.[5]

That same year, the European Greens picked up the theme of a Green New Deal as the party's political platform and published a detailed plan called *A Green New Deal for Europe: Towards Green Modernisation in the Face of Crisis*.[6] The report was the policy document that the European Greens took into the 2009 EU elections as their playbook, and it was championed by the EU's most prominent green leaders, Claude Turmes and Daniel Cohn-Bendit, both colleagues with whom I had worked closely over the years.

The United Nations Environment Programme (UNEP) jumped into the fray that year with a scholarly report written by Edward Barbier titled *Rethinking the Economic Recovery: A Global Green New Deal*.[7] The report helped move the new narrative across the UN agencies and departments and quickly spread to nations around the world, bringing new players into the Green New Deal narrative.

South Korea also joined the ranks in 2009 with its own Green New Deal, signing off on a $36 billion initiative over a four-year period to build out low-carbon projects and create 960,000 new jobs, primarily in the fields of construction, rail, fuel-efficient vehicles, retrofitted buildings, and energy conservation.[8]

In 2011, I coauthored a book with the famed Spanish architect Enric Ruiz-Geli titled *A Green New Deal: From Geopolitics to Biosphere Politics*, focusing on the greening of architecture and the built environment in a climate-changing world.[9]

A few years later, the European Federalist Movement took the Green New Deal forward with a petition titled "New Deal 4 Europe: Campaign for a European Special Plan for Sustainable Development and Employment" and used it to launch a 2015 European-wide citizen initiative to mobilize support for a transition into a zero-carbon green economy.[10] The Green New Deal narrative continued to gain momentum over the years, becoming a theme in the 2019 European elections.

Meanwhile, in the United States, "the Green New Deal" became the moniker for the US Green Party and the presidential run of Jill Stein in 2016.[11]

Bringing the Green New Deal up to date, Data for Progress, a think tank that provides research and polling on left-leaning issues, published its own extensive report in 2018 titled *A Green New Deal: A Progressive Vision for Environmental Sustainability and Economic Stability*.[12] In the fall of 2018, both the fledgling Sunrise Movement and US Representative Alexandria Ocasio-Cortez joined the Green New Deal ranks with their own declaration.[13]

To sum up, the ground had been laid for a Green New Deal movement over a period of a decade. That movement is now coming to fruition with the ascendance of a powerful new millennial- and Gen Z–driven political revolution in both the European Union and the United States.

■ ■ ■

As noted, at the heart of the Green New Deal transition are the four sectors that make up the Second Industrial Revolution infrastructure—ICT/telecommunications; energy and electricity; internal combustion mobility and logistics; and the residential, commercial, industrial, and institutional building stock. In just the past decade, all four of these infrastructure sectors have begun to decouple from the fossil fuel civilization and recouple with green energies, clean technologies, sustainable efficiencies, and the accompanying processes of circularity and resilience that are the central features of an ecological society, leaving stranded fossil fuel assets everywhere. In 2015, Citigroup sent shockwaves through the energy industry and the global economy by predicting $100 trillion in stranded fossil fuel assets if the Paris Climate Summit succeeded in establishing a binding commitment by the nations of the world to limit global warming by 2°C.[14]

The mention of $100 trillion in stranded fossil fuel assets caught the attention of the global business community. Again, stranded assets are assets that have been prematurely written down before their expected life cycle runs its normal course. Stranded assets are part of the normal day-to-day operations of the market. But occasionally, an entire class of assets can suddenly and unexpectedly become stranded. This generally happens when a revolutionary new class of technologies and accompanying infrastructure platforms suddenly enter the marketplace, producing what Joseph Schumpeter termed "creative destruction," quickly depreciating the value of existing assets, killing them off and moving them from the asset column to the liability column on the balance sheet. These types of disruptions most often characterize the great paradigm shifts in communication technology, sources of energy, modes of transport, and changes in habitats—for example, the shift from postal communication to the telephone, or from the horse and buggy to the automobile.

Stranded assets are usually a subject of interest only to accountants. However, lately the term has suddenly burst into the public arena, at least within financial circles and corporate suites, where management is witnessing an epic battle emerge, pitting the dying energies, technologies, and infrastructure of a twentieth-century fossil fuel civilization against the emerging green energies and accompanying digital technologies of a smart twenty-first-century Third Industrial Revolution.

Much of the early pioneering work in examining the trajectory and impact of stranded assets within industries and across supply chains has come from the Smith School of Enterprise and Environment, an interdisciplinary hub of the University of Oxford, and particularly the research of Ben

Caldecott, who directs the Oxford Sustainable Finance Programme.

Shortly after Citigroup dropped the $100 trillion bombshell, Mark Carney, the governor of the Bank of England, informed industry leaders in a speech delivered at a Lloyd's of London dinner that investors might be subject to "potentially huge" losses from agreed-upon climate change targets set by the nations of the world, resulting in massive reserves of oil and gas being "literally unburnable," and stranding assets across the fossil fuel civilization. Carney cautioned that "once climate change becomes a defining issue for financial stability, it may already be too late."[15]

Three years later, in 2018, the issue of stranded fossil fuel assets was no longer tied to nation-states' climate target agreements, which, by this time, were voluntary and often not upheld. Rather, the more serious question that had now entered the public dialogue centered around the falling cost of solar and wind technologies and green power generation and storage in the marketplace, which is driving the four principal sectors of the Second Industrial Revolution to decouple from the fossil fuel infrastructure at a speed and a scale that would have been unthinkable just a few years ago, leaving potentially trillions of dollars in stranded fossil fuel assets behind and abandoned. Here's a current look at the unfolding disruption.

ICT and the Communication Internet

When we think about which sector of the global economy uses the most energy and emits the most global warming gases, we usually tick off electricity, buildings, heat production, transportation, and maybe, as a tentative afterthought, throw agriculture into the mix. The ICT sector, which includes telecommunications, the internet, and data centers, rarely comes up. In fact, even researchers monitoring energy use and global greenhouse gas emissions seldom turn their thoughts to the ICT-related industries, as evidenced by the virtual lack of studies, at least until very recently.

Now, with the exponential rise and use of ICT devices, and especially tablets and smartphones, the introduction of more network equipment, and the proliferation of data centers, as well as the embedding of billions of sensors in the Internet of Things, the amount of sheer data being generated, stored, and sent is escalating—and along with it, the amount of electricity used in the process.

A 2018 study assessing global warming emissions' footprint ran the numbers and found that, "if unchecked, ICT GHGE [greenhouse gas emissions] relative contribution could grow from roughly 1–1.6% in 2007 to exceed 14% of the 2016 level worldwide GHGE by 2040, accounting for half of the current relative contribution of the whole transportation sector."[16]

This projection doesn't even include—but should—the energy used and the carbon emissions in manufacturing all the electronic devices. Nor does it include the short life cycle of these devices in an industry compelled to bring a new generation of devices into the market, especially smartphones and tablets, every two years in the quest for larger profit margins. The use of energy in just the manufacturing of these devices accounts for 85–95 percent of the devices' life-cycle annual carbon footprint.[17] If we take still another step back in the ICT supply chain, the projection doesn't include energy used and emissions emitted in extracting and processing rare earths and embedding them into devices, nor the cost of waste disposal for literally billions of devices.

Although smartphones and tablets are big players in

energy use and are on a steep upward growth curve, it's the ICT infrastructure that consumes the most energy, uses the most electricity, and emits the most greenhouse gas emissions, accounting for 70 percent of the ICT carbon footprint. And it's the proliferation of data centers that accounts for most of the energy use and carbon footprint, which by 2020 is estimated to be near 4 percent of all of the world's power and 45 percent of the entire ICT footprint.[18] The Green New Deal agenda will have to pay close attention to the ICT sector's decarbonization as it comes to use an increasing percentage of the global electricity being generated.

The world's giant internet companies are leading the way in decoupling from fossil fuels and reinvesting in green energy in the ICT sector, with Apple, Google, and Facebook setting the pace. In April 2018, Apple announced that all of its data centers worldwide are now powered by renewable energy. The company also announced that twenty-three of its key manufacturing partners around the world have agreed to power all of Apple's production with 100 percent green energy. Commenting on this milestone, Apple's CEO, Tim Cook, said, "We're going to keep pushing the boundaries of what is possible with the materials in our products, the way we recycle them, our facilities and our work with suppliers to establish new creative and forward-looking sources of renewable energy because we know the future depends on it."[19] Google achieved 100 percent renewable energy usage in its data centers in 2017 and is currently operating twenty renewable energy projects with a total investment of $3.5 billion in renewable energy infrastructure.[20] In July 2017, Facebook announced that "all" of its new data centers from here on out will be powered by 100 percent renewable energy.[21]

The internet behemoths are out front in decoupling from the fossil fuel civilization, but many other leading ICT and telecom companies are running nearly apace. The numbers are significant. Microsoft and SAP have been 100 percent powered by renewable energy since 2014.[22] AT&T, Intel, and Cisco, among others, are quickly integrating renewable energy into their companies' business operations.[23]

Given that solar and wind are now cheaper than coal and head-to-head with oil and natural gas, and within just a few years will be far cheaper, and with the marginal cost of generating solar and wind near zero, the upfront financial commitment to decouple from fossil fuels and reinvest in renewable energies is, simply speaking, a smart business decision. Add to the equation the need to be able to secure data centers and other sensitive operations if the power grids and electricity lines go down (more likely with the increasing incidence of climate events and cyberterrorism), so that these companies' off-grid data center facilities and other operations will remain secure.

The Renewable Energy Internet

Unbeknownst to most government leaders, a large swath of the business community, and a majority of the public, solar and wind energy generation have both been on a steeply declining exponential cost curve, not unlike the exponential curve experienced earlier by the computer industry. ENIAC, the first electronic computer, was invented at the University of Pennsylvania in 1945.[24] Thomas Watson, then president of IBM, allegedly predicted that the world demand would not extend beyond five computers because of the potentially prohibitive cost. What no one could predict back then was developments in the 1970s at Intel, where engineers were successful in doubling the number of components per integrated circuit every two years, putting computer chips on a plunging exponential curve in cost. Today, over 4 billion people connect to the internet, largely due to the availability of affordable smart devices.[25]

Similarly, in 1977, the fixed cost per watt of silicon photovoltaic cells used in solar panels was $76; today, that cost has dropped to below 50 cents.[26] Currently, power and utility companies are quietly buying long-term power generation contracts for solar for as little as 2.42 cents a kilowatt-hour.[27] And according to a 2019 report released by the International Renewable Energy Agency (IRENA), onshore wind is being generated at as low as 3 to 4 cents per kilowatt-hour,[28] with no end in sight in terms of the exponentially falling cost of generating the new green energies.[29]

The impact on society of near-zero marginal cost solar and wind energy is all the more pronounced when we consider the enormous potential of these energy sources. The sun beams 470 exajoules of energy to Earth every eighty-eight minutes—equaling the amount of energy human beings use in a year. If we could grab hold of one-tenth of 1 percent of the sun's energy that reaches Earth, it would give us six times the energy we now use across the global economy.[30] Like solar radiation, wind is ubiquitous and blows everywhere in the world—although its strength and frequency vary. A Stanford University study on global wind capacity concluded that if 20 percent of the world's available wind were harvested, it would generate seven times more electricity than we currently use to run the entire global economy.[31]

According to a detailed study conducted by researchers from Stanford University and the University of California at Berkeley and published in *Joule* in 2017, the United States has the capacity to provide nearly 100 percent of its energy needs with renewables, with solar contributing 57.28 percent, wind contributing 38.41 percent, and the remaining 4 percent made up of hydro, wave, and geothermal.[32]

There are more than 3,000 electricity providers in the

United States—made up of 2,000 publicly owned utilities (POUs), 187 investor-owned utilities (IOUs), 876 cooperative electric utilities (co-ops), 9 federal power agencies, and several hundred power marketers—serving 151 million customers.[33]

It's no secret that the electricity sector is beginning to decouple from the fossil fuel industry in both the European Union and China, while still taking baby steps in most of America. The Renewable Energy Internet is comprised of five foundational pillars, all of which have to be phased in simultaneously for the system to operate efficiently.

First, buildings will need to be refurbished and retrofitted to make them more energy efficient so that solar energy technology can be installed to generate power for immediate use or for delivery back to the electricity grid for compensation. Second, ambitious targets must be set to replace fossil fuels and nuclear power with solar- and wind-generated energy and other renewable energy sources. To achieve this goal, incentives need to be introduced to motivate early adopters to transform buildings and property sites into micro power-generating facilities. Third, storage technologies, including batteries, hydrogen fuel cells, water pumping, etc., will need to be embedded at local generation sites and across the electricity grid to manage both the flow of intermittent green electricity and the stabilization of peak and base loads. Fourth, advanced meters and other digital technology will need to be installed in every building to transform the electricity grid from the current servomechanical operation to digital connectivity capable of managing multiple sources of green electricity flowing to the grid from local generators. The distributed smart electricity infrastructure will enable formerly passive consumers of electricity to become active managers of their own green electricity. Fifth, parking spaces will need to be equipped with charging stations to allow electric vehicles to secure power from the new Energy Internet.

Millions of electric vehicles connected to the Energy Internet will also provide a storage system that can send electricity back to the grid during peak demand, when the price of electricity has spiked, while vehicle owners can be compensated for contributing their electricity to the network.

The construction of a national smart grid across the country will serve as the backbone of the Energy Internet. The Electric Power Research Institute (EPRI) provides a comprehensive definition of what makes up the national smart grid:

> Today's power system . . . is primarily comprised of large central-station generation connected by a high voltage network or Grid to local electric distribution systems which, in turn, serve homes, business and industry. In today's power system, electricity flows predominantly in one direction using mechanical controls. . . . The Smart Grid still depends on the support of large central-station generation, but it includes a substantial number of installations of electric energy storage and of renewable energy generation facilities, both at the bulk power system level and distributed throughout. In addition, the Smart Grid has greatly enhanced sensory and control capability configured to accommodate these distributed resources as well as electric vehicles, direct consumer participation in energy management and efficient communicating appliances. This Smart Grid is hardened against cyber security while assuring long-term operations of an extremely complex system of millions of nodes.[34]

Back in 2011, EPRI estimated that the national smart grid and accompanying storage technology would cost upwards of $476 billion over a twenty-year period to construct but that the grid would create between $1.3 trillion and $2 trillion in overall economic benefits. EPRI also estimated that the installation of a national smart grid could cut emissions by "58 percent relative to 2005 emissions."[35]

But that study was done in the very early years of the transformation of the electricity sector from fossil fuels to renewable energies and at the onset of the decoupling of electric utilities, transportation, and the building sector from fossil fuels and the recoupling to renewable sources of energy for electricity. And in 2011, electric vehicles were in their infancy, and the Internet of Things was still largely a concept and had not yet rolled out across society, connecting everything with everyone in an emerging smart digital infrastructure. There was also little discussion in 2011 about a shift from gas and oil heating to all-electric heating across the nation's residential, commercial, industrial, and institutional building stock.

These new developments will dramatically increase the demand for electricity to power and move economic and social life which, in turn, will require ever-greater complexity in managing renewable energies and the generation of electricity coming into and out of the national grid from literally everywhere. The speed at which these changes are occurring suggests that at least the skeletal Energy Internet will need to be built out in a single decade rather than over the two decades projected by the EPRI study or else the system will not be able to handle the demands placed on it by the greater use of electricity over just the next ten years. Failure to do so will hamper and even forestall the Green New Deal transition. If that were to happen, America would not be able to reach the decarbonization target needed to meet the IPCC deadline, set in stone, to avoid tipping over the 1.5 degrees Celsius rise in the Earth's temperature.

Moreover, the increased demands on the national grid and the growing complexity of integrating all of the components and services ups the bill for getting the national smart grid system online and operating smoothly throughout the United States.

For example, a new study published in January 2019 by the Brattle Group, a leading energy and consulting firm specializing in the energy and electricity fields, estimates that the build-out and scale-up of just the "transmission infrastructure" of the smart national power grid will cost upward of $40 billion annually between 2031 and 2050. According to a 2016 study by the National Renewable Energy Laboratory (NREL), even if solar panels were installed on every "appropriate" building in the United States, this distributed energy would only provide approximately 40 percent of the country's current electricity demand.[36] This will mean that utility-scale solar and wind generation in less-populated rural areas in the western half of the country where there is ample solar and wind will need to be brought online to send green electricity to the eastern half of the United States to complement the distributed solar and wind generated in metropolitan regions— all of which require the build-out of the high-voltage national transmission system. This investment in transmission infrastructure will be essential, according to the Brattle Group, to "ensure that the grid is robust, flexible, capable of maintaining high levels of reliability, and resilient against energy threats."[37]

Other studies are projecting differing estimates for various parts of the national smart grid infrastructure that also need to be scaled. All these studies at this point in time are best-guess scenarios given the speed at which the national electricity grid is moving from a fossil fuel–based centralized system to a distributed electricity system based on potentially millions of solar- and wind-generation sites feeding in and off a smart highly digitized nationwide power grid. There will be a need to bring together all the stakeholders at the federal, state, and local levels to begin the process of fine-tuning both the prioritization of the various components of the national electricity infrastructure, their costs over time, and how they will be integrated into a nationwide operating system over a 20-year period.

The phase-in and integration of the five pillars that make up the operating platforms of the Renewable Energy Internet transform the electricity grid from a centralized to a distributed system, and from fossil fuel and nuclear generation to renewable energy. In the new system, every business, neighborhood, and homeowner becomes a potential producer of electricity, sharing their surplus with others on a smart Energy Internet that is beginning to stretch across national and continental landmasses. America's Green New Deal will need to heed the lessons we learned in Europe and, from the get-go, ensure that all five pillars of the Renewable Energy Internet are brought together as a seamless whole or risk setbacks that will delay the successful deployment of the Third Industrial Revolution paradigm.

In Germany, the federal government established a feed-in tariff across the country to spur businesses, neighborhoods, and individuals to install solar panels and wind turbines, for which they would receive a premium price above the market price for selling their green electricity back to the grid. The incentive worked. Small and medium-sized enterprises, neighborhood associations, and farmers created electricity cooperatives, secured bank loans, and are currently generating solar and wind energy, which they are selling back to the national power grid. In 2018, all renewables claimed a 35.2 percent share of energy sources in gross German power production; nearly 25 percent of all the power was solar and wind, and much of it was being produced by small electricity cooperatives.[38]

Germany's once-powerful electric utilities—E.ON, RWE, EnBW, and Vattenfall—are producing only 5 percent of the new green electricity of the twenty-first century, taking them out of the game of "generating" green electricity.[39] To their credit, these companies were ideally suited to generate electricity from centralized sources of energy—coal, oil, and natural gas—which require large amounts of capital to extract, transport, and transform into electric power on the grid. The enormous capital requirements inevitably led to the erection of giant, vertically integrated business operations to create economies of scale and return profits to investors.

The new green energies, however, are distributed rather than centralized. The sun shines everywhere, and the wind blows everywhere, which means that they can be harnessed everywhere—on rooftops and along terrains—favoring literally millions of micro power-generating sites. The shift from fossil fuels to green energy is "power to the people," both figuratively and literally, as hundreds of millions of people become producers of their own energy and electricity where they work and live. This is the beginning of the great democratization of power in communities around the world.

Critics have long argued that Germany's love affair with renewable energy hides a darker story: the country's continued reliance on dirty coal. The fact is, while solar and wind make up nearly 25 percent of the share of energy sources in gross German power production, and are now cheaper than coal, Germany relies on coal for more than one-third of its energy needs.[40] Why is Germany still using coal? It has to do with the politics of how to bail out those regions of Germany that rely on mining coal to maintain their local economies and employments. To address this issue, a German government commission announced in January 2019 that it would embark on an ambitious plan to completely eliminate coal-generated energy over the next twenty years and, in return, compensate the coal regions with €40 billion to assist their local economies in transitioning into the green era.[41] Other countries around the world that continue to rely on coal are watching the German experiment, realizing that they, too, will have to quickly phase out coal while assisting their coal-producing regions in staying on their feet.

The International Trade Union Confederation (ITUC), representing 207 million unionized workers in 331 affiliated organizations in 163 nations and territories, has drawn international attention to the need to address the plight of stranded workers and stranded communities in what is likely to be an accelerated exit from the fossil fuel civilization. The confederation has established a "Just Transition Centre" to assist stranded workforces and disadvantaged communities in embracing the new green business opportunities and mass employment in the emerging green energy economy.

Sharan Burrow, the general secretary of the International Trade Union Confederation, warns that the "sectoral and economic transformation we face is on a scale and within a timeframe faster than any in our history."[42] Fortunately, the statistics show that even in the early stages of the transition from a fossil fuel culture to a renewable energy society, green semiskilled, skilled, and professional jobs exceed employment in the conventional energy sector in many communities and regions. Burrow makes clear, however, that local and national governments need to step up and "establish just transition funds in all countries and for vulnerable communities, regions, and sectors" to cover "investment in education, reskilling and retraining; extended or expanded social protections for workers and their families; and grant, loan and seed capital programmes for diversifying community and regional economies."[43]

The democratization of energy resulting from the falling costs of solar- and wind-harvesting technology, along with early adoption by newly established electricity cooperatives, has not only disrupted the fossil fuel workforce but also shaken the power-generation and electric utility industry, forcing a disruption in their business models. Many of the world's giant power and electric utility companies are quickly decoupling from the fossil fuel industry and moving to manage the green energy being produced by millions of individuals in cooperatives while establishing a new business model of energy services for customers.

In the new energy practice, the electricity companies will mine Big Data on electricity consumption across each client's value chains and use analytics to create algorithms and applications to help their clients increase their aggregate energy efficiency and productivity and reduce their carbon footprint and marginal cost. Their clients, in return, will share the aggregate efficiency and productivity gains with the electricity companies. Power companies will profit more from managing energy use more efficiently and selling less rather than more electricity.

In 2006, Utz Claassen, the CEO of EnBW, invited me to Germany on two separate occasions to meet with his senior staff to help lay out a strategy to transition the company out of fossil fuels and nuclear power and into the renewable energies and accompanying energy services of a Third Industrial Revolution.[44] Claassen was quick to jump onboard, informing his five hundred senior employees at a mass meeting that EnBW would lead the German power and electric utility companies into the new era of postcarbon distributed renewable energy services. In 2012, EnBW announced its plan to transition from fossil fuels and nuclear power and pay more attention to renewable energies and energy services.[45]

In 2008, I received a similar invitation from E.ON to engage in a public discussion with its chairman, Dr. Johannes Teyssen, on the new business model for managing energy services in the emerging green society. Eight years later, E.ON split into two companies, one remaining with the legacy businesses in conventional fossil fuel energies and nuclear power and the other focusing on renewable energy services, to adjust to the disruptive changes in the German power and electric utility sector that were forcing a paradigm shift.[46]

Vattenfall and RWE, the other two major German power and electric utilities, have announced similar transition strategies based on the new business model that we introduced in Europe.[47] German power companies, who just a decade earlier were among the unrivaled giants of the European power industry, changed course, recognizing that they were facing an old and outmoded energy regime and its accompanying infrastructure of stranded fossil fuel assets that was no longer a viable business model.

Nor were the German power companies an aberration. China has now entered the renewable energy field and currently leads the world in the manufacture and installation of solar- and wind-harvesting technology. In 2017, China accounted for more than 45 percent of the global total investment in renewable energy.[48]

In December 2012, the Xinhua News Agency reported that Premier Li Keqiang had read *The Third Industrial Revolution* and had instructed the National Development and Reform Commission and the Development Research Center of the State Council to read it and follow up with a thorough study of the ideas and themes it puts forth.[49] Wang Yang, then the Communist Party secretary of Guangdong—the nation's leading industrial hub—and a member of the Politburo, and shortly thereafter a vice premier of the country, also championed the book publicly, helping move the narrative across China between 2013 and 2018. (Wang Yang is currently number four on the hierarchy of the seven-person standing committee of the Politburo of China.) I subsequently traveled to China on four official visits in September 2013, October 2014, October 2015, and March 2016, meeting with Wang Yang and other top government officials from the National Development and Reform Commission, the Development Research Center of the State Council, the Ministry of Industry and Information Technology, and the China National Academy of Sciences to discuss the Chinese transition into a Third Industrial Revolution economy. During the first two visits, the vice premier expressed his government's determination to ensure that China is among the leaders in deploying a green Third Industrial Revolution.

Three months after my first visit in September 2013, the government of China announced a massive financial commitment to lay out a digital Energy Internet across China, so that millions of Chinese homeowners and apartment dwellers and thousands of Chinese businesses can produce their own solar- and wind-generated green electricity in and around their residential, commercial, and industrial buildings and share surpluses with each other on the national electricity grid. The chairman of the China State Grid Corporation, Liu Zhenya, accompanied the announcement with the publication of an article titled "Smart Grid Hosting and Promoting the Third Industrial Revolution." In the essay, Liu Zhenya described China's ambitious plan to digitalize the electricity grid and transform it into an Energy Internet. The distributed, collaborative, peer-to-peer, and laterally scaled energy infrastructure will alter the economic life of China while establishing its commanding leadership in the next great economic revolution. The announcement made by Liu Zhenya of the decision to introduce the Energy Internet as the "intercontinental backbone network" for a new economic era represents a decisive moment in the history of China. According to Chairman

Liu Zhenya, if we "can firmly grasp the historical opportunity for the Third Industrial Revolution, [it] will largely determine our position in future global competition."[50]

In November 2014, President Xi Jinping surprised the world community by announcing his country's commitment to increase the use of non–fossil fuel energies in primary energy consumption—primarily solar and wind—to 20 percent by 2030.[51] Bloomberg New Energy Finance's (BNEF) annual long-term economic analysis of the world's power sector has China benefiting from having 62 percent of its electricity being supplied by renewables by 2050.[52] This would mean that the majority of energy powering the Chinese economy would be generated at near-zero marginal cost, making China and the European Union the two most productive and competitive commercial spaces in the world.

While China followed the EU's lead in the first generation of the solar and wind energy transition, a visionary Chinese green energy pioneer, Li Hejun, the founder and CEO of Hanergy, leaped ahead in second-generation green energy adoption, becoming the world's number-one solar thin-film producer. In his 2015 biography, *China's New Energy Revolution*, Li Hejun said that he "was deeply moved [by the] powerful set of coordinates and insights" in *The Third Industrial Revolution* and was particularly struck by the contention that solar energy was "more suitable for future independent and distributed production."[53]

In September 2013, Li Hejun, who at the time was also the vice chairman of the powerful All-China Federation of Industry and Commerce, invited me to Beijing to share the vision, theory, and practical application of renewable energies—and the role China might play in the next great energy revolution—with twenty of China's key policy leaders, thought leaders, and entrepreneurs. The meeting was a seminal event that helped galvanize support behind the Chinese leadership's new commitment to establishing the green business opportunities of an ecological era.[54]

Fast-forward to 2018. Hanergy leads the world in thin-film solar power technologies. Its new "solar powered electric express delivery cars," equipped with thin-film modules, are on the road and can travel 100 kilometers a day.[55] The company, which holds the world record for solar efficiency at a 29.1 percent conversion rate, is also using thin film to power unmanned aerial vehicles, backpacks, umbrellas, and a range of other items, allowing individuals to carry the sun's energy with them wherever they go to power much of what they do.[56]

China's renewable energy sector already employs 3.8 million people.[57] The manufacturing, installing, and servicing of solar- and wind-harvesting technology and the conversion of the country's electricity grid from a servomechanical system operating on fossil fuels and nuclear power to a digital Renewable Energy Internet will spawn millions of additional jobs in the coming three decades.

The US power and electric utilities are just beginning to catch up to their European and Chinese counterparts. San Antonio, Texas, is America's seventh-largest city in population, and its public electric utility, CPS Energy, is the largest municipally owned energy and electric utility in America and a prime contributor to the revenue of the city.[58] In 2009, CPS Energy and the City of San Antonio invited our TIR team to collaborate on a master plan to transition the metropolitan region into the first zero-emission Third Industrial Revolution infrastructure in the United States. Our team included twenty-five experts from around the world and across the sectors of ICT, the renewable energy industry, global transport and logistics, architecture, construction, urban planning, and economic modeling and environmental design.[59] Aurora Geis, the chairwoman of CPS, headed up their team, and Cris

Eugster, at the time the sustainability director and now the COO of CPS, guided the day-to-day efforts.

The roadmap process took place over several months. At the time, San Antonio was pivoting between two approaches to its energy future. The company had been the first American electric utility since the nuclear reactor meltdown at Three Mile Island in 1979 to commission two nuclear power plants and had begun the planning stages toward construction before we arrived on the scene.[60] CPS was also looking at an equally bold future course that would take it into wide-scale wind and solar energy generation across the state and had begun to make forays into these new energy fields as well.

There was already opposition in the city to building two nuclear power plants nearby. In addition, there was concern that the nuclear power plants might experience the kind of cost overruns that had plagued other nuclear power plant installations, jeopardizing the revenue of CPS and the city of San Antonio. CPS had commissioned a study on the potential risks of cost overruns, and the report projected the possibility that the cost could be as much as 50 percent higher than originally estimated when the commitments were signed off.

Our consulting group, at the time, urged CPS to grab hold of the green energy option. We argued that the wind potential in Texas alone could catapult the state into a green zero-emission energy future with wind being generated at near-zero marginal cost.

Texas's claim to fame in the Second Industrial Revolution was its identification as the largest oil-producing state in the United States and, at one time, the world. We suggested that a bold shift to wind, accompanied by solar, could reposition the state as the leading renewable energy power in America in the rollout of a Third Industrial Revolution. It was during this internal conversation that CPS learned that Toshiba, the Japanese company overseeing the installation of the nuclear power plants, had just projected a cost overrun of $4 billion over the originally agreed-upon price, taking the price tag to $12 billion.[61]

A crisis ensued, and when the dust settled, the city and CPS bailed out of the nuclear deal with a substantial financial loss, swinging the door wide open to wind power. It turned out to be a good business decision. The current levelized minimum cost of energy (LCOE) per megawatt hour for building and operating a nuclear power facility today is $112, while, as mentioned, the minimum levelized cost for generating a megawatt of wind is $29, and utility-scale solar comes in at $40 per megawatt hour.[62] Still, apparently not every power and electricity company has heeded the message. The only new nuclear power plant under construction in the United States in the past 30 years is Georgia Power's Vogtle Electric Generating Plant. This nuclear power plant, originally contracted at $4.4 billion, is now five years behind schedule and has ballooned to a $27 billion project—a whopping cost overrun by any standard.[63] It's difficult to understand how some elected officials are still championing the construction of new nuclear power plants across the country.

In the meantime, in the past eight years, CPS Energy has been beating a path through Texas, making deals with ranchers to install wind farms across the plains. Today, ranchers around the state are enjoying a second income, hosting wind farms where the cattle roam.

Texas is currently the nation's leading wind-generating state and has more installed capacity than all but five countries in the world. Wind generated about 15 percent of the electricity in the state in 2017, putting it on par with the current green energy generation in the European Union.[64] On March 31, 2016, CPS Energy reported that 45 percent of San Antonio's "daily energy needs . . . were met through wind energy generated from seven contracted farms."[65]

The lesson here is that Texas accomplished most of this in less than ten years, by taking a risk and sticking to their hunch that wind power would rebrand the Lone Star State. Along with California, Texas has raised the bar and demonstrated to the other forty-eight states that they can begin playing in the same green arena, bringing America into a nearly 100 percent renewable energy regime made up of solar and wind and accompanying energy efficiencies over the course of the next two decades.

Anne Pramaggiore is another key American player leading the charge. For many years Pramaggiore has been the president and CEO of Commonwealth Edison, the giant electric utility serving Chicago, and she is now also CEO of Exelon Utilities, which, with six businesses (including ComEd) under its umbrella, is the country's largest natural gas and electric distribution company. In 2016, Pramaggiore delivered a keynote address at the Energy Thought Summit in Austin, Texas. She mentioned that two years earlier, her company had convened a group of power-sector stakeholders to brainstorm how to make the electricity grid smarter. While many of the leading energy management companies and consultancies contributed valuable suggestions and insights, Pramaggiore felt that the effort lacked a unifying concept until she read *The Third Industrial Revolution*.[66] Pramaggiore studied our twenty years of engagement in the European Union in introducing both the Renewable Energy Internet infrastructure for generating and managing the green energies and the new provider/user energy services business model that accompanies the paradigm shift, and she thought about how the approach might be adapted to the American electricity network.

In her presentation, Pramaggiore remarked, "It was kind of like having a jigsaw puzzle where you have all the red pieces in one corner, all the blue pieces in another corner and you can kind of see it coming together, but it's not there.

Then all of a sudden we started reading platform economics and the pieces started coming together. It made sense to
us."[67] Pramaggiore is the first of a new generation of American
electric utility chiefs conversant in digital platform capabili-
ties brought to the production and distribution of renewable
energies and comfortable with the new disruptive business
model that will need to be put in place to move society into a
zero-carbon future.

How disruptive will the transition be for the fossil fuel sector and accompanying electricity sector with the onslaught of
solar and wind energy into the market? IRENA (the International Renewable Energy Agency) was commissioned by the
German government to do a report on the future projections
of fossil fuel production and consumption versus renewable
energy production and consumption in preparation for its
presidency of the G20 Summit in 2017. A part of that report
ran scenarios on the potential cost of stranded assets brought
on by the accelerating transformation from a fossil-fuel-
driven civilization to a renewable-energy-powered society.

IRENA ran a two-timeline-scenario projection on the
adoption of renewable energies and the speed of energy efficiency deployment to assess how each timeline will affect the
magnitude of stranded assets across upstream energy (energy
at its source), power generation, and buildings and industry,
the "three large sectors that are responsible for approximately
three-quarters of today's direct global energy-related carbon
dioxide emissions." In the first scenario, called REMap, "accelerated" renewables and energy deployment from 2015 to
2050 "will deliver emission reductions that have a two out of
three chance of maintaining a global temperature change below 2 degrees Celsius above pre-industrial levels." The second
case, called the "delayed policy action," is a business-as-usual
scenario until 2030 and thereafter an accelerated deployment

of renewables "to ensure that the global energy system remains within the same emission budget by 2050."[68]

In the delayed policy action scenario for upstream energy, were business-as-usual capital expenditures on fossil fuel energy to continue to 2030, the stranded fossil fuel assets would total approximately $7 trillion, while under the accelerated early transition REMap scenario, the stranded fossil fuel assets would come in at $3 trillion in losses. The stranded assets would represent 45–85 percent of the assumed valuation of today's oil upstream production.[69]

In power generation, under the delayed scenario, fossil-fuel-related assets would total $1.9 trillion, while under the accelerated early transition REMap model, stranded fossil fuel assets would be $0.9 trillion.[70]

The prospect of trillions of dollars in losses is a sober reminder that when it comes to the rise and fall of great civilizations, past assets inevitably become future liabilities, imposing a bill on generations not yet here. There are times in history when new communication, energy, and mobility and logistics technology revolutions are nowhere on the horizon, leading to the collapse of a civilization. Fortunately, this time around, a powerful new green infrastructure revolution is what's pushing the old infrastructure aside, while creating the opportunity to live more lightly and sustainably on Earth.

3

ZERO-CARBON LIVING

Autonomous Electric Mobility, Nodal
IoT Buildings, and
Smart Ecological Agriculture

It is worth reiterating that the automobile was the anchor of
the Second Industrial Revolution. Much of the world's GDP
over the course of the twentieth century is traceable back to
the production and sale of hundreds of millions of internal
combustion cars and millions of buses and trucks, and all of
the industries and sectors that fed into their production and
sale, as well as all of the industries and businesses that benefited from "the Auto Age" and the build-out of new cities and
suburbs, including the real estate industry, shopping malls,
fast-food chains, travel and tourism, theme parks and tech
parks . . . the list is endless.

Near-Zero Marginal Cost Mobility

The transportation and logistics industry, which burns an
enormous amount of fossil fuels and is a major contributor to
global warming emissions, is also decoupling from the fossil
fuel industry and moving over to the production of electric
and fuel-cell vehicles powered by solar and wind electricity
from the electric utilities. Eighteen countries, including Germany, China, India, France, the Netherlands, and Ireland,

have already announced their intentions to phase out the sale and registration of new vehicles powered by fossil fuels in the next few decades.[1]

Much of the oil used for transportation is going to remain in the ground as auto companies transition to electric and fuel-cell vehicles. Bank of America projects that electric vehicles will account for 40 percent of all car sales by 2030. According to a study conducted by Fitch Ratings, one of the three major US credit rating agencies, global electric vehicles could number as many as 1.3 billion by 2040. Taking this into consideration, Bank of America concludes that "electric vehicles will likely start to erode this last major bastion of oil demand growth in the early 2020s and cause global oil demand to peak by 2030."[2]

Many of the lead cities in the world are already taking into account current projections on the swift transition underway in the auto industry from internal combustion vehicles powered by fossil fuels to electric vehicles powered by green renewable electricity. In April 2019, Los Angeles mayor Eric Garcetti made public a sweeping Green New Deal master plan that put the future of transport at the center of the city's shift into a zero-emission economy. Garcetti announced that 25 percent of all vehicles in the city of Los Angeles will be electric by 2025, and 80 percent by 2035.[3] These projections are striking for a city known for its car culture.

The oil giants are not unaware of what all of this means for their industry. In July 2017, Royal Dutch Shell CEO Ben van Beurden said that global oil demand could peak by the late 2020s as electric vehicles begin to replace en masse the internal combustion engine of the twentieth century. In an interview on Bloomberg TV, van Beurden added that he would join the ranks and buy an electric car as his next vehicle purchase.[4]

Is Royal Dutch Shell's CEO just being glib? Some of the

other global oil giants are still keeping a stiff upper lip. Helen Currie, the chief economist at ConocoPhillips, says her company ran scenarios on projected electric car demand and other factors that might affect the future prospects of the oil industry and "struggled with finding a peak" for demand, at least "anytime within the next 20 to 30 years." She added that "we readily acknowledge it's plausible, but we really tend to see oil demand being fairly strong and robust."[5] Others disagree.

Much depends on three factors revolutionizing the transportation sector: the transition from gasoline-powered vehicles to electric and fuel-cell vehicles powered by green energies; the shift to shared vehicle services; and the introduction of self-driving vehicles. Each of these shifts is revolutionary and, standing alone, would be enough to disrupt the transportation sector. Together, feeding off each other, they portend a complete upheaval of mobility and logistics around the world, leaving a trail of stranded assets, the magnitude of which is difficult to fully comprehend.

The meshing of the Communication Internet and the Renewable Energy Internet makes possible the build-out and scale-up of the autonomous Mobility and Logistics Internet. The convergence of these three internets comprises the kernel of the Internet of Things platform for managing, powering, and transporting goods and services in a Third Industrial Revolution economy.

The autonomous Mobility and Logistics Internet is made up of four foundational pillars, which, like the pillars of the Energy Internet, have to be phased in simultaneously for the system to operate efficiently. First, charging stations will need to be installed ubiquitously across land-masses, allowing electric vehicles—cars, buses, and trucks—to power up or send back electricity to the grid. Second, sensors will need to be embedded in devices across logistics networks to allow factories, warehouses, distributors, retailers, and end users to have up-to-the-moment data on logistical flows that affect their value chains. Third, the storage and transit of all physical goods across supply chains will need to be standardized—using smart, digitally enhanced containerization—so that they can be efficiently passed off to any transport vehicle and sent along any passageway, operating across the logistics system in the same way that information flows effortlessly and efficiently across the World Wide Web. Fourth, warehouse operators along the logistics corridors will need to aggregate into cooperative networks to bring all of their assets into a shared logistical space to optimize the shipment of goods, taking advantage of lateral economies of scale. For example, thousands of warehouses and distribution centers might establish blockchained cooperatives to share unused spaces, allowing a carrier to drop off a shipment at any warehouse and pass it on to another carrier from another company who might have more cargo going near the particular destination. This will ensure that all the carriers are fully loaded in their trailers at all times and that shipments are sent along the most efficient path en route to their final destination.

The Internet of Things platform will provide real-time logistical data on pickup and delivery schedules, weather conditions, and traffic flows, with up-to-the-moment information on warehouse storage capacities. Automated dispatching will use Big Data and analytics to create algorithms and applications to ensure the optimization of efficiencies along the logistical routes and, by doing so, increase productivity and reduce the carbon footprint while also reducing the marginal cost of every shipment.

By 2028, at least some of the shipments on roads, railways, and water will be carried out by driverless electric and fuel-cell transport, powered by zero-emission and near-zero marginal cost renewable energies and operated by sophisticated algorithms. Autonomous electric and fuel-cell transport will accelerate aggregate efficiency and productivity and reduce the labor cost of shipping goods toward near zero on a smart Mobility and Logistics Internet.

The technological transformation in mobility and logistics is already changing the very nature of what it means to be a transportation company. In 2016, I joined Wolfgang Bernhard, then head of Daimler Trucks & Buses, in Dusseldorf to help introduce Daimler's new mobility and logistics business model to journalists from around the world.[6]

After I took a few minutes to lay out the operating principles of the Mobility and Logistics Internet, Bernhard announced to the assembled journalists that Daimler was investing half a billion euros in its new Digital Solutions & Services unit to provide state-of-the-art smart logistics services to companies to help them better manage their logistics supply chains. At the time of the announcement, Daimler had already equipped 365,000 of its commercial vehicles with sensors, enabling the cabs to monitor and collect Big Data on weather conditions and traffic patterns, as well as up-to-the-moment availability of warehouse space. Bernhard observed that "for high-performance logistics, real-time data are essential—and our trucks supply these data. . . . This will boost our customers' performance and help them to operate their businesses safer and more environmentally friendly."[7]

Bernhard then wowed the journalists in attendance by dimming the room lights and connecting to a live video feed of a helicopter hovering over a German expressway monitoring three Daimler long-haul trucks in transit. The video zoomed into the trucks' cabs, allowing Bernhard to talk to the drivers. He asked all three drivers to take their hands off the steering wheel and feet off the gas pedal. The trucks then went into autopilot mode and platooned together in a train-like formation, transforming the extended vehicles into a mobile Big Data center, picking up relevant logistical data in real time across the expressway. The drivers, in turn, settled into their dual role as logistics analysts, monitoring their sensor feeds and feeding Big Data across the web to their logistics partners. A year later, Daimler invited its top engineers to Berlin, where we further refined the engineering model for the mobility and logistics business.

Ford Motor Company is also introducing a mobility and logistics business, with the launch of Ford Smart Mobility. Ford is partnering with lighthouse cities, working alongside city planners and civic organizations to develop new ways to move people and goods beyond the private car. The goal is to work with a full range of transportation partners to develop seamless mobility services that can partner Ford's autonomous self-driving electric vehicles with public transportation, bike-sharing and scooter-sharing services, and pedestrian walkways to ferry passengers and goods effortlessly, passing them off between the various modes of transportation to final destinations, with the objective of reducing congestion and carbon emissions.[8]

I joined Mark Fields, then CEO of Ford, in January 2017 on the opening day of the North American Auto Show in Detroit to introduce the new business model. Ford went on to sponsor the premiere of the film that our office coproduced with Vice Media, *The Third Industrial Revolution: A Radical New Sharing Economy,* at the Tribeca Film Festival and sponsored subsequent premieres of the film in Miami, San Francisco, and Los Angeles.

The erection of the autonomous Mobility and Logistics Internet transforms the very way we view passenger mobility. Today's youth are using mobile communication technology and GPS guidance on an incipient Mobility and Logistics Internet to connect with willing drivers in car-sharing services. Young people, at least in urban areas, prefer "access to mobility" over "ownership of vehicles." Future generations will likely never own vehicles again in a smart automated mobility era. For every vehicle shared, however, five to fifteen vehicles are eliminated from production.[9] Larry Burns, the former corporate vice president of research, development, and planning at General Motors, studied mobility patterns in Ann Arbor, Michigan, a midsized American city, and found that car-sharing services could eliminate 80 percent of the vehicles currently on the road while providing the same, or better, mobility at a lesser cost.[10]

There are currently 1.2 billion cars, buses, and trucks crawling along in traffic in dense urban areas around the world.[11] The mass production of gasoline-powered internal combustion vehicles has devoured large swaths of the Earth's natural resources over the course of the past hundred years. Burns' study suggests that 80 percent of the vehicles currently on the road are likely to be eliminated with widespread adoption of car-sharing services over the course of the next generation.[12] The remaining 240 million vehicles will be electric and fuel-cell, powered by near-zero marginal cost renewable energy. Those shared vehicles, in turn, will be driverless and running on automated smart road systems.

The long-term transition from ownership of cars to access to mobility in driverless vehicles on smart road systems will alter the business model for the transportation industry. While the big auto manufacturers around the world will produce fewer vehicles over the course of the next thirty years, they will reposition themselves as aggregators of the global automated Mobility and Logistics Internet, managing mobility services.

Let's go back to Royal Dutch Shell CEO Ben van Beurden's provocative prediction that oil consumption could peak in the late 2020s as electric vehicles begin to replace the internal combustion engines of the twentieth century. What are the other major players in the global energy sector and transportation sector saying?

A 2018 report conducted by the Stockholm Environment Institute that projected stranded asset risks in the European transport sector is evocative of what is going to occur in America and around the world, and is worth paying attention to. The study cuts right to the chase, estimating that the European automotive sector alone is at risk of €243 billion ($277 billion) in stranded assets as the transportation revolution unfolds on the continent. It should be noted that the total enterprise value of the European auto industry as of 2017 was €604 billion ($689 billion).[13]

A part of the reason for the steep incline in sales of electric vehicles is the rapidly declining price of lithium batteries, which cost $1,000/kWh (kilowatt-hour) in 2010 but by the end of 2017 were only $209/kWh, a 79 percent plunge in price in just seven years. The average energy density of electric vehicle batteries is also improving, at a rate of 5 to 7 percent each year.[14]

Governments are establishing more strict fuel economy standards for automobiles, which will force a sizable electrification of the automobile fleet, while simultaneously extending generous incentives for the purchase of electric vehicles. China used this carrot-and-stick approach successfully, securing 21 percent of all global sales of electric vehicles in 2017 from just six Chinese cities. Here again, Europe is going toe-to-toe with China. Daimler, Volkswagen, and Volvo have all announced ambitious deployment plans to electrify their fleets over the next ten years, accompanied by similar carrots and sticks offered up by the EU member states.[15]

As of 2018, electric vehicle sales represent only 2 percent of global vehicle sales. However, BNEF projects that worldwide sales of electric vehicles will leap from a paltry 1.1 million in 2017 to an impressive 30 million by 2030, as their price tag dips below the cost of manufacturing internal combustion vehicles. China is running ahead of the game and is projected to account for 50 percent of all global electric vehicle sales by 2025, and 39 percent by 2030, as other countries ratchet up their electric vehicle fleets.[16]

According to BNEF, the "tipping point" where the "unsubsidized cost" of electric vehicles becomes competitive with the cost of internal combustion vehicles is 2024. By 2025, the report projects electric vehicles will constitute 19 percent of all passenger vehicle sales in China, 14 percent in the EU, and 11 percent in the United States. This is the year when the rubber literally hits the road. The number of internal combustion vehicles sold per year (gasoline or diesel) begins to decline in the mid-2020s (following a similar disruption path experienced by the European electricity sector between 2010 and 2015), signaling the beginning of the endgame for the internal combustion engine and the dawn of electric vehicles powered by green electricity.[17] By 2028, BNEF predicts that electric vehicle sales will account for 20 percent of all global vehicle sales.[18] At this juncture, we will likely see the beginning of the collapse of the fossil fuel civilization. It should be noted that 96 million barrels of oil are consumed around the world each day, and transport accounts for approximately 62.5 percent of all the oil used.[19] The numbers speak for themselves.

While the shift to green-powered electric vehicles is a transformational event that, by itself, will rock the global economy in the biggest disruption since the advent of the gasoline-powered automobile, the accompanying shift to driverless autonomous vehicles in car-sharing services will have a comparable impact on changing the way we organize mobility and logistics in society.

The speed of the transformation has caught the industry and society off guard. A 2017 study by RethinkX, a leading transportation research forecaster, reports that today's car-sharing services will quickly transition into shared passenger services and electric vehicle fleets in the 2020s.[20] The increased efficiencies in vehicle utilization will be considerable. For example, consider Europe, where privately owned cars, on average, are only driven 5 percent of the time, and even then only 1.5 out of the 5 seats are occupied. The study projects that shared mobility in autonomous electric vehicles will increase vehicle utilization by ten times, extending a vehicle's lifetime by 500,000 miles, and potentially 1 million miles by 2030. The bottom line, according to the findings of the study, is that mobility as a service will make available a much lower cost of transportation than existing alternatives and be "four to ten times cheaper per mile than buying a new car and two to four times cheaper than operating an existing vehicle by 2021."[21]

A more surprising finding is that provider/user transportation in autonomous vehicles, operating with near-zero marginal cost human labor and powered by near-zero marginal cost solar and wind electricity, plunges the cost of providing mobility while simultaneously allowing the provider to commodify the time passengers spend in the vehicle by offering various types of entertainment and commercial purchases via the internet, similar to the offerings from airlines in long-distance air travel. "Other revenue sources from advertising, data monetization, entertainment and product sales will open a road to free transport," RethinkX concludes.[22]

Because each vehicle will be used on average ten times more than individually owned vehicles, fewer will be needed on the road, and less time will be lost in gridlocked traffic. In the United States alone, traffic congestion cost the economy $305 billion in 2017.[23]

The study also found that by 2030, individually owned human-driven, internal combustion engine vehicles will account for only 40 percent of the vehicles on the road and will represent only 5 percent of all the passenger miles driven. Not surprisingly, these exceptional efficiency gains will raise the annual income for US households by as much as $1 trillion by 2030. According to the report's authors, "productivity gains as a result of reclaimed driving hours will boost GDP by an additional $1 trillion."[24]

By 2030, 70 percent fewer passenger cars and trucks will be manufactured, disrupting the entire transportation and logistics sector and stranding assets on a scale never before seen in the industry. On the other hand, the study says that "the average American family will save more than $5,600 per year in transportation costs, equivalent to a wage raise of 10 percent." That's $1 trillion of additional money available to American households.[25]

Whether all the projections of the RethinkX report will materialize in the time frame projected may be open to question. What is sure is that the Great Disruption in the conception and deployment of mobility will have profound consequences for the transportation sector, the energy sector, and society.

Now, double back to Bank of America's claim that increased penetration of electric vehicles into the market "will likely start to erode this last major bastion of oil demand growth in the early 2020s and cause global oil demand to peak by 2030" and Royal Dutch Shell CEO Ben van Beurden's similar claim that global peak oil demand will come by the late 2020s.[26] Are they right? Do the other giant oil companies agree, or are they still bullish on a more extended future for their industry before stranded assets become a reality?

We may already have an answer. Bernstein Research, one of the energy industry's most respected market forecasters, warned in a research note in July 2018 that the global economy could experience an oil-price shock of $150 per barrel, topping even the $147 per barrel all-time high in July 2008 that, along with the subprime mortgage crisis, took the global economy into the Great Recession. According to CNBC,

Bernstein Research says that reinvestments in oil reserves are currently the lowest in over twenty years and the amount of those reserves is likely to last only for another ten years or so.[27] If ten more years of reserves sounds familiar, that's just about the time other studies project that global demand for oil will peak and begin a decline. A coincidence? Unlikely.

Bernstein Research acknowledges that the oil giants are aware of the meteoric rise of renewable energy and electric vehicle adoption and are privy to all the studies suggesting that global oil demand is going to peak sometime in the near future. Some companies are possibly pulling back on replenishing oil reserves beyond ten years for fear of devastating losses brought on by the exploration and capture of oil that will never be used—to wit, stranded assets. With investors already clamoring for the oil companies to return cash to shareholders rather than spend it on replenishing oil that may never be burned, the likelihood, says Bernstein Research, is that "any shortfall in supply will result in a super-spike in prices potentially much larger than the US$150/bbl spike witnessed in 2008."[28]

Nodal IoT Buildings

While the ICT/communication sector, the electricity sector, and the mobility and logistics sector are in the process of de-coupling from the fossil fuel industry, so too is the real estate sector, which also consumes a huge amount of energy and is a primary contributor to global warming emissions.

Cities, regions, and nation-states are mandating and incentivizing the retrofitting of existing buildings to reduce the amount of energy used and are enacting legislation to require that all new residential, commercial, and industrial buildings be zero emission or positive power using solar, wind, geothermal, and other renewable energies. California has established an aggressive agenda to decarbonize its building stock. In September 2018, Governor Jerry Brown signed a bill into law that prepares the ground for reducing greenhouse gas emissions from California's existing residential and commercial buildings by 40 percent below 1990 levels by 2030.[29] The California Public Utilities Commission is also preparing initiatives that will ensure that all new residential buildings be zero net energy by 2020 and all commercial buildings be zero net energy by 2030.[30]

The global real estate market in 2015 was valued at $217 trillion, nearly 2.7 times the GDP of the world, and represents 60 percent of the investment assets of the global economy.[31] Looking ahead, the construction market will grow by another $8 trillion by 2030.[32]

As alluded to earlier, the paradigm shifts in communication, energy, and mobility change the nature of the built environment. The First Industrial Revolution gave rise to dense urban built environments because of hub-to-hub railroad transportation, while the Second Industrial Revolution birthed widely spread out suburban environments off interstate highway exits. In the Third Industrial Revolution, existing and new buildings—residential, commercial, industrial, and institutional—are transformed into zero-carbon energy-efficient smart nodes and networks embedded in an Internet of Things matrix. Every building node connected to the IoT infrastructure acts as a distributed edge data center, green micro power-generating plant, energy storage site, and transport and logistics hub to manage, power, and move economic activity in a smart green America.

Buildings are no longer passive, walled-off private spaces but, rather, actively engaged entities sharing their renewable energies, energy efficiencies, energy storage, electric mobility, and a wide range of other economic activity with one another at the discretion of their occupants. But, the laying on of all the digital infrastructure depends first and foremost on decarbonizing every building.

A vast number of existing US buildings will have to undergo a complete retrofit to seal interiors, minimize energy loss, optimize efficiency, and buttress structures to be resilient to climate-related disruptions. Gas and oil heating, which is a big source of global warming emissions in buildings, will need to be replaced by electrical heating across the residential, commercial, industrial, and institutional building stock. The return on a building's retrofit investment in energy efficiency and energy savings takes place over relatively few years, after which the owner or renter enjoys a reliable stream of savings on energy costs for decades.

Transforming the building stock also means millions of jobs. Each $1 million of spending on the manufacture and installation of building improvements generates 16.3 jobs when adding together direct employment, indirect employment, and induced employment.[33] Germany's experience provides a metric for the job-creating potential in America as it embarks on a nationwide retrofitting project. The German Alliance for Work and the Environment is credited with the most ambitious project—retrofitting 342,000 apartments and, in the process, creating 25,000 new jobs and saving 116,000 existing ones; that's more than 140,000 new or saved jobs.[34] Even though German employment figures might vary somewhat from America's, they can be used to project the potential employment opportunities in the mass retrofitting of US dwellings.

Only after sealing the building envelope to make it more energy efficient can the smart IoT infrastructure be embedded, transforming the building into a smart node, ready to engage its neighbors locally and globally in collective endeavors. Early on, the Internet of Things was viewed more as an ancillary aid to industries to help them increase their surveillance of equipment and improve performance across assembly lines and supply chains—for example, embedding sensors in airplanes that could alert a company when a component needed to be replaced before standard maintenance checkups.

While the term "Internet of Things" was coined by Kevin Ashton back in 1999, the prospects for its widespread application remained unexplored for another thirteen years because of the high cost of sensors and actuators. Then, in an eighteen-month period in 2012 and 2013, the cost of radiofrequency identification chips used to monitor and track things plummeted by 40 percent, opening up the possibility of embedding sensors across the whole of society.[35]

A year later, in 2014, our office published *The Zero Marginal Cost Society*, suggesting that the IoT has a far more important role to play by becoming a smart nervous system to improve commercial and social life.[36] We argued that the IoT's ultimate application would be to embed it within and across the residential, commercial, industrial, and institutional building stock. By doing so, all our habitats would be transformed into smart building nodes that could connect with each other on a multitude of platforms to create a distributed global brain and nervous system, bringing the human family together in ever more diverse and fluid socioeconomic networks.

Silicon Valley entrepreneurs and global consulting companies picked up on the notion of "nodal buildings." Yet it was a Chinese company that quickly applied the theory in practice. Zhang Ruimin is the chairman of the board and CEO of the Haier Group. Much of the public outside China might not be familiar with the company, although their homes, offices, commercial spaces, and tech parks are likely to be outfitted with the company's smart technology. Haier is the world's leading appliance manufacturer and owns various appliance brands around the world, including General Electric appliances in the American market.

I had the pleasure of visiting with Zhang Ruimin in September 2015 on the occasion of the tenth anniversary of the company's launch of its global business plan.[37] After Zhang read *The Zero Marginal Cost Society,* he began to reenvision buildings as smart distributed nodes that could aggregate in social platforms to enrich family life and commerce.[38] Haier is now the leader in smart IoT technology embedded in appliances, which are used in buildings around the world.

Zhang Ruimin told me that the goal of his business model is to provide homes, businesses, and communities with IoT technology that reduces the electricity used and the carbon footprint.

IoT infrastructure in every building, while still nascent, is expected to grow exponentially in the next few years as the United States transforms its building stock into smart digital nodes interconnected in smart networks. Each $1 million of spending on Internet of Things technologies leads to thirteen direct, indirect, and induced jobs.[39]

The real estate sector, by any account, is the most vulnerable to becoming the biggest stranded asset in the world in the coming decades. Unlike the provisioning of energy generation for electricity, the residential, commercial, industrial, and institutional building stock is locked in, with only 2 percent of total property holdings turning over each year, making it the least agile global asset.[40] To gain a proper perspective on how difficult it will be to transform the building stock to near-zero emissions, bear in mind that in the UK, 87 percent of the current building stock will still be standing in 2050.[41]

Our experience in the European Union is that getting up to scale in across-the-board retrofits of the building stock is among the most challenging aspects in implementing a Green New Deal and requires a steadfast resolve to overcome the sociological and psychological intransigence that comes with not wanting to disrupt daily patterns of living and working. The resistance is often overcome, especially in low- and middle-income social and public housing, when occupants realize that their monthly utility bills—generally the biggest housing expense after rent—will plummet, giving them more discretionary income.

Building retrofits are absolutely necessary to decarbonizing the American and global economy and will need to be vigilantly attended to in the Green New Deal transition. If we don't aggressively get on with this task, the projected stranded asset losses in the worldwide building sector are going to be staggering. Under the IRENA delayed case, stranded assets in the global building stock would ring up at a mind-blowing $10.8 trillion, double the amount that would occur in the early accelerated-transition REMap scenario.[42]

The US Conference of Mayors, at their annual conference in Boston in 2018, passed a tough resolution calling on American cities to "focus attention on the energy efficiency of America's existing and newly constructed residential, multi-family, commercial, and governmental buildings."[43] First-mover cities are beginning to heed the call, enacting more strict mandatory requirements and incentives and penalties to accelerate the retrofits of the building stock across their governing jurisdictions in the hope of beating the climate change clock and keeping emissions locked down at 1.5°C or less.

The European Union has established a protocol that our US Conference of Mayors might want to adopt, called the Energy Performance of Buildings Directive; it provides a mechanism for monitoring, incentivizing, and penalizing all the parties that need to be engaged in retrofitting the building stock, installing renewable energy on-site, and creating a smart energy infrastructure with adequate energy storage. This law mandates that every building across the twenty-eight member states hold an Energy Performance Certificate and be responsible for monitoring its own heating and air conditioning. Two members of the faculty of the Department of Architecture and Built Environment at Northumbria University, Kevin Muldoon-Smith, lecturer, and Paul Greenhalgh, associate professor, explain the importance of this act:

> Energy Performance Certificates (EPCs) have a significant relationship with climate-related stranded assets in real estate. They are a key enabler of building improvements, as they influence decision-making in real estate transactions and provide cost-optimal recommendations for energy performance improvement.... They provide the opportunity for governments to enforce minimum energy performance standards, and they are an important information tool for building owners, occupiers, and real estate stakeholders.[44]

The governments of England and Wales have used the EPCs to create an enforceable report card, called Minimum Energy Efficiency Standards (MEES), for nonresidential privately rented property. If a property's MEES score is below E (meaning it has a score of F or G), it would be illegal to rent out. A similar rule is used for residential property. Around 10 percent of residential property, worth £570 billion, and 18 percent of the commercial stock, worth £157 billion, are below the threshold. Both governments are looking at elevating the minimum threshold over time to incentivize physical improvements within buildings.[45]

There are many additional and valuable benefits in issuing minimum energy efficiency standards reports: for example, publicly naming and shaming owners of substandard buildings, not to mention depreciating the value of the property on the market. Continually updated energy performance certificates issued for every building across a city, state, or nation also provide the data set that could be used to determine the value of the property for purposes of assessing property taxes, with more energy efficient properties and properties generating solar electricity receiving tax deductions and less energy efficient properties receiving tax hikes.

Unfortunately, the financing mechanism that accompanies MEES—called, interestingly enough, the "Green Deal Finance Model," which would incentivize the owners of dilapidated residential property to make the efficiency changes—was taken away by the government and never even introduced for commercial property, leaving owners with a penalty but without an incentive to upgrade their properties.[46] Again, the lesson learned over and over is that transitioning the built environment away from the fossil fuel culture and toward a green renewable energy culture, by necessity, must provide equally powerful carrots and sticks to ensure success.

Preparing the American Workforce for the Green Era

The decoupling of the communication sector, the electricity sector, the mobility and logistics sector, and the building stock sector from the fossil fuel civilization has barely begun in the United States. Yet the shift in the makeup of the labor force brought on by the transition to a Third Industrial Revolution economy is already showing up in the rise in employment across the four industries that make up the nervous system of the new green economy. The statistics are impressive. According to the 2017 US Energy and Employment Report compiled by the US Department of Energy, close to 1 million Americans work in the energy efficiency, solar, wind, and electric vehicles sector, which is nearly five times the employment in the fossil fuel electric industry.[47] If part-time workers in the construction industry engaged in retrofitting buildings are included, the number climbs to 3 million Americans "working in part or in whole for the energy efficiency, solar, and wind sectors."[48] These employment numbers are going to grow exponentially as the nation turns its attention to a Green New Deal to transition into a zero-emission Third Industrial Revolution economy over the next two decades.

Preparing a nationwide workforce for the various competencies that will be needed to transform the entire infrastructure of the country into a smart green paradigm will require massive training and/or retraining, on the scale of what the United States did at the beginning of World War II, when the country's male workforce was suddenly deployed to the war effort and women were called forth to manage American industries on the home front. This seemingly impossible task was accomplished in less than eighteen months across every industry. Of late, there has been growing discussion around a similar mobilization and training of high school and college graduates in the form of apprenticeships in communities and industries cued to the build-out and scale-up of the green infrastructure.

According to a Brookings Institution study, there are currently 14.5 million infrastructure workers across the fifty states. They are mostly male, which does not reflect the racial or gender diversity of the population at large. Fewer than 20 percent of the workers in the green energy and energy efficiency fields are women, and people of color make up less than 10 percent of the workforce.[49]

Brookings notes that "the transition to the clean energy economy will primarily involve 320 unique occupations spread across three major industrial sectors: clean energy production, energy efficiency, and environmental management." Most of these jobs will require some level of both vocational and professional training in design, engineering, and mechanical knowledge. Interestingly, hourly wages in the new green jobs exceed the national average by 8 to 19 percent; equally important, workers at the lower end of the income ladder can make $5 to $10 more per hour than in comparable jobs in the old economy.[50]

The problem is that much of the existing infrastructure workforce is nearing retirement, posing the question of how to prepare a new generation with the skills necessary to transition America into a postcarbon green era. State, municipal, and county governments are just now beginning to establish *infrastructure academies* whose purpose is both to retrain the existing workforce and to prepare a younger generation for the new infrastructure jobs that accompany the shift into a Third Industrial Revolution economy. For example, in 2018, Washington, DC, mayor Muriel Bowser established the DC Infrastructure Academy, a joint initiative between the city and public-private partners, including Washington Gas, DC Water, and Pepco, the electric utility, to train workers living in the city's most disadvantaged neighborhoods for the new green employment opportunities.[51]

The Green New Deal has opened up a conversation across the country about establishing green apprenticeships in the form of state and national service programs—a Green Corps, a Conservation Corps, a Climate Corps, an Infrastructure Corps—that will provide a living wage and professional certification upon completion of service and allow a younger generation of Americans to advance careers in an increasingly green economy. There is ample precedent for these initiatives. The Peace Corps, VISTA, and AmeriCorps have proved invaluable in encouraging public service and providing opportunities for young people to learn new skills, which have helped them find career paths and employment. Unions, local governments, universities, community colleges, and trade schools will play an important role in partnering with the various service corps in preparing the new green workforce of the twenty-first century.

Smart Ecological Agriculture

Although the four key sectors that make up a society's critical infrastructure are the juggernaut for managing, powering, and moving economic activity, social life, and governance, and together carry a hefty carbon footprint, we would be remiss in leaving the agricultural sector out, because it is a key consumer of energy and brings with it a big carbon footprint.

The cultivation, irrigation, harvesting, storing, processing, packaging, and shipping of food to wholesalers and retailers uses a huge amount of energy. Petrochemical fertilizers and pesticides account for a significant portion of the energy bill. Operating farm machinery is also a major energy expenditure. In the European Union, the cultivation of crops and animal rearing use the most energy in the food value chain, making up one-third of the energy bill. Industrial processing adds another 28 percent of total energy use. Packaging and logistics comprise 22 percent of the total energy expended. Final disposal of food waste represents about 5 percent of total energy use.[52] The statistics for American farms are likely comparable.

Let's go back to animal rearing for a moment. People would likely be shocked to learn that cattle are responsible for much of human-induced agricultural greenhouse gas emissions, according to the United Nations Food and Agricultural Organization.[53] Livestock, primarily cattle, graze on 26 percent of our planet's ice-free land.[54] There are approximately 1.4 billion cows currently on Earth, and they are a major emitter of methane, a greenhouse gas that has 25 times the global warming potential of carbon dioxide (CO_2).[55] Cows also emit nitrous oxide in their feces. Nitrous oxide has 296 times more global warming potential than CO_2.[56]

But that's just the beginning of the story. In the United States, more than half of crop production by mass is used for animal feed, according to a study by the Institute on the Environment.[57] When compared to the production of common plant-based protein sources, "beef and other ruminants ... require more than 20 times more land and generate more than 20 times more greenhouse gas emissions than pulses [i.e., legumes] per unit of protein consumed," making intensive cattle production and related animal husbandry incredibly inefficient.[58] And then there is the sad fact that the major cause of deforestation in many countries around the world is to provide grassland for grazing cattle, which means far fewer trees to absorb global warming emissions.

Still, it is encouraging that the millennial and Gen Z generations are now becoming aware of the beef issue and beginning to transition their dietary regime toward a more vegetarian or even vegan diet, and fast-food chains are beginning to introduce vegetarian alternatives. In April 2019, Burger King announced that it would be selling plant-based patties at all 7,300 of its locations nationwide by the end of the year.[59]

Unfortunately, the agriculture and food sector around the world has lagged woefully behind other commercial sectors in decoupling from fossil fuels. In Europe, for example, only 7 percent of total energy used in agriculture comes from renewable energy sources, in sharp distinction to 15 percent in the overall energy mix.[60] Weaning the food sector off fossil fuels and petrochemical-based farming in Europe, America, and the world is a demanding task.

The food sector is, however, beginning to turn its attention to the challenge. Replacing petrochemical farming practices and especially the use of petrochemical fertilizers and pesticides with organic ecological-based farming practices is spreading across Europe, while the United States is still trailing. Currently, 6.7 percent of the farmland in the twenty-eight member states of the EU has been given over to organic farming, while only 0.6 percent of agricultural land in the United States is being used to produce organic crops.[61]

However, the retail sales of organic food are increasing, amounting to $45.2 billion in the United States in 2017.[62] Consumer demand is pushing the transformation. A growing number of Americans are willing to pay higher prices for organic and sustainable foods. As the market for organic food grows, more farmers will transition into ecological agricultural practices, bringing the price of organic food down at the retail level.

Farmers are also joining together in the creation of electricity cooperatives and beginning to install solar, wind, and biogas energy technologies.[63] Some of the green electricity is being used on the farm, and the rest is being sold back to the Energy Internet, creating a second source of income.

Farmers might also enjoy a third source of income by "carbon farming." Cover crops, crop rotation, and no-till farming are all simple, long-proven ways to keep carbon sequestered in the soil. For example, a simple planting of cover crops—rye, beans, oats—between rows of vegetables helps hold carbon, nitrogen, and other organic nutrients in the soil. Carbon farming provides a double benefit. It absorbs CO_2 from the atmosphere and stores it in the soil, where it aids in the growth of plants and increases yields.[64]

If the US Department of Agriculture were to reorder just a small amount of its massive aid to American agriculture, which currently totals $867 billion, and provide incentives to encourage farmers to use carbon farming across their fields, it would have a demonstrable impact on carbon capture and storage, addressing climate change while farmers profit from increased yields.[65] Farmers might also be compensated with federal and state tax credits for reforesting part of their land and creating additional carbon sinks to capture and sequester CO_2 emissions.

While the erection of solar and wind installations for generating green electricity on farms and carbon farming for sequestering CO_2 will be important contributions to greening society, a far bigger opportunity exists to expand both efforts on the nation's federally owned land. One-third of the entire landmass, and all of the off-shore land, remains in the federal government's hands.[66] In recent years an increasing percentage of that land has been leased to the fossil fuel industry to extract coal, oil, and gas reserves. Astonishingly, global greenhouse gas emissions from fossil fuels extraction on federal public lands accounted for 23.7 percent of all CO_2 emissions in the United States from 2005 to 2014.[67] At present, a meager 5 percent of the country's renewable energy is generated on public land.[68] The Green New Deal should reverse the priority. The leasing of federal public lands for extracting fossil fuels should be eliminated. At the same time, the opening up of public lands to solar and wind generation on a much larger scale should be encouraged to secure the green energy to power America in the twenty-first century.

Moreover, America's public lands—its forests, grassland, and shrubland—currently sequester only around 15 percent of the CO_2 emissions from fossil fuel extraction on the same public lands.[69] By eliminating fossil fuel extraction entirely and reforesting, where applicable, public lands will become America's lungs for absorbing industrial CO_2 emissions during the transition years into the green era.

The shift from mechanical to digital operations on farms is also beginning to change the way food is grown, harvested, stored, and shipped. The phase-in of the Internet of Things infrastructure promises huge gains in aggregate efficiency and productivity for American farmers, food processors, wholesalers, and distributors. Farmers are already utilizing the emerging IoT by placing sensors across their agricultural fields to monitor weather conditions, changes in soil moisture, the spread of pollen, and other factors that affect yields. Automated response mechanisms are also being installed to ensure proper growing conditions.

As the IoT infrastructure is phased in with the implantation of sensors across supply chains to track every moment of the ag journey from the planting of crops to the final destination at retail stores, farmers, processors, wholesalers, and distributors in the United States will be able to mine the Big Data flowing across their value chains and, in doing so, increase their aggregate efficiency and reduce their marginal cost and ecological footprint in the managing and powering of farms and in the processing and transporting of food, taking the food industry out of the chemical era and into an ecological era mediated by new smart digital interconnectivity.

The Age of Resilience

The way we communicate, harness the Earth's energy, move around, shelter ourselves, and eat are so basic to the organization of economic and social life that we often take them for granted until a fundamental disruption in the way we think of them and use them forces a revolution in our social orientation and the way we perceive the world around us. The transformation in the way we live our lives in a digitally enhanced ecological society is already proving to be very different than our forebears' way of life in a mechanized fossil fuel civilization. In this sense, the Green New Deal infrastructure is as much about a change of consciousness as it is about a change in infrastructure.

Writing at the onset of the fossil fuel era, a French aristocrat, the Marquis de Condorcet, captured the essence of the new consciousness at the height of the French Revolution with a passage full of hope that has metamorphosed into a haunting reminder of where we've come from over the past two centuries. He opined:

> No bounds have been fixed to the improvement of the human faculties.... The perfectibility of Man is absolutely indefinite.... The progress of this perfectibility, henceforth above the control of every power that would impede it, has no other limit than the duration of the globe upon which nature has placed us.[70]

Condorcet's vision became the philosophical frame of what has become known as the Age of Progress. We now know better, surrounded by the carnage wrought by the fossil fuel civilization. Spirited odes to the Age of Progress and the "perfectibility of Man" are seldom heard, and even then in muted tones. The Age of Resilience is upon us. The Green New Deal infrastructure is designed for this reality. Its components, applications, and operations will enable us to adapt to a once pacified and domesticated nature that is now rewilding—and hopefully to survive the escalating climate events that now envelop the Earth.

That's why a prospective Green Corps, Climate Corps, Infrastructure Corps, and Conservation Corps, made up of millions of young Americans, is more than just a career ladder to new business opportunities and employment. These proposed agencies, at the federal, state, and local levels, will be among the first responders to climate events and in the disaster relief and recovery missions that will increasingly be a constant reality rather than a rare anomaly. Every community will need to be continually vigilant and engaged in disaster mode if we are to successfully adapt to the rewilding future that is now here. In this new world, national security is more about climate catastrophes than about military threats. Already, the

Pentagon and state National Guards are reformulating their core missions and increasingly prioritizing critical operations around deployments to address climate events. The new reality is that every community is vulnerable to a radically changing climate. Nobody escapes from the planet's wrath. The Green New Deal's smart Third Industrial Revolution infrastructure is our first line of defense in adapting to climate change. In a sense, it's our lifeline to the future.

4

THE TIPPING POINT

The Collapse of the Fossil Fuel Civilization, Circa 2028

The decoupling from fossil fuels by the four primary sectors responsible for much of the global warming emissions and their realignment with the emerging renewable energies of a Green New Deal is quickly edging society to the collapse of the fossil fuel civilization. In June 2018, *Nature Climate Change* published a detailed and extensive study conducted by scientists from the Cambridge Centre for Environment, Energy and Natural Resource Governance at the University of Cambridge, which concluded that the question of the carbon bubble was no longer tied to governments' emission targets but rather to an ongoing technological revolution, which "remains robust even if major fossil-fuel producers [e.g., the US] refrain from adopting climate mitigation policies."[1] "Our conclusions," say the authors of the report, "support the existence of a carbon bubble, which, if not deflated early, could lead to a discounted global wealth loss of between $1–4tn, a loss comparable to the 2007 financial crisis," but "further economic damage from a potential bubble burst could be avoided by decarbonizing early." The authors go on to say:

Irrespective of whether new climate policies are adopted or not, global demand growth for fossil fuels is already slowing down in the current technological transition. The question then is whether under the current pace of low-carbon technology diffusion, fossil-fuel assets are bound to become stranded due to the trajectories in renewable energy deployment, transport fuel efficiency and transport electrification. Indeed, the technological transition currently underway has major implications for the value of fossil fuels, due to investment and policy decisions made in the past. Faced with SFFA [stranded fossil fuel assets] of potentially massive proportions, the financial sector's response to the low-carbon transition will largely determine whether the carbon bubble burst will prompt a 2008-like crisis.

The authors of the report suggest that the competitive advantage of solar and wind energy prices could force a weakened oil industry to drop the price of oil on world markets—despite the losses—in order to extract the maximum amount of remaining oil from under the ground and the sea and minimize remaining stranded assets. To quote from the report, "Low fossil-fuel prices may reflect the intention of producer countries to 'sell-out' their assets, i.e. to maintain or increase their level of production despite declining demand for fossil-fuel assets." If this scenario were to happen, it would mean a potentially catastrophic increase in global warming emissions, taking the world far beyond the 1.5°C threshold.

20-20-20 in 2020

Let's back up and revisit the series of events that began with governments mandating targets for the reduction in global warming emissions and the subsequent rapid technological innovations that led to a dramatic plunge in the cost of renewable energies.

As briefly mentioned in chapter 2, by 2007 a consensus was emerging, both at the European Commission and within the European Parliament, that weaning the EU off a fossil fuel culture would necessitate legally binding targets across three interrelated domains that all member states would need to accept and adopt: a dramatic increase in energy efficiency; a historic shift to renewable energies; and a huge reduction in global warming emissions. Each of these mandated targets would feed off the other, helping the EU take its first step toward the ultimate goal of a complete transformation into a postcarbon economy by 2050.

The eureka moment came in November 2005 with the election of Angela Merkel as chancellor of Germany. What was most notable about the election is that it led to a grand coalition government between Merkel's Christian Democratic Union (CDU) party and the Social Democratic Party (SPD) and the elevation of Frank-Walter Steinmeier to foreign minister and Sigmar Gabriel to minister of the environment, nature conservation, and nuclear safety.

Germany was already the undisputed world leader in addressing climate change and anxious to transform its economy from fossil fuels to green energies. Both political parties had been nudged to take a more aggressive stance on climate change by the fledgling Green Party that had emerged in the 1980s and had become a major player in German politics. The Green Party narrative eventually metamorphosed into a green agenda that was largely taken up by the Social Democratic Party and the Christian Democratic Union.

The coming together of the CDU and the SPD in a grand coalition, shadowed by the Greens, opened the door to the possibility of a political breakthrough that could change the narrative and future direction of Europe, making it the leader of a green transformation around the world.

By sheer serendipity, Germany was positioned to take over the presidency of the Council of the European Union between January 1 and June 30, 2007 (each member state assumes the presidency in rotation). Germany has always been a prime mover in the EU, and in 2007 three of the five major political parties in Europe were ideologically aligned in the country—the CDU, the SPD, and the Greens. This presented us with a unique opportunity to change course in Europe and move the continent toward a postcarbon green paradigm. All we needed was a similar coalition of the five major parties represented in the European Parliament to come together and pass a written declaration that would call for the EU to mandate strict legal targets for decarbonizing its member states. The six-month German presidency would be the defining moment.

Angelo Consoli, who directs our office in Brussels, and I met with Jo Leinen, a senior member of the European Parliament from Germany and a leading voice of the SPD, to strategize a plan of action that could unite all five major political parties at the European Parliament: the European People's Party–European Democrats (EPP–ED), which is composed of Christian Democratic parties across Europe; the Party of European Socialists (PES); the Greens–European Free Alliance (Greens/EFA); the Alliance of Liberals and Democrats for Europe (ALDE); and the European United Left–Nordic Green Left (GUE–NGL). The objective was to coalesce around an EU parliament written declaration to increase energy efficiencies, generate green energies, and reduce global warming emissions and to make its targets mandatory requirements in the member states.

The passage of a formal written declaration in the European Parliament is a rare occurrence. The rules require passage within a very narrow ninety-day window, making it an extremely difficult and grueling task. Our parliamentary team recruited supporters across the five major EU political parties and began meeting with literally hundreds of parliamentarians and their legislative directors and chiefs of staff, soliciting support. The declaration, which was passed just days before the deadline, reads as follows:

> The European Parliament,
> —having regard to Rule 116 of its Rules of Procedure,
> A. whereas global warming and costs of fossil fuels are increasing, and having regard to the debate launched by the European Parliament and the Commission on the future of energy policy and climate change,
> B. whereas a post-fossil fuel and post-nuclear energy vision should be the next important project of the European Union,
> C. whereas the five key factors for energy independence are: maximising energy efficiency, reducing global-warming gas emissions, optimising the commercial introduction of renewable energies, establishing hydrogen fuel-cell technology to store renewable energies and creating smart power grids to distribute energy,
> 1. Calls upon the EU Institutions to:
>   - pursue a 20% increase in energy efficiency by 2020,
>   - reduce greenhouse gas emissions by 30% by 2020 (compared to 1990 levels),
>   - produce 33% of electricity and 25% of overall energy from renewable energy sources by 2020,
>   - institute hydrogen fuel-cell storage technology, and other storage technologies, for portable, stationary and transport uses and establish a de-

    centralised bottom-up hydrogen infrastructure
by 2025 in all EU Member States,

- make power grids smart and independent by 2025 so that regions, cities, SMEs and citizens can produce and share energy in accordance with the same open-access principles as apply to the internet now;

2. Instructs its President to forward this declaration, together with the names of the signatories, to the Commission and the governments and parliaments of the Member States.[2]

The European Parliament's declaration reinforced the European Commission's similar mandates that were being formulated, giving Germany the needed support to secure the 20-20-20 formula for decarbonizing the European Union.

In June 2007, in the last few days of the German presidency of the Council of the European Union, Sigmar Gabriel asked me to join him and give the keynote address at the German presidency's closing conference of the twenty-seven environmental ministers, officially inaugurating the EU's new postcarbon journey.

It needs to be emphasized that it was the three mandatory targets set in stone by the European Union that led each member state to establish its own plans to reach each of the targets set forth. The most important of these targets was the one mandating that 20 percent of the energy used in the EU needed to be renewable energy, particularly solar and wind, by 2020.[3] To fulfill the mandate, other countries began following Germany's lead by introducing feed-in tariffs, which prompted early adopters to produce green energy for sale back to the grid at a premium price above market value.

The real value of the feed-in tariffs lies well beyond Europe reaching its renewable energy targets. This incentive not only encouraged a flood of small green energy producers to enter the market—primarily in the form of electricity cooperatives—but also propelled companies to rev up R&D to a fever pitch, fostering new technological innovations that dramatically reduced the fixed costs of generating solar and wind electricity, moving them to near parity and even below parity in some instances with the conventional fossil fuel energies a decade later. Setting legally mandated targets, combined with feed-in tariffs to promote the growth of competitive renewable energies, was the Great Disruption that has now brought the fossil fuel civilization to the edge of an imminent collapse.

The Great Disruption: Crossing the Green Line

But how do we know that Europe and the world are within striking distance of the endgame for the carbon era? First, the feed-in tariffs, which were in place for less than a decade, are already being phased out across the EU and in other regions around the world because of the falling price of renewable energies brought on by the rush of new innovations in solar and wind technology and deployment.[4] Following on the heels of the EU, the People's Republic of China entered the game, subsidizing its own solar and wind technology industries, allowing them to mature and drop the price of generating renewable energy even further, making solar and wind energies a prime mover in powering society.

While the subsidies for solar, wind, and other renewable energies phased in and are now phasing out in a very short period of about ten years, fossil fuel energies, even after a two-hundred-year run as the primary energy source, still enjoy an eye-popping $5.3 trillion in post-tax subsidies per year (as of 2015) around the world despite the fact that they are now quickly moving over to the stranded asset column on the global accounting sheet. (Post-tax subsidies are, for the most part, the calculation of "environmental damages from energy consumption [which] are just as real as are supply costs ... and any failure to fully internalize them means that some of the damages from fossil fuel use are not borne by fuel consumers and this constitutes a form of subsidy.")[5]

The question being asked with growing urgency by some and with incredulity by others is how the fossil fuel civilization could be close to an endgame because of the upstart solar and wind energies when the latter made up only 3 percent of global energy capacity in 2017.[6]

There is a rule of thumb in economics that is little known and mostly ignored, even by the titans of the financial community and business sectors. Yet it is remarkably prescient in predicting Schumpeter's "creative destruction."

Investors, on the whole, are not swayed as much by the size of an enterprise or sector as by its growth curve. They will continue to stay onboard as long as their investment shows increasing growth. If that growth loses momentum, they take notice and often lose interest. When new challengers emerge, even if they are seemingly inconsequential, if they begin to exhibit accelerating growth or even an exponential growth curve, investors begin to shift allegiance to the challenger. The key is the threshold. That is, when a challenger captures just 3 percent of the market from an incumbent, the incumbent's sales often peak and begin to decline, signaling its eventual demise.[7] Kingsmill Bond, who is the lead energy strategist for the Carbon Tracker Initiative, the previously mentioned UK research organization of specialists tracking climate risks, observes that this rule of creative destruction holds across all areas of commerce but is particularly telling when analyzing the transitions in energy paradigms over history. For example, gas lighting demand peaked when electricity accounted for only 3 percent of the lighting.[8]

Once again, the correlation to consider is not the size of the market vis-à-vis an incumbent and a challenger but rather the sales growth of each player. Even when the challenger enjoys only a tiny 1 percent of the market but a 20 percent growth rate, the challenger is likely to gobble up all of the incremental growth by year ten. Or, to take it from another angle, if the challenger has an exceptional growth rate of 30 percent and the market growth rate is only 1 percent, then the sales of the incumbent will likely peak at the point where the challenger's market share is only 3 percent.[9]

Kingsmill Bond describes four stages in the current energy transition in Europe and around the world. Stage 1 is where solar and wind climb to provide about 2 percent of the electricity. This is the initial innovation phase. Stage 2 is where solar and wind have captured 5–10 percent of the energy market. This is the peaking phase. Stage 3 is where solar and wind comprise 10–50 percent of the market, the rapid change stage. The death knell is where solar and wind cross over to more than 50 percent of the market.[10] The peaking stage is the turning point for the financial markets because that's when the demand for fossil fuel energies peaks and the industry begins to lose market share.

An additional factor needs to be added to the equation to understand the full implications of a Great Disruption in energy. In 2017, 43 percent of the primary energy in the world was used to generate electricity.[11] Over the coming decades, the electricity sector is going to use an increasing amount of global primary energy as the transport sector decouples from fossil fuels and moves to electric vehicles powered by the electricity grid.

According to the Carbon Tracker Initiative, the transitional moment is when 14 percent of global electricity will be supplied by solar and wind.[12] Europe passed the 14 percent tipping point in 2017 when 15 percent of electricity generation was made up of solar and wind. The United States in 2017 was only at 8 percent, China was at 6 percent, Latin America at 5 percent, India at 5 percent, Africa at 2 percent, and the Middle East at less than 1 percent. Solar and wind supplied 6 percent of all global electricity in 2017.[13]

When will this transitional moment and tipping point occur on a global scale, stranding trillions of dollars in fossil fuel assets and bursting the carbon bubble? The two crucial variables in projecting global future energy supply are the growth rate of global energy demand and the growth rate of solar photovoltaic (PV) and wind supply.[14] In the view of Kingsmill Bond:

> If we make assumptions for these two factors, it is possible to calculate the date at which fossil fuel demand peaks . . . assuming total energy demand growth of 1.3% (assuming a slight fall from the 5-year average) and solar PV and wind supply growth of 17% (assuming a continued S curve of supply growth, with growth rates falling over time from the current level of 22%). The date of peak fossil fuel demand is then 2023.[15]

Bond concedes that the Carbon Tracker Initiative's "view of 1.3% energy demand growth and 17% solar PV and wind supply growth is open to question" and therefore offers a number of scenarios with a global growth rate of energy demand of 1–1.5 percent and growth of solar PV and wind supply of 15–20 percent. All these scenarios "give a range of 2020 to 2027 for the date of peak fossil fuel demand."[16]

The US growth rate in combined solar and wind, at least, is spot on with the Carbon Tracker trajectory. Solar and wind made up 4 percent of the electricity generated in the United States in 2013, and in each succeeding year the figure has risen by approximately 1 percentage point. In 2017, solar and wind constituted 8 percent of the electricity, a figure that is projected to reach 10 percent by the end of 2019.[17] Assuming this rate of increase continues, the United States will likely reach 14 percent of solar and wind electricity generation by the end of 2023 and be at or near the tipping point.

The carnage is palpable. Solar and wind costs are, in many cases, already below the running cost of current coal- and gas-fired power plants.[18] With more and more solar and wind electricity coming onto the grid every day, operating coal- and gas-fired power plants is becoming uncompetitive, forcing utilities to shut them down, meaning their capital investment will never be paid off.

Early on, the natural gas industry argued that a new generation of gas-fired power plants would need to be installed, offering up two seemingly convincing rationales: first, that natural gas is the least onerous of the fossil fuels and emits less CO_2 than coal and oil and is therefore an appropriate bridge fuel on the way to a low-carbon society; second, natural-gas-fired power plants need to be in place when the sun isn't shining and the wind isn't blowing, providing backup storage, especially at peak electricity times. Worried that this might be the case, electric utilities began installing new gas-fired power plants, ostensibly to back up variable renewable energies.

The electric utilities should have known better. By 2011, 68 percent of all *new* electricity generation in Europe was coming from solar and wind power.[19] In reality, there was already enough solar and wind coming onto the EU electricity grid by 2011 that the gas-fired power plants that were hastily installed would be only infrequently used or not used at all, meaning, once again, that their capital costs would never be paid down. The green route was on. It is now well recognized that the exit ramp from a fossil-fuel-based electrical system to a solar-and-wind-based electrical network appears when the latter crosses over the 14–15 percent barrier of penetration that, as mentioned, the EU reached in 2017.

The notion that variable solar and wind energy will require backup conventional fossil fuel power to prevent power lapses for decades to come has become a kind of modern-day urban myth, spread to a large extent by the gas industry. It's just not true. Battery storage and hydrogen fuel-cell storage at rapidly declining costs can easily provide backup power to compensate for the variability of solar and wind generation. Choosing the appropriate mix of solar and wind power, recognizing the variability of each of these energies during different seasons relative to the variability in power demands at different times of the year, also helps maintain a dependable flow of electricity. Better demand-side management, upgrading the grid code, and hastening the transition from a servomechanical to a digital grid, making it smarter and more efficient at integrating electricity between base and peak load times, are equally suited to the task of maintaining the stability of electricity demand.[20]

When the terms "stranded assets" and "carbon bubble" are thrown around, the dire implications of what these emerging realities might mean for the world economy and civilization are often lost in the esoterica. However, knowing the extent of the bad news is important so that humanity can prepare for the jarring and unprecedented economic destabilization and accompanying social disruption that will come with the collapse of the fossil fuel civilization.

We should also bear in mind that in this instance, the bad news is the good news. The sooner the collapse of the fossil fuel era comes, the brighter the prospect that humanity might be able to quickly scale up a smart, global green infrastructure that will take us into a postcarbon ecological civilization, hopefully in time to save our species, our fellow creatures, and the Earth we inhabit.

Missing the Warnings

What, then, will the collapse of the old energy order and the birth of the new energy regime look like? We can already get an inkling of what's in store for society because we have a precedent. The European Union is embroiled in the transformation at this moment and is the canary in the mine.

The powers that be were late in recognizing the Great Disruption coming in Europe. This was the first systemic failure. There was a twofold crisis taking hold in the first decade of the twenty-first century right under the nose of global institutions, nation-states, and the global business community who, for the most part, seemed naïvely unaware of or unconcerned about the dark forces that were surfacing. From the mid-1980s until the fall of 2003, crude oil was selling at a steady price of about $25 per barrel and was of little concern to the business community, workers, and their families. From then on, the price of oil began a steady upward climb and didn't stop until it reached a record peak of $147 per barrel in July 2008.[21] It wasn't until oil went over $90 per barrel in 2007 that global regulatory institutions, national governments, and the business community began to take notice. This came when food riots broke out in the poorest countries in the world because of the high price of staples like wheat, corn, soybeans, and rice due, in part, to the rising price of oil. The average price of rice skyrocketed by 217 percent, wheat by 136 percent, corn by 125 percent, and soybeans by 107 percent.[22] Panic set in as millions of the world's poor went without sufficient food.

What everyone else began to realize is that when the price of oil started to climb beyond $90 per barrel, prices for everything else in the economy began to go up as well. While in the highly industrial countries we make much of increased gasoline prices affecting transportation, the public is far less aware that the price of fossil fuels affects the price of almost everything else we produce and consume in society. Our pesticides and fertilizers, construction materials, pharmaceutical products, packaging, food preservatives and additives, synthetic fiber, power, heat, light, and so on are made out of or moved by the carbon deposits we extract from beneath the ground and the ocean floor. Purchasing power began slowing with the rising price of oil in the spring of 2007. The global economy was beginning to shut down. The oil bubble was far from inconsequential, dragging down businesses and weakening the purchasing power of people around the world, especially in the developing economies. Needless to say, the major oil companies reaped record profits, while millions of businesses went under because of the high price of oil in the materials they used across their supply chains.[23]

I have firsthand experience here. My father owned a small manufacturing company that transformed polyethylene film into plastic bags. The company, which employed about fifteen people, was in continuous operation for more than fifty years. When the price of oil shot up in 2007 and 2008, the cost of polyethylene film went through the roof, followed in quick succession by the economy careening into recession territory, meaning less demand for packaging. The family business went under during the Great Recession, ending a half century of operation.

The slowing economy was hit a second time, with a knockout punch, when the subprime mortgage bubble burst in the summer of 2008. The financial world and business community claimed they didn't see it coming either, although I suspect that's disingenuous and fails the smell test. More likely, they turned a deaf ear, caught up in what the economist John Maynard Keynes called the "animal spirit" of a bull market that looked like its steep upward climb was inevitable and irreversible. The bankers made a killing.

The shutdown of the global economy and the ensuing

Great Recession slowed the demand for electricity everywhere, leaving the power and electricity sector with prior investments in power plants that were less utilized and partially stranded.

The other systemic failure was not understanding the full implications of the European Union's decision in 2007 to transition the world's largest economy out of fossil fuels and into renewable energies, accompanied by greater energy efficiencies and a reduction in global warming emissions. The European Union's new legally binding mandatory targets for renewable energy generation, along with the generous subsidies in the form of feed-in tariffs, brought millions of new players into the energy game, selling back to the grid green electricity captured by solar panels on their roofs and wind turbines on their land.

My office was, to my knowledge, the first to use the term "zero marginal cost renewable energy." The concept didn't seem to register among power producers, who for several years were anxious to explain to me that the marginal cost of solar and wind was never really zero although it was patently obvious that the sun and the wind, unlike coal, oil, and natural gas, are nearly free to capture once the fixed cost of installing the technology is paid back.

Zero marginal cost renewable solar and wind energy soon became the bête noire of the power and electric utilities. Not only is the marginal cost near zero in generating solar electricity, but the generation of the power also usually peaks in the afternoons when the demand for electricity peaks and the electric utilities reap their largest profit margins. In Germany, solar PVs reduced the peak price for electricity by 40–60 percent. Overall, the average daily price of electricity declined by 30–40 percent between 2007 and 2016, eroding profits for the electric utilities.[24]

With the fixed costs of solar and wind electricity plummeting on an exponential curve, the marginal cost of generating the new green energies near zero, and the feed-in tariffs providing a premium price for green electricity above the market price, the conditions were ripe for creating the perfect storm. The profitability of gas- and coal-fired power plants plummeted, and so did their utilization. They became stranded assets.

It's worth remembering that the fossil-fuel-based power and electric utilities in EU countries collapsed when renewable energies comprised only 14 percent of the total market, leaving a heap of stranded assets behind. The losses totaled more than €130 billion ($148 billion) in the European electricity sector in just the six-year period from 2010 to 2015. The disruption in the European power and electric utility market is going to be even more disorienting in the coming years. Already, the discrepancy between the "book value" of property, plant equipment, and goodwill and the "enterprise value" of just Europe's leading twelve utilities is reason for concern. The market value is only 65 percent of the book value, a wide disparity, suggesting that dire losses are yet to come. With the total book value of the twelve largest utilities listed at €496 billion ($560 billion), it's not inconceivable, according to one study, "that 300–500 billion euros of these assets are exposed to the risk of getting economically stranded."[25]

Apparently much of the rest of the world has failed to heed what has taken place in the European Union. The major gas-producing nations are upping natural gas production, installing pipelines across continents, and establishing cross-ocean supply lanes in a frenzied race to capture the global market. The Energy Information Administration (EIA) of the US government projects that natural gas production in the United States "grows 7% per year from 2018 until 2020."[26] In large part, the growth is coming from increasing demand within the electricity sector to transition from coal to gas in order to reduce CO_2 emissions and lower costs, because gas is now cheaper than coal. While that is undeniably true, the more important development is that solar and wind are now competitive with natural gas and, in some instances, even cheaper, which changes the equation once again, this time in favor of the cleaner renewable energies.[27]

According to 2018 research from Bloomberg New Energy Finance, "coal and gas are facing a mounting threat to their position in the world's electricity generation mix as a result of the spectacular reduction in the cost not just for wind and solar technologies, but also for batteries" (to store these variable energies). Elena Giannakopoulou, head of energy economics at BNEF, notes that some coal and gas plants with sunk costs might be sparingly used, but she goes on to say, "The economic case for building new coal and gas capacity is crumbling, as batteries start to encroach on the flexibility and peaking revenues enjoyed by fossil fuel plants."[28]

Price competition aside, the power and electricity industry continues to argue that variable renewable energies are a nonstarter without natural-gas-fired power plants backing them up with stored energy to maintain sustainability on the grid. Far from being apologetic, the gas industry is bullish on the future of natural gas. Richard Meyer, in charge of government affairs at the American Gas Association, says, "I think it's a safe bet that the use of natural gas will continue to support a low-carbon future and that natural gas could increase in the [power] sector."[29]

If that were the case—and certainly the expenditures in natural gas pipelines, power plants, and accompanying facilities suggest that, at least for now, the "gas rush" still has momentum—it would mean a dramatic overshoot of the red line the United Nations Intergovernmental Panel on Climate Change has laid down for keeping global warming emissions under a 1.5°C ceiling.

But that's not likely going to happen, and this time it's not because governments around the world have established binding targets on CO_2 emissions. The fact is, for the most part, they didn't. Rather, it's because the marketplace has already determined the outcome of the process, with solar and wind technology becoming ever cheaper on a steep curve, now followed by the falling cost of battery storage. And we can all thank the European Union for that. By the member states of the EU committing to binding legal targets a decade earlier, with short-term feed-in tariffs to encourage early adoption, businesses were set loose to improve the operating performance of solar and wind and their efficiencies, dramatically reducing the costs. China then followed, with its own companies bringing on innovations in efficiencies and further lowering the costs of generating solar and wind electricity.

As mentioned, China soon eclipsed Europe, becoming the leading producer of cheap, efficient solar and wind technology, which it began exporting all over the world. In its thirteenth Five-Year Plan, which commenced in 2016, China also turned inward, with the massive production, sale, and installation of cheap solar and wind technology in the domestic market.[30] The new focus on installing and harvesting solar and wind energy inside China coincided with the digital upgrading of China's electricity grid, enabling Chinese businesses and communities to generate their own near-zero marginal cost renewable energy and use it off the grid or sell it back to the grid.

Is it possible that the energy companies and power and electric utility companies and, for that matter, countries around the world are oblivious to the Great Disruption that has unfolded in the European Union and the People's Republic of China? Doubtful! I regularly meet with energy companies and power and electricity companies in Europe, Asia, and the Americas. They know. They see the numbers. They do the math. They watch what's happening in Europe and China. Yet they continue pushing forward a forty-year infrastructure build-out of gas pipelines across continents and installing numerous gas-fired power plants, upping the tally of global warming emissions and future stranded assets.

Turning a Blind Eye in North America

So the "gas rush" is on and two of the biggest players are in North America. The United States is now the leading producer of natural gas on the planet, and its Canadian neighbor is the fourth-largest producer.[31] While the Trump administration is at least up-front about its avowed commitment to exploit every possible opportunity to bring natural gas online for both domestic consumption and export, the Canadian government uses every public opportunity to flaunt its leadership in decarbonizing Canada and its prominent role in rallying the world to address climate change. But when it comes to issuing permits and underwriting gas projects, Canada has missed no opportunity to be at the head of the pack. The negative economic consequences of these misguided policies to keep the fossil fuel spigot wide open in North America are ominous, for the United States, Canada, and the world.

What might these emerging trajectories mean for stranded fossil fuel assets, a North American carbon bubble, and the destabilization of the US and Canadian economies? Turning to the United States, the Rocky Mountain Institute (RMI), which has advised the US government's Department of Defense and Department of Energy, as well as other governments around the world, issued a detailed and extensive 2018 report titled *The Economics of Clean Energy Portfolios: How Renewable and Distributed Energy Resources Are Outcompeting and Can Strand Investment in Natural Gas-Fired Generation*.

Working backward, the report concludes that the frenzied

rush to natural gas in the US electricity system "could lock in $1 trillion of cost through 2030." To begin with, the US power grid, once the envy of the world, is aging. More than half of the thermal power plants that are more than thirty years old will be retired by 2030. The current low cost of domestic natural gas has spurred a huge investment in a new generation of natural-gas-fired power plants, expected to reach $110 billion by 2025. By 2030, the electric power industry will have to spend upward of $500 billion to replace all the aging power plants scheduled for retirement. It will cost an additional $480 billion for the fuel to operate those power plants, for a total of approximately $1 trillion in costs through 2030. This at a time when the plummeting price of solar and wind energies is already competitive with natural gas and in a few short years will be far cheaper, with a near-zero marginal cost and zero global warming emissions.[32]

The toll is mind-boggling and grim. This will saddle the US power and electricity industry not only with a potential trillion dollars in stranded assets but also with 5 billion tons of CO_2 emissions by 2030 and nearly 16 billion tons by 2050.[33]

RMI ran a comparative study of two planned combined-cycle gas turbine power plants and two planned combustion turbine power plants being readied for peak-hour operation against optimized and region-specific renewable energy and distributed energy sources that can provide comparable services. The study found that in all four cases, an optimized clean energy portfolio is more cost-effective and lower in risk than the proposed gas plants. The implications are stunning. The data showed that "the same technological innovations and price declines in renewable energy that have already contributed to early coal-plant retirement are now threatening to strand investments in natural gas."[34] The RMI study is a potential thunderbolt for the US power and electricity sector in the United States and, if acknowledged soon enough, could quickly allow it to make the shift from fossil fuel to green energies in as little as a ten-year span. It's worth sharing RMI's conclusion at length:

> Our analysis reveals that across a wide range of case studies, regionally specific clean energy portfolios already outcompete proposed gas-fired generators, and/or threaten to erode their revenue within the next 10 years. Thus, the $112 billion of gas-fired power plants currently proposed or under construction, along with $32 billion of proposed gas pipelines to serve these power plants, are already at risk of becoming stranded assets. This has significant implications for investors in gas projects (both utilities and independent power producers) as well as regulators responsible for approving investment in vertically integrated territories.[35]

The United States' northern neighbor, Canada, is also investing heavily in natural gas exploration, extraction, and sale. While Canada is regarded as a country fiercely dedicated to the environment and protection of its natural resources, there is another, darker Canadian persona deeply tied to fossil fuel energies. Like the United States, the Canadian government, several of the provinces, the financial community, and businesses are awash in fossil fuels.

In recent years, much of the criticism by environmental organizations has centered on tar-sand extraction in the province of Alberta, with periodic protests, lawsuits, and legislative battles attempting to rein in one of Canada's most lucrative economic enterprises. Canada is the fourth-largest producer of crude oil in the world, after the United States, which is ranked number one, Saudi Arabia, and Russia. Canada extracts and refines more fossil fuels than Iran, Iraq,

China, the United Arab Emirates, Kuwait, Brazil, Venezuela, and Mexico, which I suspect will come as a surprise to most of the rest of the world.[36] Less known is that British Columbia has entered the fossil fuel arena, with deep natural gas reserves in the northern tier of the province. Technical breakthroughs in the fracking of natural gas over the past decade, accompanied by the discovery of rich natural gas reserves, have led to a rush into fracking across the region.

British Columbia is a good case study in competing visions: one deeply committed to a fossil fuel future and the other to a green postcarbon era. Vancouver, surrounding cities, and many of the First Nations bands in the northern regions of the province are among the fiercest proponents of a conservation-oriented green Canada. The Vancouver metropolitan area is often cited as one of the greenest governing jurisdictions in the world. These competing visions make the region a lightning rod in the struggle between the old and new energies, the outcome of which will give us a good indication of the course other regions in Canada might take as they find themselves caught between these two approaches to the future.

On October 2, 2018, Canada flexed its fossil fuel muscle in a very public way. Prime Minister Justin Trudeau joined British Columbia's premier John Horgan and representatives of LNG Canada, a consortium of oil and gas companies led by Royal Dutch Shell and including Mitsubishi Corporation, Malaysian-owned Petroliam Nasional Bhd, PetroChina, and Korea Gas Corporation, to announce the construction of a liquefied natural gas (LNG) pipeline.[37] The pipeline will stretch across 670 kilometers, taking gas from Dawson Creek in northeastern British Columbia to a processing plant on the coast in Kitimat to be shipped to China and other Asian markets.[38] The C$40 billion ($30 billion) investment by LNG Canada is the single largest private-sector investment in

Canadian history. Trudeau announced that the federal government would be providing C$275 million ($207 million) in support of the deployment.[39]

The LNG pipeline faced bitter opposition and protests by environmental organizations and First Nations. Less known by the public is that energy forecasters and analysts who have scoped the project are reticent and even guardedly pessimistic about the wisdom of locking British Columbia and the rest of Canada into a natural gas future that will be amortized over many decades.

The Brattle Group published a nuanced report on the future prospects of LNG back in January 2016—two years and eight months prior to the formal announcement of the project—raising serious concerns about Canada shipping LNG to China, in light of the blitzkrieg competition there from solar and wind energies. Its reticence should have raised some red flags but apparently was either ignored or not taken seriously. The report pointed out that in Germany and California, "where renewable penetration has been high, gas demand growth has already been stunted by the penetration of renewables in the generation mix (causing a reduction in gas demand growth for power generation)."[40]

Now, China is following a similar path, with a short-term push in natural gas production to accompany the phase-out of coal and a simultaneous increase in solar and wind energy production, with the goal of eliminating virtually all fossil fuels from the energy mix over the next several decades. Like the experience in the EU, much will depend on when the plummeting costs of renewable energies in China will force a disruption in the Chinese energy market, leaving billions of dollars of stranded natural gas assets in its wake on the way to creating a green energy infrastructure across the country.

The disruption is already beginning to happen. As already noted, China is now the number-one producer of solar and wind energy technology and boasts the cheapest prices on world markets, making it the leading exporter.[41] Moreover, the current thirteenth Five-Year Plan has set ambitious targets for the installation of solar and wind technology across every region of China, rivaling the earlier deployments in the European Union.

The Brattle Group report alludes to the trends in China that are mimicking the earlier disruptions in the European energy market, noting that if the costs of domestic production and deployment of renewable energies continue to drop precipitously, China's demand for imported liquefied natural gas could dry up.

> If the cost of renewable generation is low enough over-seas (i.e. below the cost of new gas-fired generation burning LNG from North America) it could dampen the attractiveness of North American–sourced LNG as a fuel for electric generation.[42]

The report concludes on a cautionary note about the potential long-term implications of investment in LNG infrastructure now being laid out in British Columbia to export gas to the Asian market.

> The investment risk of these proposed LNG export projects is increasing because there is a significant possibility that, over the 20 years of a typical LNG contract, power production from renewable energy sources will become less costly than the LNG sales prices needed to justify the upstream LNG investment cost (even without considering the value of avoided greenhouse gas emissions)....The competition between LNG-fueled gas-fired generation and renewable resources represents a risk to participants

in the LNG industry in that higher than expected renewables penetration could reduce future natural gas
demand growth (and LNG demand growth) in some
of the key overseas Pacific Asian markets. Both investors in LNG infrastructure and buyers of LNG under
long-term contracts will want to consider these risks
before making large and long-term commitments to
buying or selling LNG.[43]

For both the United States and Canada, the commercial
case for the continued introduction of large-scale natural gas
projects no longer exists because of the ever-cheaper cost of
generating solar and wind electricity. Nonetheless, the fossil
fuel industry continues to defend these investments, arguing
that natural gas is at least not as onerous as coal in CO_2 emissions. Equally egregious, the industry continues to tout the
"technology" known as "carbon capture and storage" as a way
to use the fuel without emitting harmful CO_2 emissions into
the atmosphere when, in reality, this technology is already a
stranded asset. Carbon capture and storage technology should
not be confused with natural carbon sequestration brought
on by carbon farming, reforestation, and other organic processes that absorb CO_2 from the atmosphere. A quick Google
search of every single carbon capture experiment to date and
the reams of scientific reports published on their technical
and commercial unviability should put the so-called promise
of this technology to rest. We had this debate around carbon
capture and storage technology in the EU for more than a decade, and it might be helpful to share our experience as this
techno-theme has recently been touted in the United States
by the fossil fuel industry and some elected officials.

Carbon capture and storage technology is a three-part
process, beginning with the capture of CO_2 emissions produced from electricity generation and in industrial processes.

The captured CO_2 is subsequently transported by road tanks, ships, and pipelines to storage facilities. The carbon is then stored deep under the ground in geological rock formations.

After the expenditure of hundreds of millions of dollars in establishing pilots to test the feasibility of this technology, the EU threw up its hands, realizing that the process was unable to meet either the technical or commercial expectations.[44] Energy historian Vaclav Smil summarized the commercial consensus after years of failed efforts. He made the point that "in order to sequester just a fifth of current CO_2 emissions, we would have to create an entirely new worldwide absorption-gathering-compression-transportation-storage industry whose annual throughput would have to be about 70 percent larger than the annual volume now handled by the global crude oil industry, whose immense infrastructure of wells, pipelines, compressor stations and storage took generations to build."[45]

Unfortunately, America appears to be repeating the EU's failed experiments. Southern Company embarked on a carbon capture and storage project for its coal-powered electricity in 2010 at its Kemper power plant in Mississippi to prove the viability of carbon capture and storage. After years and years of effort and cost overruns that took the project from an initial $2.4 billion budget to a total bill of $7.5 billion, Southern Company canceled the project and passed on $1.1 billion of the cost to its rate payers.[46]

Whether it is the rush to invest massive amounts of finance capital in natural gas extraction and power generation or in carbon capture and storage technology, when the former is no longer cost-competitive and the latter is not technologically feasible or commercially viable, it brings to mind the old adage, "if you find yourself in a hole, stop digging." Just leave the fossil fuels in the ground.

Rather than focus on futile and failed carbon capture

technologies, some industry players have begun to turn their attention to decarbonizing what are called the hard-to-abate sectors. These are the most challenging industries and businesses because there are not yet commercially viable alternatives to the use of fossil fuels in their processes, product lines, and services.

Much of the CO_2 abatement in these industries will come from plugging into a smart Third Industrial Revolution infrastructure that will allow them to power their production with renewable energy and to manage their transport and logistics supply chains with short-haul electric vehicles powered by green electricity and with long-haul hydrogen-fuel-cell-powered transport on road, rail, and water routes. Big Data and algorithm governance of supply chains and logistics operations will also increase these companies' aggregate efficiencies in ever more circular business processes.

When it comes to plastic packaging and to steel, cement, and other construction-related materials, it will also be necessary to find fiber-based biological substitutes. Recently, some of the world's leading chemical companies have begun to join together with genetics and life science companies in accelerated R&D efforts designed to find cheaper alternative biological-based products and processes. Again, as in other industries, the chemical company leaders are keen to reduce CO_2 emissions to slow down climate change and are increasingly alarmed about the prospect of stranded assets going forward. Products from these R&D initiatives are beginning to reach the market. For example, airlines including United, Qantas, and KLM already use some bio-based fuels but will require much more extensive R&D to fully transition into powering air travel with a cost-effective bio-based energy.[47]

Bio-based materials are replacing petrochemicals in such key areas as bioplastics, bio-based food and feed ingredients, biosurfactants, and biolubricants. There is vast market potential for replacing petrochemicals with biological-based materials in a wide range of products and processes, including clothing, film, filters, beverages, animal feed, snack foods, household detergents, industrial cleaners, and automotive and industrial lubricants.[48]

DowDuPont Inc., the world's second-largest chemical company, is among the leaders engaged in research involving hard-to-abate processes and product lines. In October 2018, I joined Dow's executive team at its European Innovation Summit in Frankfurt to discuss new R&D efforts to expedite the introduction of biological-based substitutes into the market to hasten the transition into a zero-emission economy. Two of our Third Industrial Revolution roadmap test regions—Hauts-de-France and the Metropolitan Region of Rotterdam and The Hague—are currently involved in cross-industry initiatives to bring biological substitutes quickly to market. Regions and industries should be motivated with generous carrots and equally onerous sticks to advance this critical transformation in the economy.

The Curse of Black Gold

In the last two years or so, the issue of stranded fossil fuel assets has been coming up with greater frequency in corporate boardrooms, financial institutions, government ministries, and think tanks around the world. This is not the normal conversation about the ebb and flow of markets and short-term government tweaks of economic policies, or simply about resetting agendas, but something more disconcerting that goes beyond even the occasional downturn into bear markets or deep recessions. There is a sense that something far bigger is occuring, affecting not only the global economy but our very existence and how we understand the world we live in, as well as the reliable future we took for granted.

The notion of stranded assets is more than just an economic accounting of the entropy debt for two centuries of burning carbon to create an industrial society. The stark reality of all this growing angst can be felt in a very personal way in the carbon-rich nations of the world, whose very economies depend on the extraction and sale of fossil fuels.

There is a favorite saying in the Middle East that I've heard countless times during my visits and meetings there over the years. It's attributed to Sheik Rashid bin Saeed al Maktoum, who was both the vice president and the second prime minister of the United Arab Emirates and the ruler of the Emirate of Dubai. His reign extended from 1958 to his death in 1990.

The saying goes like this: "My grandfather rode a camel, my father rode a camel, I drive a Mercedes, my son drives a Land Rover, his son will drive a Land Rover, but *his* son will ride a camel." Sheik Rashid was worried that the euphoria in the Emirates upon the discovery of oil in the late 1960s would come back to haunt his people, and he predicted that the country would run out of oil within a few generations—and then what? He saw oil more as an addiction and a curse and worried that if his country became a single-resource economy and society, there would be a day of reckoning when the oil spigot ran dry. He spent a lifetime diversifying the economy, turning Dubai into a regional hub for global trade between East and West. The oil hasn't run out, but it is fast becoming a stranded asset. Most of the oil that is left will remain forever in the ground.

It's not just the Emirates at risk. It's also carbon-rich countries around the world whose economies are so utterly dependent on the extraction, refining, and sale of oil, gas, and coal. To say that the world's banks, insurance companies, sovereign wealth funds, and private equity funds are worried would be an understatement. In 2018, the World Bank issued a report titled *The Changing Wealth of Nations 2018: Building a Sus-*

tainable Future, which laid out a somber analysis of what's in store for carbon-rich nations.

The World Bank pointed out that while private-sector investors and companies in the fossil fuel sector can always divest and reinvest in other more profitable and sustainable enterprises, carbon-rich sovereign nations tied to territorial boundaries are far more constrained and far less agile. Of the 141 nations that enjoy some carbon wealth, 26 of the countries have at least 5 percent of their wealth in fossil fuels, and most of them derive more than half their revenues from oil, gas, and coal. These are also among the poorest countries in the world, and ten of them are in the Middle East and North Africa, regions in crisis, with failed states and authoritarian regimes.[49] The potential of hitting the wall with stranded assets and loss of carbon revenue would be devastating for these countries.

To get a sense of the magnitude of the pending crisis, the World Bank reports that "the top 10 state-owned carbon-resource companies account for $2.3 trillion of state-owned produced assets related to extraction and processing of fossil fuels."[50] With fossil fuels trending toward peak demand and the beginning of slower growth, the World Bank is beseeching the carbon-rich and carbon-dependent countries to quickly diversify their economies to ensure a sufficient tax revenue to make up for the losses.

Some of the countries are attempting to divest and reinvest in green technologies, but their efforts have been minuscule. The World Bank concludes its report on the carbon-wealthy nations on a pessimistic note, saying that while divestment and reinvestment would be the best course to follow, unfortunately, "as the data show, governments have failed to use their fossil fuel wealth sustainably over the long term."[51] Try to imagine the chaos across the Middle East and North Africa in as little as five to ten years when oil is expected to peak in demand and slow in growth.

The Financial Community Sounds the Alarm

To get a sense of where things stand in regard to stranded assets in the fossil-fuel-related sectors, it's always best to follow the money—which means looking to the banking sector and insurance industry. Citigroup and Mark Carney, the governor of the Bank of England, were among the first to sound the alarm back in 2015; now the alarm bells are ringing everywhere, which should be a wake-up call across the global economy.

The World Bank is only one of several leading financial institutions to address the issue of fossil-fuel-related stranded assets and how they are fast changing the financial landscape and the rules of the game in the investment community. Lazard issued its own report in November 2018 comparing the cost of fossil fuel energies to the new green energies. Like reports from many of the world's leading energy consultancies, and even some of the oil giants, Lazard's study shows that "in some scenarios . . . alternative energy costs have decreased to the point that they are now at or below the marginal cost of conventional generation."[52] George Bilicic, vice chairman and global head of Lazard's Power, Energy, and Infrastructure Group, drives home the point:

> We have reached an inflection point where, in some cases, it is more cost-effective to build and operate new alternative energy projects than to maintain existing conventional generation plants.[53]

With reports like these, stranded fossil fuel assets have become an inextricable part of the climate change debate.

The Prudential Regulation Authority (PRA) at the Bank of England published the results of a survey of 90 percent of the UK banking sector in September 2018, representing £11 trillion ($14.2 trillion) in assets. The PRA found that 70 percent of the UK banks recognized that climate change is now posing a risk to a wide range of assets across almost every field, "and they have started to assess how the transition to a low-carbon economy driven, for example, by government policy and technical change, may impact the business model of companies that banks are exposed to." More disturbing, however, despite the awareness of the issue, only 10 percent of the banks were currently managing these risks "comprehensively," and 30 percent of the banks "still only considered climate change a corporate social responsibility issue."[54]

Concerned that the banking sector might not be fully aware of how quickly climate change is affecting investment risks across virtually every sector of the global economy, including potential stranded assets in the fossil fuel sector and closely coupled industries, Mark Carney stepped in a second time.

Aside from his role as governor of the Bank of England, Carney also served as chairman of the Financial Stability Board (FSB) until the end of 2018, an international body that makes recommendations on the oversight of the global financial system. The FSB includes all G20 major economies and the European Commission. Carney realized that the banking system was ill prepared for the barrage of stranded assets coming its way. So he and the FSB established the Task Force on Climate-Related Financial Disclosures (TCFD), chaired by Michael Bloomberg. Its thirty-two members include representatives from large banks, insurance companies, asset managers, pension funds, and accounting and consulting firms, and it was commissioned "to develop voluntary, consistent, climate-related financial disclosures that would be useful to investors, lenders, and insurance underwriters in understanding material risks."[55]

The TCFD released a set of recommendations in June 2017, beginning with an acknowledgment that the majority of banking institutions perceived climate change as a phenomenon whose effects are felt over the long term and are not relevant to financial investments made today. In other words, there was almost no understanding of the disruptions already unfolding and the forecasts coming from some of the leading energy consultancies on imminent tipping points in the 2020s, and therefore little sense of urgency about reassessing their approach to current investment decisions.

The task force recognized that increases in energy efficiency and the targeted reduction in global warming emissions, coupled with the accelerated replacement of fossil fuel energies with ever-cheaper green energies, "could have significant, near-term implications for organizations dependent on extracting, producing, and using coal, oil, and natural gas." But the authors of the report hastened to add that "in fact, climate-related risks and the expected transition to a low-carbon economy affect most economic sectors and industries," not only the energy sector. They cited a study by The Economist Intelligence Unit estimating that the risk to the total global stock of manageable assets could be as high as $43 trillion over the course of the next eighty years.[56]

The report also emphasized that the Great Disruption creates "significant opportunities for organizations focused on climate change mitigation and adaptation solutions." The report cites an International Energy Agency estimate that the transition to a low-carbon economy will require around $3.5 trillion in new investments per year for the foreseeable future in the new energy sector to reach the goal of a low-carbon society over the course of the next three decades.[57]

The entwined relationship between climate change risk across the entirety of the global economy and the risk of stranded assets in the fossil fuel sector was not lost on the authors of the Economist Intelligence Unit report. Here's how they put the conundrum:

This means that global investors are currently facing a stark choice. Either they will experience impairments to their holdings in fossil fuel companies should action on climate change take place, or they will face losses to their entire portfolio of manageable assets should little mitigation be forthcoming. Charting a path away from these two options should be a strong motivation for long-term investors to engage with companies in their portfolios and to shift investments towards a profitable, low-carbon future.[58]

The TCFD realized that it was necessary to establish a set of guidelines that could be used by investors, lenders, banks, and insurance companies to model risks and opportunities to mitigate damage caused by stranded assets, as well as to initiate projects more aligned with reducing global warming emissions and prepare the appropriate criteria and data-collecting disclosure information to which companies would need to comply. Its disclosure recommendations focused on four areas that reflect how organizations function: governance, strategy, risk management, and metrics and targets. Within these thematic categories, financial institutions were asked to disclose information on the "oversight of climate-related risks and opportunities . . . over the short, medium, and long-term," describe how the organization went about "identify and assessing climate-related risks," and explain "the metrics used . . . to assess climate-related risks and opportunities."[59]

In 2018, at the One Planet Summit in New York City, Mark Carney announced that "climate-disclosure is becoming mainstream. . . . Over 500 companies are now supporters of the TCFD, including the world's largest banks, asset managers, and pension funds, responsible for assets of over $100 trillion."[60] This was a clear sign that the financial community was beginning to understand the Great Disruption that was closing in on it.

PART II

A GREEN NEW DEAL RISING FROM THE ASHES

5

WAKING THE GIANT

Pension Power Finds Its Voice

Increasing concern over climate change, loss of confidence in the long-term financial stability of the fossil fuel industry now facing the prospect of stranded assets, and the growing competitive advantage of emerging solar, wind, and other renewable energies are triggering a reevaluation of funding priorities within the global financial sector, with an escalating number of funds transitioning capital away from fossil fuels and into green energies and the clean technologies of the twenty-first century.

A 2018 survey of UK fund managers with portfolios totaling £13 trillion ($17 trillion) conducted by the UK Sustainable Investment and Finance Association and the Climate Change Collaboration found that they believe that "International Oil Companies (IOCs) will be negatively revalued within a few years because of climate change related risks." In the report, 62 percent of fund managers "see peak demand for oil impacting valuations in the next 5 years and peak demand for gas impacting valuations in the next 10 years." Over half of the respondents (54 percent) said that "the reputational risks of IOCs are already negatively impacting their valuation." Seventy-nine percent said they will have an impact in the next two years. Fund managers cited a number of other related concerns, "such as the increasing competitiveness of alternative technologies leading to a drop in demand for fossil fuels and a shift in market sentiment as investors lose faith in IOCs ability to transition in a financially successful manner. In all, 89 percent of managers agreed that these and other transition risks would impact valuations of the IOCs 'significantly' in the next 5 years." Half of the fund managers reported that they "already offer active funds or bespoke portfolios that have 'divested from (at least) the 200 coal, oil and gas companies with the largest reserves.'"[1]

Flipping Karl Marx's Thesis Upside Down

In the United States and around the world, the question of where the money is going to come from to build out and scale up a Green New Deal Third Industrial Revolution infrastructure, customized in each region, is becoming ever more pressing. When we think of a Green New Deal, the issue of "massive federal government expenditures" is inevitably the first roadblock on the way to constructing the grand vision and narrative. Even now, when the crisis is nothing short of the very survival of life on Earth, the naysayers are apt to argue that we can't afford it, as if the issue of potential extinction is merely a line item to dispose of among the many other weighty government priorities that require attention.

Although some government funding at each level—city, county, state, and federal—will be required, it is probable that a good portion of the financing needed to build out the new infrastructure will come from global pension funds. Pension funds are the deferred wages of millions of workers in the public and private sector, payable upon retirement from their employment.

Karl Marx would never have envisioned a twenty-first

century reality where "the workers of the world" are the primary owners of global investment capital via their public and private pension funds. It might come as a revelation that pension funds were the largest pool of investment capital in the world by 2017 at $41.3 trillion. As mentioned in the introduction, the US workforce is the most powerful voice, with assets exceeding $25.4 trillion in pension funds.[2]

Worried over climate change and the prospect of their funds remaining in a fossil fuel industry beset by stranded assets, which could wipe out the retirement funds of millions of American workers, US pension funds are beginning to take the lead in the divestment process. States and cities are divesting public pension funds from the fossil fuel sector and related industries that service and/or depend on it, like the petrochemical industry, and reinvesting in the green opportunities that constitute the smart Third Industrial Revolution economy. Private pension funds are also beginning to do the same.

A growing number of union voices are also pushing for the retraining of their workforces for the new employment opportunities that accompany the transition.[3] It is foreseeable that in the future pension funds will increasingly invest in green infrastructure in regions across the United States and in other countries, with the expectation of using unionized workforces, at least in part, on the projects.

The enormous pool of pension capital has been amassed in just seven decades. While it's not a revolution in the traditional sense, and although most people, including the millions of owners of these pension funds, are unlikely to view themselves as a class representing this impressive pool of capital invested in the world, this is the new reality. In some ways, it's the best-kept secret of modern capitalist history.

The sheer economic clout that this $41.3 trillion represents, if fully embraced and controlled by the millions of individual capitalists that make up this cohort, could lead to a fundamental realignment in the relationship between the global workforce and the economic institutions that govern the international economic order.

So, to turn Marx on his head, imagine the workers of the world uniting as an army of "little capitalists." As of 2017, there were 135 million public and private sector workers in the United States, and 54 percent of them participated in pension fund retirement plans. That's nearly 73 million part- and full-time workers—an army of little capitalists.[4] And what would happen if the American pension capitalists were to join together with a legion of pension capitalists from around the world and begin to exercise control over this giant pool of capital in the global economy?

Without firing a shot, without a class struggle, without strikes, rebellion, or revolution, the tables have turned, at least on paper, with the reality that these millions of workers are the primary capitalist class today. I say "on paper" because very few of these millions of capitalists see themselves as a class or even a cohort. But what if they did step up and make a claim—a seizure of power, if you will—over how their deferred wages and retirement income are to be invested? What then?

■ ■ ■

The day was May 13, 1946, a rather ordinary day in the halls of the US Capitol. The Senate began deliberating on who should control a newly emerging form of wealth they referred to as "pension capital." A debate was gaveled into session by the president pro tempore, Kenneth McKellar. At stake was a bargaining demand made by John L. Lewis, the powerful head of the coal miners' union and a leader of the American labor movement. Lewis had called for employers to set aside ten cents for every ton of coal mined by their miners to be put in a health and welfare fund, which would then be administered by the union on behalf of its membership.

Senator Harry Byrd of Virginia was the first to take to the floor. Byrd made no pretense in expressing his opposition to the proposal that Lewis had put forth. Looking down the line, Byrd warned that "if such a privilege were to extend to all contracts made between employers and employees throughout America ... it would result in payments totaling at least $4 billion a year and perhaps more." If labor were "to use such payments in establishing funds over which nobody but the labor representative would have any control ... labor unions would become so powerful that no organized government would be able to deal with them." Eyeing the implications of unions overseeing their members' own funds and investing them on their behalf, Byrd argued that it would eventually lead to a "complete destruction of the private enterprise system of the United States."[5] Despite Byrd's misgivings, the US House of Representatives and the US Senate passed a bill, only to see it vetoed by President Harry Truman.

A year later, however, Senator Robert Taft, a prominent Republican leader, inserted an amendment in the Taft-Hartley Bill—a piece of legislation that was designed to establish how labor unions were to be regulated—calling for a jointly trusteed board in all union-bargained pension funds, with half the representatives coming from the unions and half from the employer. Taft was concerned that if union leaders were to be the sole trustees, they might use their members' funds for corrupt purposes or to exercise financial clout and political power.

Senator Claude Pepper, a Florida Democrat, took umbrage at Taft's insinuations and suggested the real reason Republican members of Congress opposed labor unions controlling their members' funds was fear that the Republicans' close friends on Wall Street might lose control over a promising new pool of investment capital that was sure to grow and become a force to reckon with in ensuing years.

The amended bill passed, and Congress was able to override a second presidential veto, making it the law of the land. An ancillary condition was inserted into the final bill: that the pension funds could only be invested in a way that maximized the returns on the investments for the beneficiaries. This limitation on how the funds could be used effectively put them exclusively in the hands of Wall Street and ensured they would only be used to advance the capital market.

In 1974, Congress passed and President Gerald Ford signed the Employment Retirement Income Security Act, known as ERISA, which further tightened the ways the funds could be invested, inserting what has become known as the "prudent man rule," ostensibly intended to protect pension funds from unscrupulous financial advisors. Instead, it ensured that the funds would only be used to advance the interests of the financial community, which would determine the scope and dimensions of what constituted a prudent investment. William Winpisinger, the head of the powerful Machinists Union, spoke for organized labor, suggesting that the "prudent man rule" was merely legalese for seizing control of workers' deferred wages to advance the interests of the banking community.[6]

Decisions made in the US Congress back in 1946 on how and who should oversee pension capital would come home to roost in the late 1970s, in ways that will be described in detail below, literally changing the fate of the fourteen northeastern and midwestern states and the lives of millions of working people. The consequences would reverberate forward to this very day, locking generations into downward mobility, poverty, abandonment, and exclusion from the great American dream.

To better understand how this change in the economic landscape of the country occurred, and its impact on the lives of millions of Americans, we need to explore the importance of new infrastructure paradigms. Infrastructure is a far more pivotal agent in dictating the well-being of individuals, families, communities, businesses, and workforces, and the distribution of the fruits of society, than is generally recognized in academia or in political discourse.

In the case of the First Industrial Revolution in the United States, railroads played a key role in the rearrangement of economic life. Hub-to-hub rail service gave birth to dense, highly populated cities along the rail routes across the northeastern and midwestern corridors. Similarly, the telegraph system, which was first used to coordinate rail traffic, was located along rail routes. Coal, the primary energy powering the First Industrial Revolution, came largely from mines in Pennsylvania and Ohio in the northern tier. The steel industry, publishing industry, and other First Industrial Revolution industries similarly lined up alongside the rail infrastructure that connected the bustling northern cities.

The build-out of the Second Industrial Revolution infrastructure between 1905 and the 1980s overlapped and eventually absorbed or replaced much of the First Industrial Revolution infrastructure. During this transition, the economic geography in America shifted again. The mass production of automobiles and the introduction of national road systems, particularly the interstate highways crisscrossing every part of the country, distributed mobility and logistics. Electricity and telephone lines were strung everywhere and extended to everyone, reaching into every nook and cranny in America. Oil, the key energy to power an automobile culture, although originally discovered in Titusville, Pennsylvania, in 1859, was quickly found in Texas, Oklahoma, and later California. Oil also made airplanes and air travel possible, as well as giant container ships, advancing trade from a national market to a global market.

Let's bring this home to the vast economic, social, and political upheaval that occurred in the United States in the mid-twentieth-century. The story starts below the Mason-Dixon Line on October 2, 1944, when a crowd of some 3,000 people in Clarksdale, Mississippi, watched with awe the demonstration of a new machine—the mechanical cotton picker. In one hour, the machine picked 1,000 pounds of cotton in the same time a single black laborer picked 20 pounds.[7] By 1972, 100 percent of the cotton in the South was picked by machine.[8] Immediately after World War II, chemical defoliants were introduced into the southern farm fields, eliminating jobs for black workers who for centuries had chopped down weeds, first as slaves and after the Civil War as sharecroppers.

Overnight, the black workforce in the South became unemployable and redundant. Thus began what Nicholas Lemann, the author of *The Promised Land,* characterized as "one of the largest and most rapid mass internal movements of people in history." More than 5 million African American families headed north in the "Great Migration," settling in the northern and midwestern states.[9] There, the men found jobs in the auto industry in Detroit, the steel industry in Gary, Indiana, and Pittsburgh, the stockyards of Chicago, etc. By the 1970s, over half of the black population of the South had migrated to the North, leaving behind a rural life of poverty and destitution governed by Jim Crow laws for employment in northern factories.[10]

The big industrial unions—particularly the United Automobile Workers (UAW), the United Steelworkers, the Industrial Union of Electrical Workers, and the Machinists Union—were becoming more vocal in the two decades following World War II, making more pressing demands in their labor negotiations with management. And these giant international unions welcomed black workers newly arrived from the South. Ford's flagship River Rouge plant in Detroit, for example, was also the home of the UAW's most activist local union, whose membership was over 30 percent African American.[11]

Similarly, in the 1950s in Detroit, 25 percent of Chrysler's workers and 23 percent of General Motors' workers were African American.[12]

Management, anxious to escape the growing demands being made by an empowered unionized workforce, developed a two-prong exit strategy. First, the automobile companies introduced computers and numerical control technologies on the factory floor—the first automated technologies—which eliminated the jobs mostly held by semiskilled black workers. The trend soon spread to other northern industries. Between 1957 and 1964, manufacturing output doubled in the United States while the number of blue-collar workers declined by 3 percent with the introduction of automation on assembly lines.[13] Second, the build-out of the highway system provided the Big Three automobile companies with a literal escape route to the new outer-ring suburbs of Detroit, where they built highly automated factories operated by a more skilled workforce that was eager to escape the inner city.

Other industries and, particularly, the industries that made up the military-industrial complex, built their new plants across the southern states. When foreign auto companies—Honda, Toyota, Nissan, BMW—established their production facilities in the United States beginning in the 1980s, they, too, were virtually all located in southern states along interstate highway exits.[14] The southern states had "right-to-work laws" designed to impede or prohibit union organizing. In the South, global companies found a more complacent white rural workforce ready to accept low wages and less than enthusiastic about organizing unions.

The Interstate Highway System connecting the country meant that companies could locate in anti-union southern states and still have access to supply chains and distribution routes across the entire country, freeing their businesses from reliance on the hub-to-hub rail system connecting major metropolitan regions across the northern and midwestern sections of the country.

Here's where the other shoe dropped, stranding the now unemployed black workforce, many of whom could not afford an automobile, in their neighborhoods. The freeways and Interstate Highway System created a new form of segregation, not much talked about to this day, except among urban planners and select academics. Mass transit, a vital means of transportation in inner cities, was allowed to atrophy across the North at the height of the auto age. Inner-city trolley systems and public bus systems were often scuttled to ensure exclusivity for automobile transport. Unemployed, on welfare, without mobility, and isolated and ghettoized, generations of African American families became wards of the state. Drug traffic, gang warfare, and the rest followed.

■ ■ ■

In 1977, my colleague Randy Barber and I began a conversation about the plight of American workers and small- and medium-sized businesses in the northeastern and midwestern tiers of the country. We saw close up the devastation wreaked on African American and white working-class communities in the inner cities by the mass exodus of companies and whole industries to the Sunbelt. We also became painfully aware of the dramatic shift in American commerce from Main Street to Wall Street, as well as the rise of global companies whose loyalties and ties were no longer restricted to the United States and whose interests, reach, and engagement now stretched across the world.

We searched for threads that might direct our future efforts to spark a deep national conversation around building a more open and democratic economy. We were particularly interested in ideas and themes that could reinvigorate the small- and medium-sized businesses at the heart of American ingenuity, create new jobs, and bring vibrant social life back to the inner cities.

Over the years, we had established close ties with local and national labor leaders who shared our concern about the disempowerment of working people at the hands of Wall Street. Randy had reached out to many labor leaders and academics and compiled a wealth of research on a growing phenomenon that had the potential to transform the economic and political dynamic in America and around the world. As Randy and I put the pieces together, we began to realize that a change was taking place in the very nature of capitalism that to date had gone unnoticed and unseen. Our conversations during those months would bear fruit in the joint authorship of a book published just a year later with the poignant title *The North Will Rise Again: Pensions, Politics, and Power in the 1980s*.

Here is the thesis we laid out in the book. First, the obvious. The sixteen northeastern and midwestern states were fast being abandoned by the very industries that made them the economic powerhouse of the world. Second, the American labor movement was watching its ranks diminish by the day in those regions as companies and whole industries searched out new opportunities in states in the South and West governed by anti-union right-to-work laws. This was no small matter, as 60 percent of all union members lived and worked in the Northeast and Midwest, while only 15 percent of union workers lived and worked in the Sunbelt.[15]

Efforts to unionize workers in the Sunbelt had repeatedly run up against anti-union sentiment among the largely rural workforce and local political establishments and chambers of commerce. Success in unionizing southern companies had been marginal at best. Stymied, organized labor found itself with little left in its recruiting toolkit.

What to do? We argued that America's labor union leaders needed to wake up from a long sleep to a new and potentially powerful and promising reality. While slumbering, their millions of workers, both in public and private employment, had part of their weekly wages deferred via collective bargaining contracts in the form of pension funds, retrievable upon retirement. Nation-states, provinces, and cities around the world had been following America's lead, establishing similar pension-fund accounts for both public employees and workers in the private sector.

In America, we said,

> pension funds are a new form of wealth that has emerged over the past thirty years to become the largest single pool of private capital in the world. They are now worth over $500 billion. . . . Pension funds at present own 20–25% of the equity in American corporations and hold 40% of the bonds. Pension funds are now the largest source of investment capital for the American capitalist system. . . . Today, over $200 billion in pension fund capital comes from the combined deferred savings of 19 million union members and the public employee funds of the sixteen states that make up the northeast/midwest corridor.

If this weren't enough to shake up the labor movement and Wall Street, we concluded with a scathing indictment of the American labor movement's leadership, as well as the leadership of state and local governments across the northeastern and midwestern tiers of the country.

> The unions and the states have, over the years, relinquished control over this powerful capital pool to the financial establishment. The banks, in turn, have used these capital assets to shift jobs and production to the Sunbelt and overseas, thus crippling organized labor and the northern economies of the United States.[16]

In other words, it was the deferred wages of millions of northern unionized workers that the banks and the financial community used to invest in America's major corporations that, in turn, were abandoning their unionized workforces and relocating in southern right-to-work states. Millions of unionized workers' savings were being invested in companies whose explicit policies were to eliminate their very jobs, and nobody seemed to be aware of it.

Randy and I then put the question directly to the states and cities of the northeastern and midwestern regions of the country and local and national labor unions: Would they "continue to allow their own capital to be used against them," or "would they assert direct control over these funds in order to save their jobs and their communities"?[17]

Although the question we posed was more pragmatic and strategic, behind it was an ideological question that has plagued capitalism since Adam Smith penned *The Wealth of Nations* in 1776. We asked, "Who should control the means of production?"[18] This question, we observed, was becoming more salient than ever as the financial community and global companies were using the deferred savings of union workers in the form of pension capital to relocate, not only to the Sunbelt but also beyond, setting up operations around the world, beggaring workforces in country after country, pitting workers and communities against each other to enlist the cheapest labor available and locating in communities where they could depend on lax or nonexistent environmental standards and few, if any, checks on the working conditions in their factories.

The reaction to the book was immediate. Tens of thousands of local and national labor leaders and rank-and-file union workers read it, as did leaders in the financial community and executives in Fortune 500 companies, all of whom had a stake in the struggle to control this gigantic pool of capital. While the book has been cited and credited over the past forty years with helping spark the movement for socially responsible investment (SRI), it's fair to ask whether nation-states, cities, and labor unions around the world have moved effectively to seize control of the trillions of dollars in pension funds whose investments dictate the direction of markets in the capitalist system.[19] Or have the efforts been more incremental and around the edges, chipping away bits and pieces of the power and securing small concessions without capturing the social capital itself?

In 1998, twenty years after the book was published, Richard Trumka, then secretary treasurer of the AFL-CIO (and now its president), convened a meeting of the nation's trade unions' secretary treasurers in Las Vegas and invited Randy and me to assess progress made. We were polite but not effusive. I should hasten to add that Trumka is one of the most vocal advocates of the themes we raised in the book, remarking that "there is no more important strategy for the labor movement than harnessing our pension funds and developing capital strategies so we can stop our money from cutting our throats."[20]

One of the more measured and tightly reasoned analyses and critiques of the successes and failures that dogged our thesis and call to action came from Richard Marens, an assistant professor of organizational behavior and environment at California State University, in an article titled "Waiting for the North to Rise: Revisiting Barber and Rifkin After a Generation of Union Financial Activism in the U.S.," published in the *Journal of Business Ethics* in 2004. Marens wrote:

> A generation ago, two community activists, Randy Barber and Jeremy Rifkin, urged a new direction for the American labor movement in *The North Will Rise Again* (1978). Their book was a response to political

and organizing setbacks that Labor had experienced in the 1970s: a 20-year decline in its share of the workforce and a demoralizing defeat of a concerted effort to reform labor law. They identified a positive counter-trend in the rapidly accumulating wealth of public and union-controlled pension plans. The job for labor was to learn how to wield this capital, both as a tool for generating investment in new union jobs and as a weapon in the fight against recalcitrant corporate management.[21]

Marens went on to say that many American unions and their leaders embraced our analysis and vision and within a decade were working side by side with newly formed SRI organizations "routinely involved in various forms of financial activism and, after another decade, investment activists working for unions could point to a long list of innovations and apparent accomplishments."[22] Shareholder resolutions multiplied on topics previously hidden behind closed doors in corporate suites, forcing changes in management practices.

Some of those shareholder resolutions opposed outrageous executive compensation while workers were summarily let go and wages remained stagnant; others focused the spotlight on Dickensian sweatshop conditions, mostly in Asia, sullying the public image of the companies and undermining shareholder value.

Still, Marens concluded in a 2007 article that while public and private pension funds became key players in advancing socially responsible investment and shareholder value, institutionalizing this new watchdog role in the oversight of corporate America, "labor's shareholder activism . . . is likely to remain a tactical weapon, albeit an intriguing and potentially useful one, for skirmishing with corporate management and publicizing grievances."[23] As for our vision of the workers of the world taking responsibility for how the pool of global pension capital will be invested on behalf of their workplaces, communities, and families, Marens suggested that the evidence, at least in 2007, was that it was unlikely. At best, he faintly hinted that the jury was still out. No longer.

Theory to Practice: The Revolution Begins

This time, it's the public pension funds of cities, states, and nations that are leading the charge, moving beyond shareholder resolutions to controlling and directing their vast investments in the decarbonization of their economies. A global movement has taken root as governments and public employee unions have begun divesting their public pensions from fossil fuels and related industries and reinvesting them in renewable energies, green technologies, and energy efficiency initiatives.

In the United States, the revolution began at colleges and universities, with students petitioning the schools' boards of trustees to "divest and invest." Bill McKibben, the head of 350.org, one of the nation's leading environmental activist organizations, played a central role in helping scale the movement. At first, only a few small, scattered municipalities—mostly college towns—made the shift in their pension fund investments. It was more a symbolic gesture. It wasn't long, however, before the investment trickle became a stream, and it is now on the verge of becoming a deluge. Bigger cities have come forward and joined all over the world—Washington, DC, Copenhagen, Melbourne, Paris, San Francisco, Sydney, Seattle, Stockholm, Minneapolis, Berlin, and Cape Town, to name just a few. Today, 150 cities and regions across every continent have taken steps to divest their public pension funds from the old fossil fuel energies and reinvest in renewable energies, electric vehicles, and zero-emission building retrofits that make up a Third Industrial Revolution infrastructure.[24]

The turning point came in 2018 when both New York City and London brought their influence to the table. On January 10, Mayor Bill de Blasio and trustees of the public pension funds of New York City announced their decision to fully divest from fossil fuels by 2023 and in a single stroke positioned America's lead city as the flagship in a worldwide transition into a Green New Deal society. New York City's public employee pension funds represent 715,000 members, retirees, and their beneficiaries, and together their funds amount to $194 billion.[25] The mayor made clear in a press conference that the decision to divest was both a moral one and a financial one. His message was unsparing. He told his fellow New Yorkers that

> New York City is standing up for future generations by becoming the first major U.S. city to divest our pension funds from fossil fuels. At the same time, we are bringing the fight against climate change straight to the fossil fuel companies that knew about its effects and intentionally misled the public to protect their profits.[26]

De Blasio went on to remind New Yorkers and the rest of America of the damage New York City experienced when Hurricane Sandy hit the five boroughs head-on in October 2012, leaving forty-four deaths in its wake and more than $19 billion in damage to property and infrastructure and in lost economic activity.[27] People around the world watched in horror as live TV coverage showed torrents of water washing over roadways, smashing through windows into department stores, and racing down into the subways. New York is one of the world-class cities most in harm's way as seawaters rise and storms and hurricanes gain in intensity and frequency, and its citizens are beginning to ask if parts of their city will be permanently submerged by the second half of the century.[28]

The loss of life and property as the city moves deeper into the century could be incalculable. The decision to divest, said the mayor, was equally an economic consideration to ensure the city's economic stability and future. The mayor's office estimated that 3 percent of its portfolio, totaling approximately $5 billion, was invested in fossil fuels and that those divested funds would need to be distributed across the city's pension investments, with a priority on finding opportunities to invest in renewable energy, retrofitting of building stock, and green infrastructure.[29]

The divestment is part of a broader decarbonization plan called One New York: The Plan for a Strong and Just City. The goal is an 80 percent reduction in greenhouse gas emissions by 2050, compared to 2005 levels, putting the city in sync with the Paris climate agreement.[30]

Sadiq Khan, the mayor of London, similarly announced plans to divest £700,000 ($903,000) in public pension funds still invested in carbon-based energies. The mayor said that the city's pension portfolio's last tie to the fossil fuel industry would be quickly severed, making it entirely free of fossil fuel investments. The city has also launched the Mayor's Energy Efficiency Fund, investing £500 million ($645 million) in greening the city's social housing, universities, libraries, hospitals, and museums.[31]

In a jointly authored opinion piece in *The Guardian,* the two mayors said, "We believe that ending institutional investments in companies that extract fossil fuels and contribute directly to climate change can help to send a powerful message that renewables and low-carbon options are the future."[32]

Just after the editorial appeared, Jerry Brown, the governor of California, signed into law a bill requiring that the state's two largest public pension fund managers, overseeing the California Public Employees' Retirement System (CalPERS) and the California State Teachers' Retirement System (CalSTRS), "identify climate risks in their portfolios and report on that risk to the public and the legislature every three years."[33] The first of its kind passed by a US state legislature, the law not only establishes a statutory definition of climate-related financial risks but also defines the legal responsibilities that the state's public pension plans need to adhere to in their investment decisions while also ensuring that their investment choices align with the state's other legislative requirements on climate change. It's worth briefly reviewing a few select passages, as they provide a boilerplate for reassessing and understanding fiduciary responsibility for states and municipalities across America, and even other countries, as governments administering public pension funds take hold of the financing of a Green New Deal and transition from a fossil fuel civilization to a postcarbon green era.

The new law states unequivocally that "climate change presents an array of material financial risks, including transition risk, physical risk, and litigation risk, that reasonable investors must take into account when making investment decisions." The law also warns that "failure to acknowledge and address these risks will result in exposure to subsequent liabilities and financial risk," and given the fact that climate change occurs over time, investment decisions must "consider both short-term and long-term effects and risks of retirement fund investments."[34]

The law concludes on a tough note designed to make clear to the trustees of these two powerful investment funds that their investment decisions can no longer simply be tied to short-term market returns, especially if those investments are in enterprises or endeavors that by their very nature contribute to climate change: "Given the potentially catastrophic consequences of climate change, the documented social and economic cost of carbon, and the emerging body of literature on the material financial risks of climate change, retirement boards simply cannot disregard financial climate risks."[35]

We need to hit the pause button and grasp the significance of this new law. CalSTRS is the largest education-only public pension fund in the world, with 950,000 members and beneficiaries, and manages financial assets totaling nearly $224 billion.[36] CalPERS is the largest pension fund in the United States, with 1.9 million public employees, retirees, and families, and it oversees financial assets totaling $349 billion.[37] Together, these two mega-giants control over $573 billion in assets, or more than half a trillion dollars invested on behalf of almost 3 million public employees, retirees, and their beneficiaries.

This law fine-tunes the fiduciary principle that guides public pension fund investments, helping asset managers better appreciate what it means to maximize the financial returns of members. The rather sophomoric understanding of the "prudent man rule" that has guided pension fund trustees for well over seventy years, in which the only criterion is a return on investments, fails to take into consideration how such investments, though they might well appear to be prudent at the moment they are made, could also trigger negative effects on other investments, with a boomerang effect that undermines the long-term maximization of the members' overall investment portfolio.

For example, take investments in fossil fuel energy companies and electric utilities whose contributions to global warming emissions exacerbate drought conditions in California and trigger wildfires that down power lines, creating power shortages and brownouts, destroy property, and disrupt commerce, potentially undermining the funds' investments in other California companies impacted by the disruptions and losses. These multiplying effects are not theoretical but very real. PG&E, a Fortune 500 electric utility in California, filed for bankruptcy in 2019 when California officials announced that the company's equipment caused at least seventeen of the twenty-one major wildfires in the state in 2017.[38]

And this is the very point Randy Barber and I made in *The North Will Rise Again* when we stated that every pension fund investment decision, regardless of its short-term return, has consequences that need to be considered, because those consequences could undermine the mid-term and long-term economic well-being of the workers whose funds are being invested. Recall, we had charged that in the past banks had invested the public and private pension funds of workers living in northeastern and midwestern states in companies fleeing those states to right-to-work states in the Sunbelt or Asian nations that have lower labor costs. This happened continuously from the 1960s to the 1990s, impoverishing millions of working people and their families, their communities, and their states. There is likely not a single worker alive today who would think in hindsight that those investments made by the trustees of the funds were "prudent," even though they showed decent returns. Investments today in companies and industries most responsible for emitting global warming gases are of a similar ilk. Prudent investments? Difficult to justify!

Lest there be any remaining doubt about the fundamental change taking place in how public and private pension fund assets are invested and assessed, the UK government—the world's fifth-largest economy in 2018—put the issue of what constitutes a "prudent" investment to the test in June 2018.[39] The UK government's Department for Work and Pensions (DWP) issued new regulations around the same time that California did. The regulations govern how future investments of public pensions are to be evaluated in the oversight of the nation's £1.5 trillion in pension assets.[40] And as in California, the issue centered on deepening the understanding of what is entailed in exercising fiduciary responsibility.

In issuing the new guidelines, Esther McVey, the secretary of state for the DWP, left aside legalities and coded references to speak directly to the British people, and especially the youth. She noted that "as we see the younger generation care more about where their money is going, they are also increasingly questioning that their pensions are invested in a way that aligns with their values. This money can now be used to build a more sustainable, fairer, and more equal society for future generations."[41] The regulations include a warning to pension fund trustees to "include climate change as a specific item because it is a systemic and cross-cutting risk . . . it affects not only environmental risks and opportunities, but also social and governance considerations . . . [adding that] the UK's commitment to the Paris Agreement on Climate Change demonstrates the Government's view that climate change represents a significant concern."[42]

Some might read these recommendations and conclude that Big Government is merely flexing its regulatory muscle to impose its own ideological will on pension fund trustees and millions of public employees; in fact, the opposite is the case. In many instances, it's the public employee unions that are pressuring the governments to come to the table.

UNISON is the UK's largest union, with 1.3 million members working in both the public and private sectors in local government, education, the National Health Service, and the energy field. Having discovered that local governments across the UK had £16 billion ($20.6 billion) invested in the fossil fuel industry, UNISON made the decision at its national convention to mobilize its nationwide members in a campaign to press local governments to divest fossil fuels from their pension fund portfolios and reinvest in green energies and other socially responsible investments. UNISON's general secretary, Dave Prentis, said in an open letter to the membership that "as the law stands, a decision to divest, taken for financial reasons—such as a view that the assets of BP, Shell, etc., will become 'stranded' in the ground and therefore worthless is an acceptable reason for a fund to do so."[43]

In July 2018, Ireland became the first country to announce that it will divest "all" public pension funds from fossil fuel companies within five years. The Irish Parliament passed a bill forcing the Ireland Strategic Investment Fund, which oversees the investment of €8.9 billion ($10.4 billion) of government funds, to divest the estimated €318 million the country is investing in the global fossil fuel industry.[44]

Just eight months later, in March 2019, Norway sent tremors across the financial community when its government announced a recommendation that its sovereign wealth fund divest from all upstream oil and gas producers. Norway is Western Europe's biggest producer of petroleum, and its sovereign wealth fund is the largest in the world.[45] The message was clear: Norway is beginning to get out!

In countries where national governments have either turned a deaf ear or dragged their heels on establishing protocols for divesting from fossil fuels, public employee unions have taken on the mission of unilaterally announcing divestment of their members' pension funds. In South Korea, the eleventh-largest economy in 2018, 46 percent of electricity is still powered by coal.[46] Frustrated by the government's intransigence, the Teachers' Pension and the Government Employees Pension System, with a combined $22 billion in assets under management, announced they would "commit to stop investing in new coal projects" and reinvest the funds being withdrawn from coal projects in renewable energies, hoping it would steer similar commitments by other investment bodies and action at the national government level to divest.[47]

While localities, regions, and national governments and their public pension funds are quickly coming onboard by divesting from the fossil fuel industry and reinvesting in green energies, some of the world's leading insurance companies are not far behind, and for good reason. Eighteen insurers, mostly in Europe, with assets of at least $10 billion each, have already begun to divest from the fossil fuel industry. Several of the biggest insurers—AXA, Munich Re, Swiss Re, Allianz, and Zurich—have either limited or eliminated insuring coal projects. AXA and Swiss RE have also limited underwriting tar sands projects.[48]

Yet, only two of the ten largest American insurance companies—AIG and Farmers—have modified their investment strategies in response to climate change, which is remarkable considering the US West Coast has been devastated by climate change–induced droughts and wildfires for years, with $12.9 billion in insured losses in 2017 alone.[49] Texas and the southeastern states of Louisiana, Florida, Mississippi, Georgia, South and North Carolina, and Virginia have been ravaged by hurricanes, and the midwestern states of Nebraska, Iowa, Wisconsin, and Missouri have experienced ever-worsening 1,000-year historic floods yearly, all brought on by climate change in just the past decade, with loss of lives and property damage. I suspect, however, that the reality of the impacts of climate change will draw American insurance companies into the divest-invest fold over the course of the next two to three years.

The pushback by trustees of public and private pension funds who remain reluctant to divest from the fossil fuel industry and industries connected to it generally centers around not wanting to compromise returns on investment to satisfy demands for "socially responsible investments" that, while noble in purpose, generally perform less well in the marketplace. This argument is often wrapped around a warning about the long-term underfunded liability of pension funds around the world, suggesting that the last thing trustees want to do is invest in socially responsible funds whose returns are low, further depleting the benefits owed to the workers.

It is true that pension funds have been traditionally underfunded, but, as suggested earlier, this is because to some extent banks and other institutions have notoriously used them as a captive pool to invest in poor-performing stocks to shore up their own balance sheets.

Both public and private pension funds in America were woefully underfunded in recent years, for the most part because of the damage the Great Recession wreaked on the entirety of investments between 2008 and 2012 before the economy began its recovery. Pension fund coffers have been filling up in recent years in the overheated bull markets, but here again we need to strike a note of caution. At midyear 2018, the average stock trading on the S&P 500 was 73 percent above its average valuation. Looking back at the history of the stock market, only two times were stocks more overvalued—just prior to the Great Depression in 1929, and in the run-up to the now-infamous dot-com bust in 2000.[50]

According to Pew Trusts research, state pension liabilities are 72 percent funded (some analysts think that figure is generous). If the market were to plunge into bear territory, given that stocks are wildly overvalued on the exchanges, the underfunded liability of pension funds would suffer, but so too would every other investment vehicle.[51]

Where the argument against pension funds divesting from fossil fuels goes completely off track is the sobering reality that oil and gas stocks enjoy the dubious distinction of being one of the worst-performing sectors of the S&P 500—certainly not a good argument for continuing to invest in fossil fuels.[52]

When we get more granular, the numbers become even more revealing. In 2016, Corporate Knights analyzed returns on investments of the New York State Common Retirement Fund, the nation's third-largest pension fund, with $185 billion held in trust for its 1.1 million members. Had the fund divested from its fossil fuels portfolio, its returns over a three-year period would have increased by $5.3 billion, with each pensioner $4,500 richer.[53] Enough said.

■ ■ ■

We need to grasp the full implications of the imminent collapse of the fossil fuel civilization. Environmentalists and social justice activists have for decades been fighting the economic power that the fossil fuel culture has wielded over the global marketplace, the governance of society, and our very way of life. In recent years, we have become more and more terrified over the toll that the fossil fuel sector and related industries have taken, bringing us to the precipice of runaway climate change and an extinction event.

Where things stand now was a long time coming. In October 1973, the Organization of the Petroleum Exporting Countries (OPEC) slapped an embargo on oil delivered to the United States. Within weeks, the price of gas skyrocketed from $3 to $11.65 per gallon at the pump, with long lines of automobiles stretching for blocks around their local filling stations with drivers desperately waiting their turn for the privilege of pumping a few gallons of gas into their vehicles.

This was the moment that the public, for the first time, felt the heavy hand of the oil giants, accusing them of being complicit with the OPEC nations by taking advantage of the embargo and spiking the price of gasoline to ensure record profits off the crisis. The public's anger was boiling over in neighborhoods across America.

With the 200th anniversary of the Boston Tea Party just weeks away, the comparison between the East India Company of two centuries ago and the big oil companies of today struck a chord. My organization, the People's Bicentennial Commission, which was established a year earlier to provide an alternative to the federal government's celebration of America's 200th birthday in 1976, reached out to local community activists in Boston and New England with a call to protest the giant oil companies. Over 20,000 Bostonians joined us in a blizzard, tracing the steps of the first Tea Partiers from historic Faneuil Hall down to the Boston wharf, where a replica of the original East India ship was docked and the mayor and national officials were huddled to open the ceremonies. Local fishermen from Gloucester sailed up into Boston Harbor and docked alongside the replica ship and climbed the masts, dumping empty oil drums into the harbor while thousands of protesters chanted "Impeach Exxon" and "Dirty oil, polluted world," initiating what *The New York Times* would call the "Boston Oil Party of 1973" in the next day's edition. This was the first protest in America against the giant oil companies, to our knowledge, but it would be far from the last.

After forty years of protests against Big Oil all over the world, suddenly the tables have turned. The fossil fuel sector, once seemingly invincible, is quickly collapsing before us. It's happening at a speed and on a scale that we could barely have imagined just a few years ago. While we will have to remain vigilant in taking on the oil industry, we will also have to quickly begin building a green culture from the ashes. We need to finance a transition into a zero-carbon economy and mobilize governmental response in every community and region to take us into an ecological era. We need a Green New Deal in America and around the world.

6

THE ECONOMIC TRANSFORMATION

The New Social Capitalism

The dramatic move on the part of public and private pension funds to pull billions of dollars of their investments from the fossil fuel sector and related industries and reinvest them in the smart green economy marks the coming of age of social capitalism. Socially responsible investment has migrated from the margins of investment decisions to the very core of market activity, providing the groundswell for the most fundamental of transitions—the exit strategy to leave the fossil fuel civilization behind.

Socially Responsible Investment Takes Center Stage

What has precipitated this leap in socially responsible investment from the periphery to the center of capitalist investments? The bottom line! Although the notion of socially responsible investment first emerged with the worldwide movement to rethink investments and divestments in industries in apartheid-era South Africa, it came home to America in the late 1970s in a more generic way, with the opening up of a conversation around worker-owned pension funds being used to undermine the workers' economic security and the well-being of their communities. Proponents of the SRI concept argued that it needed to be factored into the equation in evaluating how retirement benefits were being invested.

Milton Friedman, the late Nobel laureate economist who presided over what's referred to as the "University of Chicago Neoliberal School of Economics," shot back, arguing that any notion of exercising social responsibility in how pension funds should be invested would ultimately undermine the performance of capitalist markets, with Big Government subjecting the flow of capitalist investments to ideological constraints. The Friedman position laid down a dictum that was followed religiously by most pension fund trustees in the management of the growing pool of workers' social capital in the ensuing decades.

On the surface, Friedman's dictum seemed to hold sway, at least through the early years of the new millennium. Under the surface, however, younger generations of baby boomers, Generation Xers, and millennials pushed for measuring investments by their environmental, social, and governance practices (ESG) in shareholder battles and in the administration of workers' pension fund investments.

A new phrase entered into the public dialogue around economic investments: "doing well by doing good," a line borrowed from Benjamin Franklin. The idea was that there need not be, nor should there be, a sharp division between morally and socially good business practices and the bottom line. Rather, it was argued that this was a false dichotomy—that in reality, doing well by doing good enhances the bottom line.

With this counternarrative, unions and NGOs continued to put forth shareholder resolutions at companies' annual meetings to factor SRI into their practices. Their successes led to socially responsible investments accelerating after the dot-com bust in 2000, at the hands of a younger generation that was not shy about shaming morally irresponsible and unacceptable corporate behavior, often using social media and reputation sites to embarrass, prod, and enforce changes in corporate practices.

Today, SRI has gone mainstream. According to a report prepared by Morgan Stanley, 86 percent of millennials are interested in socially responsible investing, differentiating their cohort from its elders.[1] Reflecting this emerging shift, SRI in the United States has topped $12 trillion, much of it proffered by pension fund trustees.[2] Although SRIs run the gamut and can be found across every industry and sector, the deepening concerns over climate change, the environment, carbon footprint, and the geopolitical influence of Big Oil have catapulted divestments out of the fossil fuel industry and into reinvestments in renewable energies and green industries.

The new thrust has given rise to "impact investing," providing seed money to businesses that embed ESG into every aspect of their operations. In surveys conducted across the asset market sector, Morgan Stanley repeatedly heard from interviewees who expressed their strong conviction that the very nature of investment decisions is at an inflection point in the industry due to a shift in the kind of investments clients demand. "Doing well by doing good" has become the new mantra.

Is the enthusiasm justified? A spate of in-depth studies over the past two years, including studies prepared by Harvard University, the University of Rotterdam, and Arabesque Partners and Oxford University, show that companies with a strong ESG presence across their value chains tend to outperform their competitors, in part due to their commitment to greater aggregate efficiencies, less waste, circularity built into their supply chains, and a low carbon footprint, all of which increase their bottom line profit, and each of which is tied to their shift away from a fossil fuel civilization and into a green era.[3] Rather obvious.

Every aspect of the economy is made out of or moved by

fossil fuels. They have been the lifeblood of the First and Second Industrial Revolution infrastructures that make possible every economic and commercial endeavor. Without this carbon infrastructure, businesses and, for that matter, society as a whole, could not exist. The point is, the fossil fuel infrastructure has been, up to now, the foundation of society's prosperity and well-being.

Given that fossil fuels are the lifeblood of the current global economy, does anyone anywhere believe that we are in the sunrise or even the crest or plateau of the fossil fuel era? And what then of the infrastructure that underlies a fossil fuel culture? Can anyone claim that the infrastructure is still robust? Clearly, this period of history is closing.

Infrastructures are like living organisms. They are born, grow, mature, and begin a long period of decline, eventually ending in death, which is exactly what is happening with the carbon-based Second Industrial Revolution. Fortunately, a digitally interconnected postcarbon Third Industrial Revolution infrastructure, which is at the heart of a Green New Deal, is ascending, along with new aggregate efficiencies, higher productivity, and a dramatic reduction in carbon footprint. In turn, new businesses and workforces will be required to build out the green economy and manage it in the twenty-first century.

As to whether low-carbon investments might indeed be socially responsible but financially poor investments, S&P Dow Jones analyzed index exposure to carbon risks for a number of versions of the S&P 500 Index and concluded that "the low-carbon versions actually outperformed the benchmark over the five-year period in most cases."[4]

We saw in chapters 2 and 3 that the key sectors that make up the Second Industrial Revolution infrastructure are each decoupling from a fossil fuel civilization—ICT/telecommunication, electricity, transportation and logistics, and the building stock—and recoupling with the incipient Green New Deal Third Industrial Revolution infrastructure around the world. If trustees of pension funds are looking to maximize the lifetime financial interests of their pensioners and their beneficiaries, it would be difficult to conceive how this might be done by locking investments into a dying Second Industrial Revolution infrastructure with its stranded assets and declining business models.

The Green New Deal is all about infrastructure: Broadband, Big Data and digital communication, near-zero marginal cost, zero-emission green electricity, autonomous electric vehicles on smart roads powered by renewable energy, and nodally connected zero-emission positive power buildings, the linchpins of a Green New Deal infrastructure, are going to have to be built out and scaled up in each region and connected across every region, enveloping landmasses around the world. This infrastructure transition will have to move quickly and be at least partially in place in the coming years if we are to hold the increase of temperature on Earth to 1.5°C or below.

How Much Will It Cost?

How much investment are we talking about to mend parts of the Second Industrial Revolution and decommission other parts that move into the stranded assets column? And how much investment will we need to spend on the smart new zero-emission Third Industrial Revolution infrastructure? Oxford Economics reports that the nations of the world will need to increase the proportion of GDP to infrastructure from the 3 percent per year expected under current trends to 3.5 percent per annum—certainly doable.[5]

Some countries are stepping up quickly while others are crawling woefully behind. McKinsey reports that the United States ranks an embarrassing twelfth on the list, having invested only 2.3 percent of GDP on infrastructure from 2010 to 2015, and its ratio of investment to GDP continues to fall with each passing year.[6]

At least the public around the world seems to understand the importance of infrastructure to the general well-being, with 73 percent of respondents in a recent international survey saying that "investing in infrastructure is vital to [their country's] future economic growth" and 59 percent saying that they "do not believe enough is being done to meet their country's infrastructure needs."[7]

Now, the United States may be on the verge of catching up. Infrastructure spending has risen from near invisibility in political circles to become a controversial red-hot public issue with the growing realization that the nation's crumbling infrastructure is now at a breaking point, costing the American economy literally hundreds of billions of dollars in losses, and becoming a matter of national security. The problem is compounded by the damage inflicted by climate-related disasters on already weakened infrastructure.

President Trump is championing a $1.5 trillion infrastructure rollout over ten years—mainly to mend the aged twentieth-century Second Industrial Revolution infrastructure. All is not as it seems. The White House is offering up only $200 billion in federal financing, mostly in the form of tax credits, with the bulk of the financing to come from the states.[8] The Democrats are calling for a $1 trillion infrastructure package financed by the federal government, which would include mending the Second Industrial Revolution infrastructure and overlaying the build-out of a smart digital green Third Industrial Revolution infrastructure that can take the country into a zero-emission society and address climate change.[9]

In reality, the Trump plan is paltry but not a radical departure from the federal government's share of financing the country's infrastructure, which in recent years has averaged around 25 percent of the total cost, with the rest of the infrastructure commitment left to the states. Moreover, the federal tax breaks the president is promoting are more in line with what the government customarily does to assist the states and stimulate market forces that accompany infrastructure-related projects. But, unfortunately, the tax breaks the White House has in mind are almost universally connected to bolstering the antiquated fossil fuel infrastructure, much of which is quickly becoming stranded assets. The wiser course of action would be for the federal government to provide tax credits, tax deductions, tax penalties, grants, and low-interest loans to encourage a Green New Deal transition and let both the marketplace and the states use the incentives to quickly speed the transition from a fossil fuel civilization to a zero-carbon emission society.

However, the federal government should take a significant responsibility, along with the states, for financing some of the build-out of the national power grid, which will serve as the backbone of the Third Industrial Revolution infrastructure. There is precedent for this. The backbone of the Second Industrial Revolution infrastructure was the Eisenhower-era National Interstate and Defense Highways Act of 1956. This public works project connected the country, created the suburbs, and established a totally integrated mobility and logistics infrastructure across America. The infrastructure cost the federal government an estimated \$425 billion (in 2006 dollars) to lay out thousands of miles of roads over a period of thirty-seven years.[10] The federal government covered 90 percent of the financing, paid for by a slight increase in the gasoline tax, and the states covered the remaining 10 percent of the bill.[11] The smart national power grid in the twenty-first century, providing seamless digital interconnectivity to enable the sharing of electricity from renewable energy sources across every region of the country, is analogous to the build-out of the Interstate Highway System, which provided a seamless interconnectivity for mobility across the country in the twentieth century.

Or taking the analogy one step further, KEMA, a former leading European energy, electricity, and engineering consultancy, made the point years ago that the "smart grid is to the electric energy sector what the Internet was to the communications sector and should be viewed and supported on that basis."[12]

There is another parallel between the Third Industrial Revolution's smart digital infrastructure and the Interstate Highway System. President Dwight D. Eisenhower was keen on erecting a vast interstate highway system, in part because of his own personal experience in the military. In 1919, when he was a young colonel in the army, he participated in a motor convoy across the continental United States on the historic Lincoln Highway—at that time the first road across America. The journey was designed to focus attention on improving America's highways and took over two months to complete. Later, in an autobiography, he quipped that "the trip had been difficult, tiring, and fun," but the memory of all the delays across the country stayed with him during his military career. In World War II, General Eisenhower pondered his earlier experience after observing the German Autobahn—at that time the world's only national highway system—and later remarked that "the old convoy had started me thinking about good, two-lane highways, but Germany had made me see the wisdom of broader ribbons across the land."[13]

When Eisenhower became president in 1953, he already had in mind "the grand plan" for an interstate highway system connecting all of the American economy and society. Defense and security issues were a constant companion. He was particularly concerned about the possible mass-evacuation of urban populations in the event of a nuclear attack and the need to move military equipment, where needed, in the case of an invasion, and saw an interstate highway system as critical to national security and defense. This was not the only reason for engaging in an interstate mobility infrastructure project. In his speech to the National Governors Association in 1954, the president listed a number of other objectives, including public safety on the roads, easing traffic congestion, and improving logistics in the production and distribution of goods and services. However, in his speech to the governors, he again emphasized that defense issues were also a priority and warned the elected officials of "the appalling inadequacies to meet the demands of catastrophe or defense should an atomic war come." The final piece of legislation was called the Federal Aid Highway Act of 1956, but is popularly known as the National Interstate and Defense Highways Act.

Like the Interstate Highway System, the emerging smart national power grid is digitally connecting the American economy and society and increasing the nation's efficiency, productivity, and economic well-being, and, when finished, will also address security concerns that, at least in part, gave rise to the Interstate Highway System. In the 1950s, the threat was nuclear war. Today, the threat is cyber war. On the upside, the smart national power grid is managing an ever more diverse and complex energy infrastructure made up of literally millions of players in dense relationships on ever-shifting platforms. Yet, the very complexity of the current system makes it increasingly vulnerable to cyberattacks. Nor is this merely a theoretical issue. The nation's power grid and electricity system has already been hacked by agents of foreign countries, and there is growing concern that hostile powers as well as rogue terrorist groups are turning their attention to disabling our large electricity transformers, high-voltage transmission lines, electricity generation plants, and electricity distribution systems. If electricity were to be disabled across an entire region or the whole country over weeks and even months, the economy would collapse, society would crumble, and government would be virtually inoperable at every level.

This prospect keeps elected officials, the military, and the business community up at night wondering if and when a cyberattack might occur, knowing that we are wholly unprepared at this point in time across the entire national electricity grid. Hurried discussions are now occurring at the local, state, and federal levels and within the power and electricity industry on how to quickly harden every aspect of the emerging national smart grid, from the large power transformers and long-distance high-voltage transmission lines to the final distribution of electricity to end users. There is at a minimum an agreement on one factor—that is, the key to cybersecurity rests in deepening resiliency and, that, in turn, requires an expansion of distributed power in every community.

The installation of microgrids will be our nation's frontline insurance. Were a cyberattack to happen anywhere in the country, homeowners, businesses, and entire communities would be able to quickly go off-grid, reaggregate, and share electricity neighborhood to neighborhood, which would allow society to continue functioning. It would be difficult for anyone to argue that the threat of cyber warfare against the nation's power and electricity grid is any less a national security issue.

Just as the ever-present threat of a cyberattack demands continuous vigilance, so too does the threat of catastrophic climate events that are escalating exponentially across the country, resulting in tens of billions of dollars in damage to local ecosystems and loss of property, human life, and commerce. Cyberattacks and climate disasters are both going to escalate in the years ahead, making the questions of both cybersecurity and climate resilience the highest priority national security issues facing the country.

With the interstate highway precedent in mind, let's run the numbers to get a tentative sketch of the areas that need to be funded to lay down a smart, zero-emission Green New Deal infrastructure to address climate change and transform the American economy and society. How much funding is each area likely to need, and how will the costs be divided between the federal government and the states? It is interesting to note that the $476 billion price tag that the Electric Power Research Institute projected for building the national smart grid is nearly identical to the cost of the interstate highways, and it, too, is projected to result in economic benefits far beyond its cost.[14] Over the initial ten-year build-out of the national power grid, the federal government would only have to invest approximately $50 billion per year.

The ten-year federal government infrastructure commitment should also include an additional $50 billion a year in the form of tax credits, tax deductions, grants, and low-interest loans to spur solar and wind installations, the adoption of electric and fuel-cell vehicles, and other aggregate efficiencies that will take America's businesses, workers, and families into the green era. By way of comparison, in 2016 federal tax preferences in the form of tax credits for renewable energy were an estimated $10.9 billion, while an estimated $2.7 billion in tax preferences were given over to energy efficiency or electricity transmission.[15] The estimated tax credit for plug-in electric vehicles between 2018 and 2022 is projected at $7.5 billion.[16]

Federal tax credits and other incentives have been instrumental in encouraging the installation of solar and wind technology, creating the market for green energies in the United States. The Solar Energy Investment Tax Credit allows homeowners to deduct 30 percent of the cost of installation of solar panels from their taxes. As of 2018, more than five million homes were powered by solar electricity. Wind power has equally benefited from tax credits, with enough wind now being captured in America to power 17.5 million homes. While past tax preferences helped spawn the solar and wind market, increased energy efficiencies, and the introduction of electric vehicles, to get to scale in a wholesale transformation into a green energy era, these tax preferences need to be at least tripled over the next twenty years.

Finally, the federal government should set aside $15 billion per year to retrofit the nation's residential, commercial, industrial, and institutional building stock. A comprehensive study undertaken by the Rockefeller Foundation and Deutsche Bank estimates that the retrofitting of residential, commercial, and institutional buildings will cost approximately $279 billion over a ten-year period. That study was conducted in 2012. It's likely that today the costs will exceed $300 billion. Moreover, our global team estimates that the scope and magnitude of the retrofit is likely to take upward of twenty years to successfully complete.

The Rockefeller/Deutsche Bank study projected that this critical investment alone will result in $1 trillion of energy savings over a ten-year period, which is a savings of 30 percent annually on all the spending on electricity used in the United States. A nationwide retrofitting of the building stock would also create 3.3 million cumulative job years of employment and reduce the country's global warming emissions by 10 percent.[17]

In total, the federal government's *initial* ten-year infrastructure plan would amount to $115 billion per year: $50 billion per year in the partial financing of the national power grid; $50 billion per year in tax credits, tax deductions, grants, low-interest loans, and other incentives to stimulate solar and wind installations, the purchase of electric vehicles, the installing of charging stations, and other green components of an emerging Third Industrial Revolution infrastructure; and $15 billion per year to retrofit the nation's residential, commercial, industrial, and institutional building stock to speed the transition into a zero-carbon emission economy. The total federal budget for the ten-year infrastructure deployment would ring up at $1.15 trillion. This would give the country at least a "bare bones" national smart grid and accompanying infrastructure that is up and functioning. The price tag is not much more than the Pentagon's annual budget in 2019 alone.

Can it be done in ten years? The Brattle Group says that "major transmission projects," which are the key component of an integrated national power grid, "require 10 or more years on average for planning, development, approval, and construction."[18] So yes, it's possible.

Still, the federal government's commitment of $115 billion annually over a ten-year period represents only a partial down payment on what the country will need to do to transition into a fully operational smart zero-emission green economy. Significant additional dollars will be required to build out the Third Industrial Revolution infrastructure. As alluded to earlier, the burden of financing the transition is going to fall primarily on states, counties, and municipalities. In all the debate currently swirling in Washington political circles about the role of the federal government in building out and managing a smart new national infrastructure, the reality is that the federal government plays a small role in maintaining the nation's infrastructure. It's worth noting that state and local governments—and not the federal government—own 93 percent of the country's infrastructure and pay 75 percent of the cost of maintaining and improving it.[19]

Assuming that the Green New Deal infrastructure transition will roughly follow that same 75/25 state/federal split, this would require a commitment of around $345 billion per year on the part of the states to match the $115 billion per year commitment by the federal government, for a combined total of $460 billion per year in infrastructure spending over a ten-year time period. Recall that the Brattle Group estimates that between

2031 and 2050, an additional $40 billion in new investment annually will be required for just the scale-up in "transmission investment" for the smart grid to keep up with electricity demands. Other studies will include additional infrastructure costs in the scale-up over an extended period of time.

It needs to be reemphasized that the current infrastructure proposals being debated in Congress have a ten-year timeline. While it would be possible, in the best-case scenario, to build out a *juvenile* Third Industrial Revolution infrastructure within ten years, a *mature*, integrated, and operational zero-emission smart green infrastructure will require an additional ten years to be fully established. What we're talking about here is a twenty-year generational transformation into a nationwide Third Industrial Revolution paradigm. Assuming a continued combined investment by the federal government and states at the same level for an additional ten years, we are looking at approximately $9.2 trillion in funding over a twenty-year time period.

Even assuming that the US GDP doesn't continue to grow but remains around $20 trillion per year—the GDP for 2018—the total investment comes out to around an additional 2.3 percent of GDP annually above and beyond the 2.3 percent currently invested in just mending and maintaining the old twentieth-century infrastructure. That's 4.6 percent of GDP annually to lay out and deploy a state-of-the-art, smart, zero-carbon emission digital infrastructure to manage a twenty-first-century resilient economy. Lest the powers that be blink at a doubling of our current dismal 2.3 percent of GDP to 4.6 percent annual spending on infrastructure, it should be noted that the People's Republic of China spent an annual average of 8.3 percent of its GDP on infrastructure between 2010 and 2015.[20]

These numbers tell us what is likely in store for the United States and how its position in the world economy will be affected in the coming half-century if its annual investment in infrastructure remains so far below China's. What we're saying here is that if we want the United States to continue to be among the leading nations of the world, doubling our annual spending on infrastructure is reasonable, and the twenty-year timeline to transition into a smart zero-carbon Third Industrial Revolution economy is possible, but only if all the stars align. Again, these are estimates in a rapidly changing technological landscape, and are likely to be continuously revised and updated as the country moves through this historic infrastructure transition.

This $9.2 trillion projected cost of the smart national power grid and accompanying infrastructure scale-up over twenty years is slightly lower than cost projections in some other studies. That's because the exponential plunge in the costs of solar and wind energy technology, battery storage, and electric and fuel-cell transport, plus the accompanying aggregate efficiencies that come with the Internet of Things built environment, will likely continue unabated over the twenty-year span, dramatically reducing the overall cost of a nationwide smart green infrastructure deployment. Then, too, across-the-board tax credits, tax deductions, grants, low-interest loans and other incentives, as well as graduated penalties, working alongside falling costs, are likely to accelerate the adoption of the infrastructure in homes, businesses, and neighborhoods, and across communities. This has certainly been the history with the introduction of solar and wind energy technology, and it soon will happen with electric transport.

This is a key point that needs to be emphasized. We traditionally think of infrastructure as overarching centralized platforms financed at considerable expense by governments and laid down for use by the public at large—road systems, electricity and telephone lines, power plants, water and sewage systems, airports, port facilities, etc. All well and good.

While the Third Industrial Revolution infrastructure requires a smart national power grid—a digitally managed Renewable Energy Internet—that can mediate and manage the flow of green electricity coming and going between millions of players in their homes, automobiles, offices, factories, and communities, many of the actual infrastructure components that feed into and off that grid are highly distributed in nature and are paid for and belong to literally millions of individuals, families, and hundreds of thousands of small businesses. Every solar roof, wind turbine, nodal Internet of Things building, storage battery, charging station, electric vehicle, etc., is likewise an infrastructure component. Unlike the bulky, top-down, and static one-way infrastructures of the First and Second Industrial Revolutions, the distributed and laterally scaled infrastructure of the Third Industrial Revolution is, by its very nature, fluid and open, allowing literally billions of players around the world to assemble and reassemble, and disaggregate and reaggregate, their own component parts of it where they live and work and while they commute, in continuously evolving blockchained platforms.

Much of the smart infrastructure, then, is going to come online because of the generous tax credits and other incentives combined with the exponentially falling cost curve of the infrastructure components and processes. In the Green New Deal, infrastructure is potentially participatory and democratized and always metamorphosing into new patterns if overseen by commons governance rather than private corporate governance in each region. The $9.2 trillion price tag reflects the way this digital distributed infrastructure is likely to emerge and evolve in the coming decades.

When all is said and done, let's not forget that all these infrastructure improvements will add $3 to the US GDP for every dollar invested and create millions of new jobs.[21]

Finding the Money

So, where is the money going to come from to finance a federal and state government rollout of a $9.2 trillion twenty-year Green New Deal infrastructure across America? Let's begin by weighing in at the federal government level.

With a changing of the guard in the US Congress and at the White House, it might be possible to initiate a higher graduated tax rate for the super-rich, which America had in the 1950s and '60s, the period of our country's greatest growth and prosperity. That is certainly reasonable and justifiable, especially given the deepening gulf between the super-rich and an ever-more impoverished American workforce. According to Mark Mazur, director of the Urban-Brookings Tax Policy Center, if a marginal tax of 70 percent were imposed on the income of the super-rich—individuals making $10 million a year or more, and then only after the first $10 million in income—it would bring in an additional $72 billion in revenue per year for the federal government.[22]

Bill Gates, the second-richest individual in the world, worth $90 billion, and Warren Buffett, the third-richest, worth $84 billion, agree that the super-rich should be taxed at a far higher rate and have publicly advocated a change in the laws to address the growing inequality between the super-rich and the rest of the population.[23] In a February 2019 interview with Stephen Colbert on CBS, Gates was unequivocal on the issue, saying, "I think you can make the tax system take a much higher portion from people with great wealth," adding that "these fortunes were not made from ordinary income, so you probably have to look to the capital gains rate and the estate tax if you want to create more equity there."[24] Buffett agrees, saying, "The wealthy are definitely undertaxed relative to the general population."[25]

The revenue raised from increasing the tax rate on the

super-rich could and should be used to help fund a Green New Deal to rebuild the economy, which would create new business opportunities and the mass employment that go with the green infrastructure shift. Still, this new source of revenue won't be enough to get the job done.

We could also redeploy some of the billions of dollars that go into the Pentagon budget. That, too, seems more than reasonable. The American Society of Civil Engineers estimates that the United States will need an additional $206 billion a year beyond what we are already spending on infrastructure build-out just to get the nation up to a passing B grade.[26] This seems like a small amount of money to begin the transition into a smart green Third Industrial Revolution infrastructure to rebuild the American economy and address climate change—especially when in 2017 alone, the cumulative damage from climate disasters in the United States cost $300 billion.[27] That's just for one year!

For those raised voices saying that the US government can't afford a significant upgrade in the nation's infrastructure, consider that the defense budget for just the year 2019 is $716 billion, one of the largest in US history.[28] According to the Congressional Budget Office, funding for weapons systems takes up about one-third of the budget of the Department of Defense (DoD).[29] The United States' defense budget is larger than the total combined military budgets of China, Russia, the United Kingdom, France, India, Japan, and Saudi Arabia.[30] Surely there's something terribly wrong in the way the federal government is allocating funds to protect "the national security" of the homeland. We ought to consider reallocating at least a small part of the DoD's priorities from ever more costly expenditures on weapons systems we will never use to the military's new paramount role in protecting the country against cyber wars and managing climate-related disaster response and relief missions, which will increasingly be seen as the most important national security issues facing our communities and country in the decades to come. An additional $30 billion could be garnered for the federal government's contribution to the Green New Deal by simply cutting 12.6 percent of the overblown and outsized weapons systems budget of the DoD, which amounts to only approximately 4 percent of the total military budget for 2019. If we're not even willing to reprioritize this tiny fraction of the current DoD budget to secure a resilient smart national power grid to address cyber war and catastrophic climate events, then we're putting the country in deep jeopardy.

Additional federal revenue can come from terminating the nearly $15 billion in federal subsidies given to the oil, gas, and coal industries each year.[31] There is no longer any justification for subsidizing the fossil fuel sector, whose assets are quickly becoming stranded.

Just adding up the above numbers, here's what we get. The federal government could raise $70 billion per year on new taxes on the super-rich, $30 billion by cutting 12.6 percent of weapons development and procurement, and an additional $15 billion by ending subsidies for the fossil fuel sector, for a total of $115 billion in revenue per year available to finance the federal government's portion of the transition to a zero-emission green infrastructure.

Of course, this is just one of many potential scenarios for raising the funds necessary to deploy the federal government's contribution to a Green New Deal scale-up over the next two decades. There are many other possible combinations that could be brought to bear. For example, a small percentage of the proposed universal carbon tax revenue could be used to help finance both the federal and the state governments' contributions to the Green New Deal rollout, with the rest of the revenue being distributed to American families so that the burden of carbon taxes remains in the hands of the fossil fuel industry. But the point is this. All of these numbers are readily actionable without significant compromise to the vast wealth of the super-rich, Pentagon preparedness, and the financial well-being of millions of American families.

That said, the other, equally promising place to look for the money, at least in part, is the trillions of dollars in public and private pension funds that are just now turning their eye to the vast investment opportunities that accompany a wholesale transition into a green Third Industrial Revolution. Pension fever is already in the air in the United States and on the lips of politicians in both political parties. In February 2019, *The Hill,* the publication that keeps elected officials, the federal bureaucracy, and lobbies abreast of happenings across the government, published an opinion piece by Ingo Walter, professor emeritus of finance at NYU's Stern School of Business, and Clive Lipshitz, managing partner of Tradewind Interstate Advisors, titled "Public Pensions and Infrastructure: A Match Made in Heaven," suggesting that the giant national pool of workers' public pension funds is sparking a romance with government that will help finance an upgraded twenty-first-century infrastructure.[32] Some of this financial pool is going to come onboard and invest in the roll-out of the national power grid and in the greening of federal government–owned physical assets. This is a certainty. Figuring out how to strike the proper balance between the federal government's direct funding of the infrastructure shift and financing the build-out with pension fund capital and other sources of private capital will likely be the central dynamic that plays out in Congress and the White House between the Democratic and Republican parties. The deliberation could bring both political parties together across the aisle to get on with the inevitable transition into a zero-emission economy.

This "match made in heaven" comes with an important

caveat. Any use of unionized pension funds in green infrastructure investments and related projects must include
unionized workforces in the roll-outs, wherever possible, so
that workers' pension capital isn't used, once again, to finance
companies that are anti-union and that consciously eliminate
union jobs on their worksites. Since only 11 percent of the
American workforce is currently unionized and there will be
green infrastructure projects that can't fill workloads with
sufficient unionized workforces, there will need to be at least
a guarantee that protects the rights of workers to organize
and collectively bargain, if they so choose.

The matchmaker in the coming together of public and
private pension funds and the green infrastructure build-out
is green banks. Their mission is to provide a percentage of
available capital for the express purpose of financing large-
scale build-outs of the Third Industrial Revolution green infrastructure. Over the past decade, the UK, Japan, Australia,
Malaysia, and other countries have created green banks that
have invested in green energy to the tune of $40 billion or
more.[33] As early as 2012, the International Trade Union Confederation weighed in, urging the creation of green banks that
could act as clearinghouses to bring together the vast pool of
workers' global pension funds with green infrastructure investments.[34]

In the United States, Chris Van Hollen, then a congress-
man and now a senator from Maryland, introduced the
Green Bank Act of 2014, the first of its kind at the federal
level. (Chris Murphy of Connecticut introduced its Senate
companion bill.) It authorized an initial $10 billion issue of
US Treasury bonds to capitalize a bank that would provide
"loans, loan guarantees, debt securitization, insurance, portfolio insurance, and other forms of financing support or risk
management" to finance green infrastructure-scale projects

and jump-start the transition into a green infrastructure.[35] Van Hollen's bill was never enacted into law, but he succeeded in breathing life into the idea of green banks in America. By 2016, New York, Connecticut, California, Hawaii, Rhode Island, and Montgomery County, Maryland, all had green banks up and running, and other jurisdictions were in the process of establishing them.[36]

Since states are responsible for most of the infrastructure, it became clear that any federal initiative to institutionalize a national green bank would have to modify its modus operandi to adjust to the many state green bank initiatives already well underway. So, when Van Hollen reintroduced legislation calling for a national green bank in 2016, the new bill did not allow the federal government to directly finance green infrastructure; rather, it mandated that the US green bank be restricted to lending funds to state and municipal green banks, who would then be responsible for directly underwriting green infrastructure initiatives.[37]

By 2019, the establishment of green banks had spread around the world. In March of that year, officials from twenty-three mostly developing countries, representing 56 percent of the world's population and accounting for 26 percent of global GDP and 43 percent of global CO_2 emissions, held a Green Bank Design Summit in Paris with the purpose of establishing their own green banks.[38] Institutional investors were at the table, and pension funds and other investment funds were ready to scale.

The new push to establish green banks in developing countries and transition into a smart Third Industrial Revolution infrastructure is a clear sign that the Green New Deal vision is universal in appeal. Interestingly, there is a growing consensus that this smart green infrastructure revolution can move even more quickly in emerging nations, for the simple reason that their liability is also their asset. In other words, lacking infrastructure, developing countries are finding that they can move more quickly to deploy a virgin green infrastructure accompanied by the appropriate codes, regulations, and standards than highly developed nations that have to decommission or build on an older Second Industrial Revolution infrastructure. Solar and wind installations are mushrooming across the developing world.

Back in 2011, Dr. Kandeh Yumkella, then director general of the United Nations Industrial Development Organization (UNIDO), and I began a conversation on how the developing countries could begin embracing and deploying the smart Third Industrial Revolution vision. We jointly introduced the concept in 2011 at UNIDO's biennial General Conference. Yumkella declared, "We are at the beginning of a Third Industrial Revolution," and then asked, "How do we share knowledge, share capital and investments around the world, to make this revolution really happen?"[39] UNIDO took up the challenge of bringing the UN and developing countries into a green postcarbon narrative and infrastructure deployment.

Green banks are proliferating in developing countries and industrialized nations. However the financial mix is put together, pension fund capital will be a driving force in the transformation. It's a win-win for the Green New Deal deployment.

Tens of millions of workers will invest their pension funds in their countries' future, ensuring unionized workforces when possible, protecting the rights of workers to organize, securing reliable returns on their pension funds, addressing the issue of climate change head-on, and spurring the vast new business opportunities and employment that accompany a transformation of their nations' infrastructure in the emerging green era.

Here in the United States, irrespective of whatever green national bank bill might be enacted into law, public pension funds, and even a growing number of private pension funds, are going to do some of the heavy lifting in financing a Green New Deal at the federal level. Still, their primary interest is going to be in underwriting the much bigger green infrastructure investment at the state and local levels, to the tune of $345 billion annually over the next twenty years.

But first, there is a spoiler at the party that needs to be addressed. Let me explain. Since infrastructure is, by its very nature, a public good that every citizen needs to access and use, infrastructure services were always thought of as a public service provided by local, state, and national governments. However, a shift has taken place at the state and local levels, with more and more existing public infrastructure being sold off or leased as concessions to the private sector and new infrastructure being privatized from the get-go. These are called "public-private partnerships." Part of the explanation for the shift lies in the change in the political landscape that began in the early 1980s with the ascent to power of Margaret Thatcher and Ronald Reagan, both of whom embraced privatization and deregulation. The rationale was and still is that government agencies overseeing and operating government-financed and -managed infrastructure, without competition biting at their heels, eventually become lethargic bureaucracies, slow to innovate, and poor managers when they finally do so.

This is part and parcel of what has become the neoliberal ideology that favors privatizing these key infrastructure services and letting the "open marketplace" take a run at managing them henceforward. I should add, in passing, that no good evidence was ever provided to back up this claim that infrastructure would be better served in private hands. The rail service, the electricity grid, the postal service, the public health service, public television, and other government services seem to function very effectively, at least in the more developed nations. Still, the politicization of public infrastructure captured the public's attention, at least enough to embolden neoliberal governments, from Thatcher and Reagan to Blair and Clinton, to hand over many of their traditional infrastructure responsibilities to the private sector and the whims and caprices of the marketplace. I suspect that if ever an extensive history of this period were done, we might find that the private sector, already sated in the conventional markets, was anxious to grab hold of these potentially lucrative public infrastructure services that came wrapped up with a built-in captive audience that had little choice but to use them—a princely proposition for the marketplace.

In more recent years, there has been a second wave of privatization of infrastructure, primarily in response to an increase in public debt and, in some countries, the public desire to reduce tax commitments in an era where wages, especially among the middle and working classes, have not kept up with the cost of living. It's not surprising, then, that local and state governments have looked to privatizing more and more of their public infrastructure. However, private companies overseeing infrastructure are often far more aggressive in squeezing profits out of what they regard as more of a business than a service, which often leads to what industry watchers call "asset stripping." This is a common problem, experienced over and over again, with privately run prisons, toll roads, schools, and the like.

Taking Back the Infrastructure

The entrance of pension funds into the investment of infrastructure brings a new class of owners onto the field, different in many respects from private companies in how they relate to infrastructure. Pension fund trustees are more likely to see themselves as custodians or stewards, allowing them to take a more socially responsible approach to how they invest. Trustees of public pension funds in particular, but now private pension funds as well, have been among the trailblazers in adopting the ESG principles of socially responsible investing, prodded, in large part, by their members and union leaders. These pension funds bring a different mentality, potentially more responsive to investing "social capital" in infrastructure projects.

In the last several years, pension funds have begun to reposition their portfolios away from traditional investments in equities, which are viewed as overvalued, risky, short-term investments subject to gyrations between overheated bull markets and ever-deeper recessions. Pension fund trustees are becoming more interested in less volatile and more secure long-term investments in green bonds with predictable returns, and infrastructure fits the bill. A recent study conducted by PwC and the Global Infrastructure Investor Association (GIIA) titled *Global Infrastructure Investment* makes this very point, saying that "the last decade has seen a transformation in the world's economic infrastructure . . . driven by an influx of capital seeking long-term stable returns," with much of it coming from pension funds.[40]

For public employee pension funds, investment in public infrastructure is a no-brainer: the very employment of their members is in the public sector, and therefore, they have an intimate appreciation of the importance of public services. But both public and private pension funds are more likely to be responsive to investments in infrastructure, especially if it's in the same region where members live and work, since the investment secures an additional benefit of improved infrastructure services for them and their families.

This is already occurring. The giant Quebec pension fund Caisse de dépôt et placement du Québec (CDPQ) assembled sufficient financial resources to develop and operate the light rail system in Montreal.[41] Dutch pension funds have joined into partnerships with local engineering companies and invested in new road construction in their regions.[42]

In the long run, pension funds' investment in public infrastructure is going to be a better way to go than global corporations privatizing infrastructure and running it as a solely for-profit business.

Now I'd like to get personal on why I've delved into such detail on the question of global companies privatizing infrastructure versus direct investment by pension funds in the build-out of public infrastructure. Recall the Google initiative in Toronto, where the company is hoping to privatize, build out, and manage a smart infrastructure that will eventually oversee the comings and goings of an entire population in a metropolitan region. Although disturbing, this is the next big market for the giant internet companies and ICT companies. Larry Page said it himself, apparently so enamored with digital technologies' inherent efficiencies and benefits that he did not consider even for a moment that the public might be repelled by the notion. I can tell you, from experience working with regions across the EU in the deployment of their long-term green infrastructure roadmaps, that the privatization of public infrastructure in the hands of giant global companies, especially the internet, ICT, and telecom companies, is a universal nonstarter.

On the other hand, public financing of infrastructure comes with its own problems. Up front is the government's need to minimize the ratio of debt to GDP on its books. It's a requirement across the EU. In America, local and state governments are mindful of the same restraints and are aware that the kind of investment needed will not come just from a commensurate hike in taxes or a dive into deeper debt. How, then, do we navigate through the maze and find a pragmatic formula to finance a twenty-first-century smart green infrastructure? The message heard with more resonance across the financial community is that we should look to the trillions of dollars of investment opportunity coming from the untapped pool of public and private pension fund capital.

For their part, pension funds are willing and eager to invest. But there is a catch. The real problem is a lack of camera-ready large-scale Third Industrial Revolution infrastructure projects in which to invest. This is not unique to the American market. This is a problem around the world, where cities, regions, and countries are tinkering with thousands of small, unconnected pilot projects with little initiative to scale an infrastructure transformation. For example, in the UK, at present, there is only one mega-infrastructure project being deployed that is financed by a consortium of pension funds: London's £4.2 billion "super-sewer," known as the Thames Tideway Tunnel, billed as the "biggest overhaul of the capital's waste plumbing system since Victorian times."[43]

Chris Rule, the chief investment officer at the Local Pensions Partnership, which oversees a £12 billion Lancashire County pension fund, bluntly says, "My perception is that pension funds are quite receptive to investing in UK infrastructure. [The problem] is supply and demand. There is more money seeking investments than there are available. That is pushing down yields." Adrian Jones, a director in the infrastructure debt team at Allianz Global Investors, echoes the theme heard by both pension investors and insurance companies, the other major players seeking investment opportunities in big infrastructure developments: "We don't see that there is a need for radical reform to get more money into infrastructure. What we need are more investible projects."[44] The universal complaint coming from pension fund trustees is *No more pilots! Give us some big-scale Third Industrial Revolution infrastructure deployments to invest in over a period of time with stable returns and we're in.*

To sum up, with municipal, county, and state governments

across the United States uneasy about increasing their debt-to-GDP ratio or raising taxes to finance large-scale infrastructure projects, and pension funds eager to invest at scale, the conditions exist for a long-term collaboration that can transition regions across America quickly into a green zero-carbon public infrastructure.

There is another snag that needs to be addressed to get America to the starting line for a Green New Deal. Most of the infrastructure investment at the local level in the United States is financed with tax-exempt municipal bonds. This poses a problem. Local governments will often choose to finance infrastructure projects via public procurement, rather than enter into financial arrangements with private companies in public-private partnerships, because the up-front tax-exempt municipal bonds are cheaper and more palatable, and an easier sell to a public that is understandably skittish about privatizing infrastructure. But private companies, in turn, complain that they often can't compete with cheaper investments made possible by tax-exempt municipal bonds and can't justify the smaller returns on investments they would have to accept to win a public-private partnership deal.

Pension funds, however, have shown a greater willingness to invest in green municipal bonds, and even accept lower returns for the opportunity to become investment partners with local governments, because their primary interest is guaranteeing a stable return for their pension fund members. Nonetheless, they are not wholly sold on diving into the tax-exempt municipal bond market, because pension funds are also tax-exempt and therefore do not secure any additional value by investing in tax-exempt municipal bonds. Now, however, pension fund advisors are floating a new proposal that is gaining traction as cities and states attempt to lure the pool of public and private pension funds into the purchase of green public bonds. The idea is to provide an incentive to pension funds in the form of a tax credit for investing in green public bonds.

David Seltzer of Mercator Advisors introduced the idea at the National Conference on Public Employment Retirement Systems in 2017. Seltzer suggested that "pension funds could monetize tax credits attached to debt or equity investments." He explained that "pension funds could convert nonrefundable tax credits to cash by applying them against their liability to the US Treasury to remit retiree withholding tax on paid benefits."[45]

Unlike the numerous tax advantage schemes in the federal tax code that benefit global corporations, a slew of subsidized industries, the financial community, and the very wealthy, this tax credit, though small in comparison, is designed to merely provide a sufficient return to allow pension funds to invest in green bonds funding American infrastructure projects. The extra benefit is that if the tax credit were to be instituted to allow billions of dollars in pension funds to divest from the fossil fuel industry and reinvest in the Green New Deal Third Industrial Revolution infrastructure, it would not only help secure the retirement of 73 million American workers but also ensure the well-being of their heirs in a climate change world.

Although tax credits would certainly draw hesitant pension funds to invest in green municipal bonds, there is still the issue of cities and states being saddled with increasing public debt. To temper the public debt, cities and states will have to entertain some form of public-private partnerships. But here again, horror stories abound of governments entering into agreements with private companies to privatize infrastructure—substandard performance and management, cost overruns, asset stripping to maintain profits, and bankruptcies. The overriding interest of corporations that are privatizing the public infrastructure is to look out for their bottom line first, which invariably means making cuts wherever and whenever they can in the name of reducing costs, but ultimately at the expense of the efficient operation of the infrastructure they are charged with building and managing.

ESCOs: The Business Model for a Green New Deal

There is, however, an alternative course that would allow Green New Deal public-private partnerships to flourish, and it has a twenty-five-year track record of success. The business model is the "energy service company" (ESCO). It's a radical approach to conducting business that relies on what's called "performance contracting" to secure profits and is a counterintuitive business method that upends the very foundation of seller/buyer markets—a key underlying principle of capitalism.

Performance contracts do away entirely with seller/buyer markets, replacing them with provider/user networks in which the ESCO takes 100 percent of the responsibility for financing all of the work and secures a return on its capital investment based on its success in generating the new green energies and energy efficiencies being contracted.

The emergent public-private partnership between governments and ESCOs puts the technical expertise and best practices of private enterprise at the service of the public, in a win-win mode, creating a powerful new dynamic between the public and private sectors. Pension funds, in turn, are the best partner to finance many of these public-private partnerships. The financing will come from the deferred wages of millions of American workers who will benefit from a stable and reliable return on their pensions, the prospect of millions of new jobs in the emerging green economy, and a near-zero-carbon green future for their children and grandchildren. For the first time, this new economic model brings together local and state governments, the business community, and American workers into a powerful partnership, each enabling the other to transform the very nature of the social contract.

Here's how the new collaboration works. First, local and state governments issue a call for tender. ESCOs bid for the contract to build out part or all of the infrastructure, with the following conditions. The company that wins the bid is responsible for funding the infrastructure build-out. The ESCO's return on capital investment comes from the revenue earned from the installation of solar and wind technologies and the generation of green electricity and the efficiency gains in electricity transmission in the build-out and management of the smart national power grid, as well as the energy efficiency gains brought on by other types of performance-contracting work: retrofitting buildings; installing energy storage equipment in and around facilities; installing IoT sensors to monitor and improve energy efficiencies; installing charging stations for electric vehicles; and reconditioning production facilities, processes, and supply chains to upgrade aggregate efficiencies at every stage of business operations; etc.

Governments and ESCOs can also enter into a variation on the performance contract. For example, the government agency can secure the financing for the performance contract with the help of the ESCO, which often has open channels to financing such projects. In this variation, the government agency is responsible for the repayment of the financing, but the ESCO is still liable for the savings guarantee that covers the payments and cost of the project. Any losses still fall on the shoulder of the ESCO. The appeal in this second route is that government agencies enjoy a tax exemption on their public projects, making it more attractive to both the ESCO and the government agency.[46]

Performance contracts can also allow for the client to begin sharing the benefits of the green energy being generated and the energy efficiencies coming online while the work is being done and before the ESCO's investment is fully paid back. These modified performance contracts are called "energy savings contracts." Generally, the ESCO will receive the lion's share of the harvested energy as well as energy efficiencies attained—usually 85 percent—until the company's investment is fully returned and the contract terminated, after which the client receives all future benefits.[47] The city, county, or state, in return, ends up with a smart, efficient low-carbon infrastructure without liability for either the capital investment or any financial losses incurred during the project. Socially responsible pension funds committed to doing well by doing good are the appropriate financing mechanism for ESCOs engaged in green energy production and energy savings build-outs.

ESCOs operate in the private realm as well as the public realm. Privately held residential real estate and particularly low- and moderate-income housing, older commercial business districts, which are often in disadvantaged communities, and industrial and technical parks will have to transition their infrastructures into a green Third Industrial Revolution paradigm. The ESCO business model operates the same way whether in the government space, the commercial domain, or civil society. Generous tax credits and graduated tax penalties will need to be established for residential, commercial, industrial, and institutional infrastructure transitions in every municipality, county, and state to encourage the Green New Deal transformation.

Whether we are talking about transitioning the public or private infrastructure from a dirty fossil fuel–laden society to a clean green society, the overwhelming reality is that the poorest communities are the most vulnerable and least-considered in the process. And it's here that the public-private partnership between local governments and ESCOs is likely to have the biggest impact, by helping these at-risk communities transition into the Green New Deal infrastructure and take advantage of the new business and employment opportunities that accompany it, while simultaneously addressing the growing public health emergency precipitated by climate change.

In a landmark county-by-county study on how climate change is likely to affect every community in America published in the journal *Science* in June 2017, the authors report that the nation's poorest communities across the South and southern Midwest will suffer the most from rising temperatures, with loss of GDP by the end of the century that could be as much as 20 percent of their income. Solomon Hsiang, the lead author and professor of public policy at the University of California, Berkeley, warns that "if we continue on the current path, our analysis indicates it may result in the largest transfer of wealth from the poor to the rich in the country's history."[48]

Not surprisingly, climate change is also having a dramatic impact on public health in America, again affecting the poorest communities, whose populations have the least access to adequate health services and to the financial wherewithal to undertake remediation and adaptation initiatives brought on by climate change events. Already, the radical change in the climate is exacting an ever-mounting adverse effect on public health, with exposure to ozone and particulate matter pollution brought on by greenhouse gas emissions leading to diminished lung function, most notably asthma, and exposure to smoke from spreading wildfires; increased exposure to allergens with warmer seasonal temperatures; heat-related sickness and death, including heat stroke and cardiovascular disease; and increased exposure to vector-borne diseases brought on by a shift in the geographic range of insects; et al.

The inseparable relationship between climate change and a growing public health emergency has become real for the millions of people in the United States and around the world who have been subjected to the hurricanes, floods, droughts, and wildfires caused by climate change. Aside from the immediate threat to life posed by these disasters, there is the secondary effect caused by the contamination of water.

In many older communities across America, sewage systems serve a dual purpose, combining wastewater being sent along to wastewater treatment plants with stormwater drainage. But now, more severe storms and hurricanes are flooding the sewage/drainage infrastructure, forcing untreated sewage and storm runoff to back up and overflow into homes, businesses, neighborhoods, and local streams and rivers in many parts of the United States, posing a serious threat to public health. And it's only going to get worse with the ever-changing climate.

Unfortunately, this is happening at the same time that the municipalities have been selling off their freshwater and sanitation systems to private companies which are often reluctant to upgrade antiquated water, sewage, and drainage systems for fear of declining profit margins.

Cities in the United States and elsewhere are becoming aware of the threat to public health and safety posed by the conjunction of dilapidated water, sewage, and drainage systems with climate change–induced floods and have recently begun to re-municipalize these critical infrastructures to gain back public control over what has traditionally been one of the most critical public services administered by government to safeguard public health.

Here again, the poor are the most vulnerable because their communities generally have the oldest and most compromised infrastructures, the least access to adequate public health services, and are the least serviced by remediation and adaptation programs.

For all these reasons, ESCO intervention on the part of

both local and state governments and the private sector should be prioritized in the most disadvantaged communities and among the poorest populations in the country. Performance contracting is as much about adapting to climate change, making sure nobody is left behind and ensuring the public health of the community by building resilience into every aspect of a community's economic and social life, as it is about efficiency, productivity, and GDP. Indeed, in the context of performance contracting, they are indistinguishable.

This is a new breed of capitalism that blends a social commitment into its very business plan. The ESCO is continuously in pursuit of new technologies and management practices that will return its investment, and the community benefits from this in a number of ways: cheaper utility bills for their homes and businesses; clean renewable energy to power their homes and businesses at near-zero marginal cost; green electricity to power electric and fuel-cell vehicles; a less polluted environment to advance public health; and new business opportunities and employment, with the revenue and benefits recirculating back into the community to enhance its economic and social well-being.

Last but not least, the success of performance contracts is wholly dependent on the training and deployment of potentially millions of semiskilled, skilled, and professional workers who retrofit the residential, commercial, industrial, and public building stock across America, build out the national smart power grid, install the solar and wind technologies, lay the broadband cable, embed the IoT technology, produce the electric and fuel-cell vehicles, manufacture and install the electric charging stations and energy storage facilities, and lay out the smart solar roads across the country. Energy service companies operating in performance contracts equally benefit the ESCO, the workforce, and the community.

Performance contracting is not just a new sidebar of

capitalism but rather a fundamental disruption of the capitalist model, forcing a paradigmatic transition in how society structures economic life in the twenty-first century. I remember my first day in marketing class at the Wharton School back in 1963. The marketing professor wrote on the blackboard the Latin phrase *caveat emptor*, "let the buyer beware," and informed the students that if they learned nothing else in his class, they should remember this cardinal rule. The saying refers to what economists call "information asymmetry," meaning that the seller never wants the buyer to know all the information he or she has on the product or service, including its real costs, actual performance, life cycle, and so on. This lack of transparency built into the system puts the buyer at a distinct disadvantage. Some of the asymmetry in the relationship is tempered by company warranties, but these inevitably fall short of protecting the buyer.

Performance contracting eliminates this bias of market transactions between sellers and buyers and, with it, the unequal and weighted advantage that always accrues to the seller, by eliminating sellers and buyers in markets altogether and replacing the traditional capitalist model with providers and users in networks.

It's worth repeating that in performance contracting, the ESCO can only recoup its investment by ensuring its own performance. This means, for example, achieving sufficient gains in energy generation and aggregate efficiencies to make the investment pay off. The user, in turn, gets a free ride. Once the ESCO's investment makes its return, the user enjoys a steady stream of green energy and energy efficiencies accruing from the equipment installed and accompanying efficiency processes put in place.

The underlying feature of ESCOs is that their services are designed to increase the aggregate efficiencies, productivity, and generativity of their clients' business operations and, by doing so, reduce the fixed and marginal costs of their operations, reduce their carbon footprint, and hone circularity and resilience deep into every aspect of the clients' business practices. Many ESCOs extend their services after the initial performance contract has paid out, especially in the commercial and industrial sectors, by managing the continuous upgrade of the services for their users.

ESCOs, to date, have played more of a niche role, often scaling small, siloed projects. Now, however, the urgent need to scale up a Green New Deal Third Industrial Revolution infrastructure across neighborhoods, cities, regions, and continents in less than a generation has ramped up the ante as well as the cachet of this new business model.

Navigant Consulting published a report ranking the current top ESCO performers in 2017. (Navigant is a partner in the TIR Consulting Group LLC consortium.) The top ten companies were (1) Schneider Electric, (2) Siemens, (3) Ameresco, (4) NORESCO, (5) Trane, (6) Honeywell, (7) Johnson Controls, (8) McKinstry, (9) Energy Systems Group, and (10) AECOM.[49] Both Schneider and Siemens have participated in TIR Consulting LLC's regional roadmaps over the past decade.

In 2013, Siemens CEO Peter Löscher invited me to the company's annual meeting to talk with the board of directors, and later to have an extended conversation with the twenty global division leaders, on how to begin creating the business models and scaling opportunities for the build-out of a Third Industrial Revolution infrastructure. When I met with the division heads, it became clear that they were, for the most part, working independently from one another. Siemens' divisions include IT, energy, logistics, and infrastructure, all key components for deploying a smart green infrastructure. The timing of the meeting was fortuitous, as the company was in the process of rebranding as a "solution provider" to help create smart sustainable cities. The infrastructure build-out provided the story line for the various divisions at Siemens to leave their silos and become a more cohesive and inclusive solution provider.

At the meeting, we discussed the ESCO performance-contracting model as a new business mechanism for scaling up smart infrastructure across metropolitan and rural regions. Five years later, Siemens was ready for prime time. The company invited me to New York City on February 8, 2018, to present the Third Industrial Revolution narrative to its assembled clients, customers, developers, members of infrastructure organizations, investment banks, and policy advisors. The conference was appropriately titled "Investing in Tomorrow: Digitalizing North American Cities." Part of the conference was dedicated to performance contracting for Third Industrial Revolution rollouts.

Although Siemens ranked sixty-sixth among the Fortune 500 Global Companies in 2018, no single company will be able to go it alone and scale up a twenty-year construction site in every city, region, and country to transition the world economy into a zero-carbon Third Industrial Revolution paradigm. More likely, Siemens and hundreds of other large companies will join with thousands of regional, high-tech small- and medium-sized enterprises, blockchained in cooperatives, in an ESCO performance-contracting business model, financed by a consortium of global and national pension funds, working with local municipalities and regions to provision the scale-up of a smart Green New Deal infrastructure. This distributed ESCO blockchain model is likely to be the favored approach to quickly transitioning local and regional economies, given the tight fifteen-to-twenty-year time frame hovering over us.

Left at the wayside is the old neoliberal model of global companies going it alone, using conventional business practices to build out and manage the new green infrastructure as a private venture, giving them leverage and control over both the infrastructure and accompanying services.

The new performance-contracting model, by contrast, is a hybrid affair, in which both the control over the build-out of the new infrastructure and its ownership remain in the hands of municipal, county, and state governments as "commons" serving the general welfare of communities, while shifting responsibility to private ESCOs to shoulder the financial responsibility to ensure the success of the erection and management of the infrastructure. The "buyer beware" in seller/buyer markets gives way to the provider "doing well by doing good" in provider/user networks.

This is the essence of "social capitalism" and represents a pragmatic business model that can speed the transition into a near-zero emission era in the short time horizon before us. If the seller/buyer market was the appropriate business model for a fossil fuel civilization and the Age of Progress, ESCO provider/user networks engaged in performance contracts are the signature business model for building and managing a sustainable green civilization in the emerging Age of Resilience.

7

MOBILIZING SOCIETY

Saving Life on Earth

It's heartening to watch the Green New Deal spread across America, Europe, and the world. To this degree, ideas do indeed have consequences. We are a storytelling species. We live by our narratives and the stories we share, and by doing so, come to know ourselves as a collective social being. The Green New Deal is a "story line" that has evolved and matured over the years, taking on ever more sophisticated and nuanced meanings. And now humanity finds itself in the throes of either a potential endgame or, hopefully, a new beginning. The Green New Deal gives us our collective voice and a shared sense of our common mission. What we so desperately need now is to turn the story line into a powerful narrative that can take us forward.

To this end, America's entrance into the conversation is crucial. While the "can-do" attitude is in our cultural DNA, it's the "American spirit" that unleashes it. That spirit has always been hopeful of a better future, with successive generations willing to pledge their lives, their fortunes, and their sacred honor to noble tasks, even at times to the point of reckless disregard for the practicalities and obstacles along the way. We see this time and again in the unleashing of the entrepreneurial spirit, not just in the marketplace but also in civil society. Americans' most unique quality is not fearing failure, be it pecuniary or social in nature. Often when I visit friends and colleagues in other countries, their conversation slips to America's risk-taking attitude and willingness to fail and start over, to learn from defeat, to never quit.

This is exactly the attitude humanity needs now to weather the climate storm that's coming—a fearless resilience in the face of the unknown, willingness to meet it head-on, and, when pushed down, to stand up again. But this time around, the tomorrows are not going to be like those we experienced in the past. Anyone who tells you that the Green New Deal is going to preserve the way of life we know, sugarcoating the greening of society, is kidding you. Our tomorrows are going to be fraught with escalating climate events that are going to take an immense toll on our communities, our ecosystems, and our common biosphere.

We are entering into a frontier of a new kind. Nature is rewilding, and we have to learn how to live with the uncertainty while adapting moment to moment to its surprises. We are going to need to cast aside any notion previously entertained about pacifying nature and molding and shaping it to serve humanity. Now we will need to regroup, gather our collective strength, learn to live by our wits, and find within ourselves the deep resilience that will allow us to survive and carry on into an unknown future that awaits our species and fellow creatures here on this little blue oasis in the universe. The sudden willingness of a younger generation of Americans and young people all over the world to do battle on climate change is a welcome turn of events, and long overdue.

A Missive from Europe

Mindful of the powerful Green New Deal clarion call sounded at the beginning of 2019 by a younger generation of activists and newly elected officials at the local, state, and national levels here in the United States, I'd like to bring my fellow Americans up to date on the most recent developments around the Green New Deal in Europe, announced just months before this writing by the European Commission, so that European and American activists can share notes on the great mobilization ahead.

On November 28, 2018, the European Union unveiled the next stage of its journey to decarbonize the continent and bring on a more sustainable future. The European Commission is calling for a climate-neutral Europe by 2050, a zero-emission ecological society stretching across the entire expanse of the European continent.[1] The twenty-eight member states are all coming along, some more enthusiastically, others with a grumble, but everyone realizing that this is not the time to retreat but, rather, to redouble our efforts.

Here is a brief run-up to the EU climate-neutral 2050 game plan. We began in August 2016 by getting the EU member states comfortable with the new climate targets that would be proposed by the end of 2018. I joined EU Commission vice president Maroš Šefčovič in Slovakia on July 9, 2016, during Slovakia's presidency of the Council of the European Union. Šefčovič introduced the outline of the new directives and goals of the EU Energy Union, tying the new renewable energy targets, energy efficiency targets, and CO_2 reduction targets for 2030 and 2050 to the smart Europe rollout. I was asked to present the case for a smart infrastructure transformation that could bring the EU into a postcarbon era before midcentury.[2]

We followed up the next year, on January 31, 2017. I delivered a similar message cued to the financial community in a presentation at the European Central Bank with the theme "A History of the Future—The World in 2025."[3]

A week later, on February 7, Vice President Šefčovič and I

joined Markku Markkula, the president of the Committee of the Regions, in a high-level conference hosted by that committee titled "Investing in Europe: Building a Coalition of Smart Cities & Regions."[4] It was important to bring the EU's powerful but often overlooked 350 governing regions into the fold, given that the ultimate success of the plan to decarbonize Europe and transition to a green era by 2050 would lie with the scale-up of a smart green infrastructure customized to each region. Šefčovič emphasized that a sustainable future "relies on regions and cities to deliver" on the EU's targets for increasing renewable energy, accelerating energy efficiency, and reducing the carbon footprint. We briefed the representatives of the regions on the progress being made in the three green lighthouse regions we were working with in Hauts-de-France, the twenty-three cities from Rotterdam to The Hague in the Netherlands, and the Grand Duchy of Luxembourg.

With the Council of the European Union, the EU's Central Bank, and the Committee of the Regions briefed and enthusiastic, Šefčovič and his team spent the next twenty-two months working on the much-anticipated EU Commission 2050 report, which was delivered on November 28, 2018, by Šefčovič, Miguel Arias Cañete, the commissioner for climate action and energy, and Violeta Bulc, the commissioner for transport.

Vice President Šefčovič informed the EU member states that "our strategy now shows that by 2050, it is realistic to make Europe both climate-neutral and prosperous." Commissioner Cañete made note of the historic importance of this EU milestone, saying that "today, we are stepping up our efforts as we propose a strategy for Europe to become the world's first major economy to go climate neutral by 2050."[5] According to the report, renewable energy consumption had spiked from 9 percent in 2005 to 17 percent in 2018 and was on schedule to meet the 20-20-20 target of 20 percent renewable energy consumption across the 28 member states along with the other two targets of a 20 percent increase in energy efficiency and a 20 percent reduction in CO_2 emissions, by the 2020 deadline.[6]

Going forward, the plan requires joint action earmarked in seven strategic areas: energy efficiency; deployment of renewables; clean, safe, and connected mobility; competitive industries and a circular economy; infrastructure and interconnections; bioeconomy and natural carbon sinks; and carbon capture and storage to address remaining emissions.

With 2020 targets in reach, the EU has set still even more aggressive new targets of 32 percent renewable energy, a 32.5 percent increase in energy efficiency, and a 45 percent reduction in greenhouse gas emissions, all by 2030, and a target to be nearly carbon-free by 2050.[7] But the report acknowledged that although the EU was leading the world into a zero-emission postcarbon era, efforts were still far too slow, given the newly released IPCC report warning that the world's nations only have twelve years left to transform their economies out of a carbon culture or risk sliding over the 1.5°C rise in Earth's temperature and into an inevitable free fall, taking us deeply into the sixth mass extinction.

I'd like to share the first few lines of the EU Commission report, which I think will resonate with the Green New Deal activist message moving across America:

> The Strategy therefore outlines a vision of the economic and societal transformations required, engaging all sectors of the economy and society, to achieve the transition to net-zero greenhouse gas emissions by 2050. It seeks to ensure that this transition is socially fair—not leaving any EU citizen or region behind—and enhances the competitiveness of the EU economy and industry on global markets, securing high quality jobs and sustainable growth in Europe.[8]

These lines are particularly moving. The EU has transitioned from having a laundry list of projects to articulating "a vision of the economic and societal transformations" that will usher in a new era in the European Union. This is Europe's key message to America's Green New Deal activists and activists around the world. The vast majority of cities, regions, and nations are still mired in siloed green projects and initiatives tucked inside the body of an outdated twentieth-century fossil fuel economic paradigm and its accompanying business model and form of governance.

Many of the Green New Deal declarations, manifestos, reports, and studies being scrutinized in the public debate read more like a story line at best, or a shopping list at worst. Each of these items alone seems so very technical and scanty. They fall short of steering the kind of shift in consciousness that can take us on the journey before us.

Thinking Like a Species

At this critical juncture in history, the Green New Deal story lines need to be put together in a coherent economic and philosophic narrative that can create a sense of our collective identity as a species and bring humanity into a new worldview, giving us a glocal heartbeat. Absent the story, all the ideas get lost in a jumble of items, none of which connect to the others. Every idea becomes a fought-over non sequitur, sapping us of the strength for the imaginative leap needed to take us into the next era of history.

All of which takes us back to chapter 1, "It's the Infrastructure, Stupid!" The great paradigm changes in human history are infrastructure revolutions that change our temporal/spatial orientation, our economic models, our forms of governance, our cognition, and our very worldview. The convergence of new communication technologies, new sources of energy, and new modes of mobility and logistics to manage, power, and move the economy and society changes the way we think about the world around us.

Forager/hunter primitive infrastructures, which dominated most of our 200,000-year history, were remarkably similar in their narratives, each exhibiting what anthropologists call a "mythological consciousness" and tribal governance. The advent of agriculture 10,000 years ago and the subsequent emergence of the great hydraulic agricultural infrastructures in Sumer in the Middle East, the Indus Valley in India, and the Yangtze River Valley in China gave rise to "theological consciousness" and centralized governing empires. The First Industrial Revolution infrastructure in the nineteenth century gave rise to "ideological consciousness" and the birth of national markets and nation-state governance. The Second Industrial Revolution global infrastructure in the twentieth century gave rise to "psychological consciousness" and the beginnings of global markets and global governing bodies. The Third Industrial Revolution glocal infrastructure emerging in the twenty-first century is giving birth to "biosphere consciousness" and peer assembly governance. The biosphere, stretching up into the atmosphere and down through the lithosphere and into the oceans, is where all the creatures on Earth live, interact, and flourish.

Each of these great paradigm shifts was accompanied by the evolution of our empathic impulse to larger collectivities and worldviews. In forager/hunter societies, empathy extended only to blood ties and kinship and the sharing of a common ancestral worldview. In the great hydraulic agricultural civilizations, empathy extended to those who shared a common religious affiliation. The great religions formed during this era, giving rise to non-blood-related "figurative families" based on religious ties. All converts to Judaism began to empathize with fellow Jews as their extended figurative family. The same with Hindus, Buddhists, Christians, and Muslims. In the First Industrial Revolution in the nineteenth century, empathy extended to figurative families based on a collective sense of national loyalty to the Motherland or Fatherland. Citizens began to empathize with each other based on their nation-state identity. In the Second Industrial Revolution in the twentieth century, empathy extended to like-minded cosmopolitan and professional ties in an increasingly borderless world. In the emerging Third Industrial Revolution, a generation of digital natives Skyping in global classrooms, interacting on Facebook and Instagram, gaming in virtual worlds, and obsessively traveling the physical world are beginning to see themselves as a planetary cohort inhabiting a common biosphere. They are extending empathy in a more expansive way, coming to think of themselves as members of a threatened species and empathizing with their common plight on a destabilizing Earth. And a growing number of young people are beginning to take a final step beyond, empathizing with all the other creatures with whom we share an evolutionary heritage.[9]

A younger generation beset by climate change is waking up to a reality that is both unnerving and revelatory at the same time. We are beginning to understand that the Earth is embedded in an untold number of interacting agencies—the conjoined movements of the hydrosphere, lithosphere, atmosphere, biosphere, and magnetosphere; the temporal sequencing of the Earth's circadian, lunar, and circannual rhythms and the changing of the seasons; and the ebbs and flows of nature brought on by the continuous interactions of the Earth's myriad creatures—all bumping up against each other in an array of feedbacks so subtle that we can barely begin to take in how each encounter changes the dynamics of the system as a whole. Yet, somehow the Earth seems to continually evolve, readjust, adapt, and maintain its equilibrium, much like a planetary organism. At least up until now!

We have suddenly been sensitized to the consequences of disturbing the burial grounds of a previous geological era. We dug up the remains of earlier life that once existed on the planet and that was transformed into coal, oil, and natural gas. We have been living off this stored "body" of energy for the past two hundred years while casting off the waste in the form of CO_2 emissions into the atmosphere. The great disruption triggered positive feedback across the Earth's agencies, bringing us to the sixth extinction event in our planet's history.

We now know that every piece of coal, every drop of oil, and every cubic foot of natural gas that twelve generations of human beings have used to create our carbon-based industrial civilization have had consequences that are now reshaping the dynamics of the Earth. What we are learning from climate change is that everything we do affects the workings of everything else on Earth and has consequences for the well-being of all the creatures with whom we cohabit this planet.

Awareness of the planetary agencies that affect our very existence is a humbling experience and the central lesson that climate change is teaching us. Learning to live among rather than rule over these agencies that traverse the Earth is what takes us from dominion to stewardship and from human-centric detachment to deep participation with the living Earth. This is the great shift in temporal-spatial orientation that gives us a biosphere perspective.

This fundamental transformation in human consciousness is the silver lining—the imaginative breakthrough—that, if truly internalized and harnessed, is what will give us a fighting chance of riding out the great climate disruption and surviving and maybe even flourishing in new ways over eons to come in a world very different than the one we all know today.

The Three Elephants in the Room

The EU, with its 512 million citizens, has, until recently, led the charge into a zero-emission green economy. The People's Republic of China, with its nearly 1.4 billion people, has roared onto the field in recent years with its plan to transition into a postcarbon era. And now the United States, with its 325 million citizens, is poised to join the herd. Without all three elephants marching in sync, sharing best practices, establishing common codes, regulations, standards, and incentives, and reaching out together to bring the rest of humanity into the fold, the race to a zero-carbon civilization in less than twenty years will be lost.

In working with the leadership in both the European Union and China, I've come to see that both governments are on the same path to address climate change. They both understand that the mission is the quick decoupling of every sector and industry from the Second Industrial Revolution infrastructure and their recoupling in the emerging Third Industrial Revolution infrastructure. The EU calls the Third Industrial Revolution "Smart Europe," and China calls the Third Industrial Revolution "China Internet Plus." They are similar plans, and, despite the two governments' squabbles, disagreements, and occasional suspicions of each other, they share common ground.

First, recall that the EU is China's largest trading partner, and China is the EU's second-largest trading partner and relatively soon will likely be its largest, binding the two governing giants in a common commercial domain.[10] Second, both the EU and China share a common Eurasian landmass stretching from Shanghai to the Port of Rotterdam, binding them together across the largest contiguous geographical space in the world. Third, both the EU and China are clear about their role at this moment in world history: to address climate change and preserve life on Earth. Fourth, both the EU and China are reaching out beyond their borders to assist other regions in making the transition to a postcarbon civilization. On this last point, China has taken a commanding lead with its Belt and Road Initiative. The initiative was announced by President Xi Jinping in 2013 and takes its inspiration from the ancient Silk Road, the trade route that connected China, Asia, and the West.[11]

The vision is to build out a twenty-first-century smart digital infrastructure that can connect all of Eurasia, creating the largest integrated commercial space in history. The Belt and Road Initiative is more than just a new global trade initiative combined with conventional infrastructure investment to ensure adequate transport and logistics corridors and speed commerce across Eurasian supply chains and markets. Rather, it is part of a bigger philosophical agenda on the part of China to establish what it calls an "ecological civilization."[12]

In 2012, the Chinese Communist Party signaled an extraordinary shift in its governance and worldview by embedding the term "ecological civilization" into the heart of its constitution and making it the theme of its twelfth Five-Year Plan, and all Five-Year Plans thereafter. In practice, the Chinese government has stipulated that all future economic planning and development in China must adhere to and harmonize with the guiding principles of nature and the Earth's operating systems.

The ecological civilization is the core not only of China's domestic policy but also of its Belt and Road Initiative. The vision takes China from a geopolitical worldview that dominated the politics of nations through the First and Second Industrial Revolutions of the nineteenth and twentieth centuries in a fossil fuel civilization to a biosphere worldview that will increasingly guide international affairs in the Third Industrial Revolution of the twenty-first century at the dawn of an ecological era.

This is not to suggest that traditional geopolitics suddenly disappears with the Belt and Road Initiative. The struggle between geopolitics and biosphere politics among China, the European Union, the United States, and, for that matter, the rest of the nations of the world will be protracted over the remaining course of the twenty-first century. But what is sure is that the geopolitical worldview wedded to a fossil fuel civilization is dying, and the biosphere worldview of an ecological civilization is emergent and represents the next stage of the human journey. This is the larger picture in which a green vision, narrative, and transition are emerging, not only in China, but also in the European Union and now just getting off the ground in America and throughout the world.

In September 2018, the European Commission and the High Representative of the Union for Foreign Affairs and Security Policy published a joint communication, "Connecting Europe and Asia Strategy," outlining the EU's approach to creating a seamless Eurasian smart infrastructure. The EU made it clear that its efforts to assist communities and countries across Eurasia, like China's Belt and Road Initiative, will focus on the building out of smart digital networks that bring together telecom and internet connectivity, the revving up of renewable energy generation, the decarbonization of transport and the digitization of mobility, the prioritization of energy efficiencies across the building stock, and all of the other infrastructure components of the Third Industrial Revolution.[13]

The EU joint communication notes that indispensable to the success of a digitally connected smart Eurasia infrastructure will be developing universally accepted codes, regulations, standards, incentives, and penalties, agreed upon by all the participating nations, in a spirit of "transparency," that would enable the deployment of an integrated smart commercial space across the world's largest landmass.

The EU-China collaboration is vital to divesting from the fossil fuel civilization and reinvesting in the ecological civilization. Both superpowers are already far along in the transformation. While critics can rightfully argue that China is still pouring investment dollars into fossil-fuel-related infrastructure across the Belt and Road Initiative, it is quickly pivoting to renewable energy, smart electricity grids, and electric transport networks that make up a Third Industrial Revolution paradigm.

In May 2017, the Chinese Ministry of Environmental Protection, the Ministry of Foreign Affairs, the National Development and Reform Commission, and the Ministry of Commerce issued an unprecedented "Guidance on Promoting the Green Belt and Road" as the very foundation of the Belt and Road Initiative, with the goal of bringing nations, regions, and localities into a global collaboration to build an ecological civilization. China is putting its money where its mouth is, with scaled green infrastructure projects being launched across all of Asia. I encourage readers to download the "Guidance" and judge for themselves both the intent and the merit of the protocol.[14]

I took part in several of the early discussions on advancing the green Belt and Road Initiative at the National Development and Reform Commission, the State Council, China's National Academy of Sciences, and the Ministry of Industry and Information Technology and shared with the Chinese leadership our efforts and initiatives at the European Commission and in the EU member states and regions in transitioning into a green Third Industrial Revolution. In 2017, at the request of China's Ministry of Industry and Information Technology, I wrote an introduction to its publication of *Digital Silk Road: The Opportunities and Challenges to Develop a Digital Economy Along the Belt and Road,* the government's plan to invest over $1 trillion to assist nations and regions across Eurasia in transitioning into a green zero-emission digitally connected infrastructure.[15]

The Belt and Road Initiative is just the beginning of the great transformation that will connect the human race across the globe over the course of the next half century. Feasibility studies and deployment plans on laying out smart, digitally enhanced high-voltage power grids across entire continents to share renewable energies are already in play. A 2019 feasibility study on a proposed Pan-American interregional power grid that will stretch from Alaska to Chile and potentially be in place by 2030 has sparked a conversation across the Americas on how this intercontinental technological alignment will likely affect the economy, social life, and governance of nation-states in this region of the world.[16] Another report published in 2019 details plans to lay a submarine power cable between Europe and North America to trade solar- and wind-generated green electricity across the Atlantic Ocean.[17] Similar feasibility and deployment plans to establish an Africa-wide power grid and a European–African power grid are afoot.

We are in the early stages of creating a global interconnected electricity power grid—a digital Pangaea—that is likely to come online in bits and pieces between now and the late 2030s, connecting the human race for the first time in history. Individuals, families, communities, and entire countries will be freed from the geopolitics of the oil era, characterized by conflict and war in a zero-sum game, and become increasingly engaged in a biosphere politics of deep collaboration in sharing the free sun and wind that bathe the Earth.

Connecting the human family on a glocal scale across a smart digital infrastructure is a singular event in the way humanity conducts its economic affairs, social life, and governance. Still, there is growing concern and even fear that China might seize this moment in history to fund and build out the smart infrastructure and use it for leverage in the form of surveillance and intervention, allowing it to exercise control over the lives of much of the human race. From my own experience in China, I don't think this is the intent. Even if it were, any such effort would fail if localities, regions, and countries along the Belt and Road were to exercise caution at the get-go and ensure that the build-out of the infrastructure and its subsequent ownership and management within their jurisdictions were under their various governments' strict control.

Then, too, we need to remember that the very nature of the Third Industrial Revolution digital infrastructure favors distributed rather than centralized control, and, to achieve network effects, it works best if the networks are open and transparent rather than closed and proprietary, and scale laterally rather than vertically to optimize aggregate efficiencies and circularity. The engineered platforms favor flexibility and redundancy, the two key elements in establishing regional resilience in a climate change world.

Were the intention of any nation-state or renegade group to surveil, control, cripple, or take down the networks, cheap, simple technology components built into the system at the end user's door will allow families, neighborhoods, communities, businesses, and local and regional governments to go off-grid at a moment's notice and decentralize and reaggregate their operations. There is no conceivable path by which a superpower could hold hostage several billion people in millions of communities if they chose to simply go off a Eurasian power grid, or for that matter a global power grid, and go it alone in harvesting their solar and wind energy in their neighborhoods and surrounding communities.

Humanity is moving toward a glocal, digitally interconnected green world. The EU and China are currently leading the way. The United States needs to come to the table. These three elephants in the room need to begin to cooperate and help build in the safeguards and assurances that will enable this transition into a Green New Deal. The politics of the biosphere era will inevitably cluster around the codes, regulations, and standards of operation that allow for transparency across this emergent digital infrastructure and accompanying networks, always with the focus on the freedom of every locality and region to govern its infrastructure as a public commons.

A last word on this matter. If the three elephants can't put geopolitics behind them and begin to collaborate along a biosphere gradient, recognizing that we are an imperiled species on an imperiled Earth, we are doomed. While our respective loyalties and commitments are diverse, climate change is forcing us to think of ourselves as an "endangered species" for the first time. Living with that new reality brings the human race together in a common bond that we've never before experienced.

The younger generation gets it. They are staring down into a potential environmental chasm. They don't want to hear their practical-minded, hardened, and even cynical elders say that a Green New Deal is unrealistic or a fantasy and that life is a zero-sum game. At this moment in history, we need to trust each other, all of us, beyond political boundaries, and begin to think as a species.

What does all this mean for the excitement building around a Green New Deal for America and other countries not yet fully engaged in either the narrative or the process? What lessons can we learn? First and foremost, the climate crisis is here and the transition to a zero-carbon society must be fast, because we're running out of time. But second, we need to realize that there is a gaping difference between 1932 and the present. This may be hard to hear for activists who want to repeat the New Deal agenda of the 1930s. It isn't going to happen the same way this time. Today, market forces are deconstructing the fossil fuel civilization. The speed and scope of the disruption are without parallel. The old fossil fuel energies are creating a carbon bubble that is unlike any economic disruption in human history. The key sectors of the economy—ICT/telecommunications/internet, electricity, transport, and buildings—are quickly decoupling from fossil fuels and recoupling with renewable energies, establishing the pathway to a Third Industrial Revolution.

This decoupling of sector after sector from fossil fuels and recoupling to cleaner renewable energies and green technologies is speeding us out of the fossil fuel culture. Some studies project that tipping point as early as 2023 and others as late as 2035. Balancing the various scenarios and projections, the inflection point is likely going to occur somewhere down the middle with a collapse of the fossil fuel civilization coming at or around 2028.

The thing to bear in mind is that the collapse of the fossil fuel civilization is inevitable, despite any efforts by the fossil fuel industries to forestall it. Market forces are far more powerful than whatever lobbying maneuvers the fossil fuel industry might entertain. This, too, might be difficult to hear for those activists still wedded to the idea that the market is never on the side of the people. I am certainly aware that this is often the case, and for a lifetime I have been critical of various aspects of market capitalism. This time, however, and with this disruption, the market is a guardian angel looking over humanity.

But the invisible hand alone will not steer us into the Age of Resilience. Building a new ecological civilization from the ashes will require a far more collective response that marshals our public capital, market capital, and social capital at every level of governance and engages the deep participation of the entire body politic.

In the Age of Progress, we could each aspire to go it alone

in the marketplace, or at least that's what the powers that be wanted us to believe. In the climate change world that is now here, we already know that the Age of Progress is history and our future lies in an Age of Resilience that will require a collective effort in every community on a scale never before experienced in our short history on Earth.

From here on out, the name of the game is "thoughtful speed." We need to expedite the transition into the green era brought on by the sectorial decoupling from fossil fuels and accelerate the build-out of a Green New Deal zero-carbon infrastructure across America and around the world.

The Twenty-Three Key Initiatives of the Green New Deal

A consensus has been emerging around twenty-three key themes and initiatives that need to be enjoined simultaneously to begin the Green New Deal journey. Here they are.

> **First,** the federal government should impose an immediate across-the-board aggressive rising carbon tax, with a significant portion of the revenues returned to US citizens through lump-sum rebates so that families, especially the most vulnerable, will receive more in carbon dividends than they pay in higher energy prices, and the remainder of the revenue used by the federal government and the states to help finance the Green New Deal infrastructure.
>
> **Second,** the federal government should establish a quick phasedown and elimination of the $15 billion in annual fossil fuel subsidies.
>
> **Third,** the federal government, in tandem with the fifty states, should prepare and deploy a seamless national smart power grid across the United States to provide sufficient green electricity capacity to power a nationwide

smart distributed Third Industrial Revolution infrastructure. The federal government should finance a significant portion of the build-out of the national smart
grid, while the states pick up the remaining financing. A
juvenile bare-bones national smart grid infrastructure
should be operational by 2030, and a fully mature operational power grid should be online before 2040.

Fourth, the federal, state, municipal, and county governments should provide tax credits and other incentives to
encourage the accelerated installation of solar and wind
technologies, where viable, across the built environment
and landscape to transition the nation into zero-emission
green energies generated at near-zero marginal cost. The
mix of solar and wind installations should prioritize
neighborhood and community microgrids to build flexibility and resilience into the infrastructure. Microgrid
cooperatives should be able to easily disconnect from the
main power grid during or after a climate event or cyberterrorist attack and share locally generated solar and
wind power in their neighborhoods. The federal government should also reprioritize the use of public lands and
immediately phase out all fossil fuel concessions and
phase in a vast increase in solar and wind installations.

Fifth, the federal, state, municipal, and county governments should provide tax credits and other incentives for
the installation of energy storage technology in homes,
commercial buildings, and industrial and institutional
facilities to provide backup power both to manage intermittent energy across the power grid and to provide
the on-site supply of emergency power should the power
grid be compromised because of a climate disaster or a
cyberterrorist attack.

Sixth, the federal, state, municipal, and county governments should introduce broadband and the Internet of

Things, conditional on the potential health and environmental impacts of wireless versus cable connection. The states should prioritize broadband installation in rural communities and disadvantaged communities.

Seventh, all industries using data centers should receive federal tax credits for installing 100 percent renewable energies on and around their data center facilities by 2030, allowing them to run totally off-grid to ensure the security of data if the power grid is crippled or goes down due to climate-related events or cyberterrorism.

Eighth, federal and state tax credits should be granted for the purchase of electric vehicles, and graduated tax hikes should be imposed on the purchase of internal combustion vehicles. To speed the process, vouchers to be used to purchase electric vehicles should be offered for trading in clunkers (internal combustion vehicles). The vouchers should exceed the trade-in value of the internal combustion vehicles. The federal government should immediately set a date of 2030 for eliminating the sale and registration of all new internal combustion vehicles—cars, trucks, and buses.

Ninth, the federal government and state, municipal, and county governments should provide tax credits for installing electric charging stations in and around residential, commercial, and industrial building sites to power electric vehicles. Real estate companies and landlords owning dwellings with multiple occupants should be encouraged to install sufficient charging stations and should receive a tax credit for doing so and an escalating tax hike over time for not providing the service.

Tenth, the federal government should mandate and finance the transition of all federal property to green zero-emission assets and infrastructure by 2030, using procurement to boost green businesses. The federal government and state, municipal, and county governments should also immediately introduce an across-the-board set of generous tax credits and deductions, grants, and low-interest loans to encourage the retrofitting of the nation's residential, commercial, industrial, and institutional building stock and the conversion from gas and oil heating to electric heating by renewable energy from the grid, with the goal of increasing energy efficiency, reducing global warming emissions, and bolstering resilience to climate-related disruptions. Additional supplementary tax credits, deductions, grants, and low-interest loans should be extended to low- and middle-income rental properties and homeowners to encourage retrofits. All federal tax credits should be contingent on the states immediately mandating targets requiring that all existing residential and commercial buildings reduce greenhouse gas emissions by 40 percent below 1990 levels by 2030 and be zero net energy before 2040, and that all new residential buildings be zero net energy by 2025 and new commercial buildings be zero net energy by 2030.

Eleventh, the federal government and state governments should establish and deploy plans to phase out petrochemical agriculture and introduce organic and ecological agricultural practices and boost regional agricultural production for local markets over a twenty-year period, with the goal of moving toward 100 percent organic certification by 2040. The federal government and state governments should provide deep subsidies and robust incentives to encourage a speedy transformation.

Twelfth, the federal government and state governments should provide tax credits and other incentives to encourage farmers to utilize carbon-farming techniques and to reforest and rewild marginal land to capture and sequester CO_2 from the atmosphere and serve as carbon capture sinks. The federal government should also re-prioritize the use of public lands by reforesting, where applicable, to capture and sequester CO_2 emissions.

Thirteenth, the federal government, states, municipalities, and counties should prioritize and finance the upgrading of all water systems, sewage systems, and stormwater drains by 2040 to be resilient to the climate change–induced hurricanes, storms, and floods that are a growing threat to public health. In drought-prone areas of the country, measures will need to be taken to install water storage via cisterns across the built environment to provide emergency backup access to water if the power grid were to go down because of a climate event or a cyberattack. Where applicable, cities should re-municipalize all water-related systems that have been privatized over the years to ensure public oversight and control of water.

Fourteenth, the federal government and state, municipal, and county governments should mandate the embedding of circularity processes into every supply chain and across every industry by 2030 to dramatically reduce carbon emissions and build resilience against climate change into all aspects of the economy, civil society, and governance, and provide appropriate incentives and penalties.

Fifteenth, the federal government, in tandem with the states, should redeploy an increasing percentage of military expenditures, without compromising national or state security, to pay for federal troops and state National Guards to manage climate-related disaster response and relief missions, from first responders to long-term restoration initiatives.

Sixteenth, the federal government should enact legislation to establish a national green bank that can provide funds to state, county, and municipal green banks that, in turn, can leverage those funds in securing sufficient financing and, especially, public and private pension funds and other investment capital for scaled green infrastructure build-outs. The national green bank's provisioning of funds to state, municipal, and county green banks should be contingent on state and local governing jurisdictions mandating a target of 50 percent of their electricity generation coming from solar, wind, and other appropriate renewable energies by 2030 and 100 percent of their electricity coming from renewable energy before 2040.

Seventeenth, the use of union pension fund capital to finance federal, state, municipal, and county Third Industrial Revolution infrastructure projects should be conditional on ensuring that unionized workforces are employed wherever possible. Since only 11 percent of the American workforce is unionized, all Third Industrial Revolution infrastructure projects must also protect the right of workers to organize and safeguard collective bargaining rights. The state, municipal, and county governments should also provide "just transition" funds for communities that are economically dependent on the extracting, refining, and distributing of fossil fuels and should prioritize the transition from these stranded industries into the new green businesses and employment opportunities of a Third Industrial Revolution.

Eighteenth, the student generation will need to learn the skills and develop the talents that will enable them to create new businesses and become gainfully employed in a Green New Deal economy. The federal government and state governments should establish service programs patterned after the Peace Corps, VISTA, and AmeriCorps. These federal- and state-financed programs—Green Corps, Climate Corps, Conservation Corps, Infrastructure Corps—will provide a living wage to high school and college graduates apprenticing with industries in communities across the country to learn the skills that will be needed to mobilize a smart twenty-first-century workforce. These new federal- and state-administered youth apprenticeship organizations will also train a younger generation to use these newly acquired skills in disaster response and relief missions, serving as first responders and in recovery efforts in local communities, working alongside federal government troops and state National Guards.

Nineteenth, the federal government, states, municipalities, and counties should prioritize Green New Deal business opportunities in the most disadvantaged communities and provide appropriate training for the new employment opportunities that come with the scale-up of the green infrastructure. Generous tax credits, grants, low-interest loans, and other incentives to upgrade all public health services should be prioritized to the poorest communities facing public health risks brought on by climate change.

Twentieth, to ensure a more fair and just society, more equitable tax laws should be enacted at the federal, state, and local levels that reduce the vast disparity between the super-rich and the rest of the population, with the revenues accrued being used to advance the transition categories that make up the Green New Deal.

Twenty-first, the various departments and agencies of the federal and state governments should reprioritize their funding and substantially increase research and development in all of the areas that accompany the transformation into green technologies and Third Industrial Revolution infrastructure deployment. Every level of government should give particular attention to funding research, development, and deployment in the hard-to-abate sectors to accelerate the transition from fossil fuel–based to biological-based processes and products. Governments should harness the best expertise and talent in public and private universities and research institutes in joint R&D collaborations to advance the transition into the green energies and sustainable technologies of a Green New Deal Third Industrial Revolution.

Twenty-second, the various departments and agencies of the federal government, in tandem with state governments, should establish an accelerated time frame for creating the regulations, codes, and standards to facilitate a seamless integration of broadband, renewable energy power generation and distribution, autonomous electric and fuel-cell vehicle transport, zero-emission Internet of Things nodal buildings, and all of the other regulations, codes, and standards necessary to ensure an interconnected and uninterrupted smart IoT Third Industrial Revolution infrastructure functioning across America.

Twenty-third, the US government should join with the European Union, the People's Republic of China, and all other willing nations in a formal ongoing collaboration to identify, support, and implement the universal codes, regulations, standards, and incentives and penalties that need to be put in place to enable both global interconnectivity and transparency in the deployment and operation of a smart green glocal infrastructure.

In the first six months of the new presidency and US Congress in 2021, Congress should enact Green New Deal laws, signed by the president, covering all of these twenty-three initiatives needed to jump-start a twenty-year emergency build-out of a green zero-emission Third Industrial Revolution infrastructure across America.

Peer Assembly Governance

We noted earlier that the design and engineering of infrastructures both enable and constrain the types of business models and forms of governance that accompany them. Recall that in the case of the First and Second Industrial Revolutions, the infrastructures were engineered to be centralized, enclosed in intellectual property, and vertically integrated to create economies of scale in order to return sufficient profits to investors because of the huge up-front costs of locating, extracting, shipping, refining, and delivering coal, oil, natural gas, and petrochemicals to end users. All other sectors, in turn, had to organize their supply chains and value chains and the production of their goods and services in a similar fashion because of their total dependence on the same energy sources and infrastructure dynamics. The temporal/spatial reach of the First Industrial Revolution infrastructure gave rise to national markets and nation-state governance to oversee them. The Second Industrial Revolution infrastructure gave rise to global markets and international organizations like the United Nations, the World Bank, the OECD, and the World Trade Organization to comanage governance alongside nation-states.

As described early on, the Third Industrial Revolution infrastructure comes with a different design and engineering construction. The platform is weighted toward being distributed in operation rather than centralized, and the system itself is optimized if it remains open and transparent to create the network effect rather than being closed off in intellectual property. Last, the distributed open and transparent nature of the system is most efficient and productive if its operations are laterally scaled rather than vertically integrated.

Giant internet companies, early on, seized hold of many of the platforms in vertically scaled global monopolies, but that is not likely to last, because they ultimately cannot compete with the millions of high-tech small- and medium-sized enterprises blockchained across competencies and operating in cooperatives overseen by commons governance. The latter's organizational style is far more agile and functions with far less overhead, while ensuring that the revenue generated stays within the cooperative enterprises and the communities where they reside, rather than much of it being siphoned off in the form of profits to outside investors.

To ensure a fair playing field, however, the federal government should vigorously enforce antitrust laws, applying the same standards in regulating the activity of ICT companies, electricity companies, and transport and logistics companies that have been used in the past to secure an open commercial space for enterprises to thrive.

The distributed, open-sourced, and laterally scaled design and engineering principles built into the Third Industrial Revolution infrastructure favor an accompanying distributed, open, transparent, and laterally scaled regulatory regime to facilitate and coordinate this new approach to commerce. Our twenty years of experience in the European Union suggest that the codes, regulations, and standards that need to be put in place to operate a green infrastructure across the continent will remain the responsibility of the member states and the European Commission. However, the build-out and scale-up of the Green New Deal economy will ultimately be the responsibility of the 350 governing regions and cities of Europe, with each customizing the infrastructure to its own goals, deliverables, and aspirations within the confines of the

EU-wide codes, regulations, and standards, allowing them to interconnect across borders in a coherent continental smart infrastructure.

This is not FDR's New Deal, with the federal government building and operating gigantic dams to generate and distribute cheap hydroelectricity across America but, rather, a distributed Green New Deal for the twenty-first century centered around locally harvested renewable energies and managed by regional infrastructures that connect across borders like Wi-Fi. In the twenty-first century, every state, city, and county in America, and indeed every locality around the world, can be relatively self-sufficient in its green power generation and resilience. The sun shines everywhere, and the wind blows everywhere. While some regions will be more blessed with ample amounts of solar and wind at any given time of the day, week, month, or season of the year, the surplus electricity can be stored and later shared with other regions experiencing lulls, guaranteeing more than enough energy to power society across continental landmasses.

The Third Industrial Revolution infrastructure works most effectively and efficiently if it's laterally scaled and connects a multitude of small players. This is not a theoretical conjecture. As mentioned in chapter 2, the four giant power and electricity companies in Germany learned this lesson the hard way and were left with billions of dollars in stranded assets in less than twelve years from the time that solar and wind energy came online. Recall that in Germany, small players—farmers, SMEs, and neighborhood associations—established electricity cooperatives, secured bank loans, and installed solar- and wind-energy-generating technologies on-site, using some of the green electricity off-grid and selling the surplus back to the grid. Today, nearly 25 percent of all the electricity powering Germany comes from solar and wind, and much of that green energy is generated by small cooperatives.[18] The Big Four power and electricity companies are generating less than 5 percent of the green energies of the twenty-first century and have, for the most part, been eliminated from renewable power generation.[19]

Distributed energy in every region goes hand in hand with distributed governance. This is what we mean by "power to the people"—fifty state economies made up of smart high-tech SMEs organized into laterally scaled cooperatives, all connected to a smart green Third Industrial Revolution infrastructure, managing, powering, and moving their goods and services across value chains at low fixed costs, near-zero marginal costs, and with a near-zero carbon footprint. While each state will be charged with the task of building out and scaling up a Third Industrial Revolution, the goals and deliverables in each jurisdiction will be customized to the specific needs of that state. But to be effective, all the states will need to connect across their borders and collaborate on a smart national power grid to create lateral economies of scale and network effects.

With this consideration in mind, the National Governors Association, the National Conference of State Legislatures, the United States Conference of Mayors, and the National Association of Counties should pass resolutions calling on each state to voluntarily establish Green New Deal "peer assemblies" made up of elected officials of the cities and counties and representatives from local chambers of commerce, labor unions, economic development agencies, public and private universities, and civic organizations. These peer assemblies, overseen by state, municipal, and county governments, will be tasked with establishing Green New Deal roadmaps to transition their economies and communities into the green era. It's not necessary for every state to sign on from the get-go, but at least to have a number of first-movers step forward in order to create a threshold effect. Other states will likely come onboard quickly as public pressure builds for a Green New Deal in their communities.

The powers that be in the nation's capital might look askance at the states, municipalities, and counties grabbing hold of the planning and deployment of the smart green infrastructure transformation for the country, but that's already begun. A quiet revolution has been occurring over the past several years below the national radar screen in states across the country. While the nation's capital wasn't looking, twenty-nine states and three territories adopted Renewable Portfolio Standards (RPS) requiring that a mandated percentage of the electricity sold by their utilities come from renewable energy sources.[20] The states are backing up their RPS with renewable energy credits to encourage both wind and solar installations.

Even though the United States government has dropped out of the Paris Agreement on climate change, nineteen states and Puerto Rico have thus far agreed to comply with the protocol, and other states are expected to soon follow.[21] A number of governors are currently developing plans to get 100 percent of their electricity from zero-carbon sources. California and Hawaii have already established a 2045 deadline to meet this mandate, and the governors of Colorado, New York, New Jersey, and Illinois have pledged to follow suit.[22] The states are on the move.

Here's what the federal government can do to maintain the momentum. Lawmakers on Capitol Hill should agree to provide each state with a one-off $60 million grant to cover a three-year period, with agreement by each state to match it. These funds should be used exclusively by state governments to establish and staff an operational center whose sole purpose is to organize and coordinate peer assemblies across their cities and counties for the express purpose of preparing Green New Deal roadmaps customized to each locality's goals, needs, and existing green sustainability programs and initiatives.

Again, while the federal government provides some infrastructure funding, states, municipalities, and counties are financially responsible for 75 percent of it. The infrastructure deployment in a federal republic like the United States is, for the most part, driven by each of the states. Anyone who is unaware of this and believes that the federal government is going to unilaterally orchestrate an infrastructure transition and impose it on the states will be in for a rude awakening.

The concept of state oversight provides the ideal governing framework for building out a distributed Third Industrial Revolution. From the very beginning of the United States of America, the states and their citizens have zealously guarded what they regard as their fundamental right to govern as they choose and have been wary of federal government encroachment on their freedoms. At the same time, states are always looking over their shoulders at their fellow states in a competitive race to be Best in Show, bringing new business opportunities, employment, and other benefits to their residents. Now that America's Big Three states of New York, California, and Texas are in a race to a green economy and society, with all the attendant benefits, other states are likely to quickly jump into the game. They won't need to be forced against their will.

We've come to realize in the European Union that the distributed nature of the Third Industrial Revolution infrastructure makes its speedy adoption and scaling more likely if it is conceptualized and introduced by the communities and regions where it will be deployed. Still, the states will have to work with each other, and with the federal government, to determine the codes, regulations, and standards of operations that will need to be put in place to ensure that the distributed green infrastructure can be quickly installed and connected across governing jurisdictions.

The key to a distributed Green New Deal will be the scaling up of energy service companies—ESCOs—and financial mechanisms for their deployment in all fifty states. Toward this end, following the 2020 national elections, the National Governors Association, the National Conference of State Legislatures, the United States Conference of Mayors, and the National Association of Counties should convene a weeklong emergency conference bringing together the key industries and businesses—from SMEs to Fortune 500 companies— whose competencies will be necessary to build out and scale up a Third Industrial Revolution infrastructure. The competencies should include the ICT sector, the telecom sector, the electronics industry, electric power utilities, the transport and logistics industries, the real estate sector, the facilities management sector, the construction sector, the manufacturing industries, the agricultural and life sciences sectors, and the travel and tourism industry, alongside representatives from the national financial, banking, and insurance communities.

The purpose of the national emergency conference of states, municipalities, and counties, and industries across all of the sectors of the economy, is to establish the ESCO business model and to set up state and local green banks to finance the development of Third Industrial Revolution infrastructures.

As of 2017, the global ESCO market was approximately $15 billion. It is expected to grow at a compound annual growth rate of 8.3 percent and amount to a $30.8 billion market by 2026.[23] Although this is an estimable growth rate in normal times, it is inadequate to the task of transforming the US and global infrastructure into a zero-emission era, given the time constraints imposed by rapidly escalating climate change.

What's needed is tenfold growth over a ten-year period, comparable to America's World War II mobilization from a peacetime economy to a wartime economy. Now, as then, all the industries, sectors, and competencies that would need to come together—this time to form ESCOs operating within and across all fifty states—already exist. They merely need to regroup across their competencies under the umbrella of the new ESCO performance-contracting business model.

Generous tax credits and a thoughtful streamlining of codes, regulations, and standards to speed up the scale of the infrastructure build-out in municipalities, counties, and states will be essential to moving forward—on a wartime-like footing—in the shift to the new business model.

Those who would argue against extending generous tax credits should be reminded that each year billions of dollars in tax credits and other incentives are dished out by states and localities to subsidize sports stadiums and conference centers and to encourage companies to locate industrial plants and commercial complexes in their communities in exchange for a few thousand jobs here and there—with a much smaller return to the economy and tax base. States and localities would be far better served by issuing state and local tax credits to accelerate the transition into a smart green zero-emission economy, with the vast opportunities that would accrue to SMEs and a redeployment of the workforce in every community.

From our experience in the EU with establishing peer assemblies, the optimum is three hundred citizens within any given region participating ad hoc and providing input and feedback at every stage of engagement. Peer assemblies are not focus groups or stakeholder groups but rather a cross-section of the public who will be intimately involved in the ongoing deliberations and the preparation of the proposals and initiatives that will be incorporated into their jurisdiction's Green New Deal roadmap.

The governor, mayors, and county executives become the facilitators and are responsible both for selecting the cross-section of participants and for overseeing the operations of the peer assemblies in their respective jurisdictions.

Each peer assembly will want to reach out and secure technical support. The states' public universities might be tasked with bringing together professional and technical talent from both their own institutions and private universities, community colleges, trade and technical institutes, think tanks, research institutes, and local charitable foundations to provide valuable expertise from across the academic and professional disciplines.

Within six months of establishing Green New Deal peer assemblies, the governor and legislature of each state should convene their own weeklong emergency conference with several thousand city and county peer assembly representatives in attendance. The conference should cover all the various aspects of a Green New Deal mobilization, including the preparation of city and county roadmaps, deployment and financing, and best practices and expert technical assistance from across the state and beyond.

The Green New Deal begins with preparing a detailed Third Industrial Revolution roadmap, which typically takes ten months. City and county peer assemblies should each prepare their own roadmap, congruent with the state's. The success or failure of a roadmap depends on whether the process itself is viewed from its inception as a truly collaborative, open, and cross-disciplinary exercise. It's recommended that every peer selected by cities and counties sign a socially responsible ethics agreement to collaborate rather than compete and to act impartially rather than lobby for a special interest or cause. The peers need to come to the task with a civic-minded community spirit if they are to succeed. Roadmaps create a community esprit de corps—a feeling among the peers that they are engaged in something bigger than themselves that will deeply affect their families, communities, and generations yet to come.

The chairpersons of city and county government peer assemblies should meet periodically with the governor's office and the state legislature to report on progress in their road-map deliberations and receive feedback and assistance. After the ten-month process, each municipality and county peer assembly will publish an extensive roadmap detailing its customized Green New Deal plan and next steps for initiating financing and local deployment of green infrastructure megaprojects. They will also share their views on the codes, regulations, standards, incentives, and penalties that need to be forthcoming from the state legislature and governor's office to expedite a statewide transition into the Green New Deal Third Industrial Revolution paradigm.

The roadmap mission is not just to create a grab bag of favorite green projects but rather to develop a comprehensive and systemic Third Industrial Revolution infrastructure plan that can be deployed across the state over a period of two decades. This integrative approach to scaling infrastructure is what's been sorely missing in Green New Deal proposals to date. It's important to visualize the build-out of a Third Industrial Revolution as a statewide multigenerational construction site that will evolve over time and branch out in many directions as circumstances dictate. Failure to understand the mission will lead to fragmentation and ultimately descend back to small, siloed favorite green projects without a transformational impact. The three Third Industrial Revolution roadmaps prepared and now being deployed in the industrial regions of Hauts-de-France, the twenty-three cities of the Metropolitan Region of Rotterdam and The Hague, and the Grand Duchy of Luxembourg are open-source and available to everyone.[24]

Many cities and counties across the United States have prepared green sustainability roadmaps, and a few have even involved some form of peer assembly in the deliberations; these localities will be an important source of expertise in sharing best practices. None of the already existing green development plans in play in municipalities, counties, and at the state level are discarded in the Third Industrial Revolution roadmap process and subsequent deployment; rather, they are embedded into the green infrastructure that connects these projects in a seamless new economic paradigm. Absent this unifying vision across each city, county, and state, we are back to thousands of well-meaning green programs that remain attached to the dying fossil fuel infrastructure of the twentieth century.

City, county, and state governments might want to establish websites to share their Green New Deal roadmap deliberations and deployments in real time across America. Engendering a nationwide dialogue on best practices and accompanying opportunities and challenges can spin off multiple collaborations across traditional political borders, creating a wholly new political dynamic beyond voting for representatives at election time. This is the very nature of peer assembly governance.

Peer assemblies continue to work beyond the roadmap stage through the entire scale-up of a zero-emissions green infrastructure transition, with peers rotating in and out of the process and across generations, ensuring continuity beyond the turnover of elected officials every two or four years, guaranteeing that the peer process itself is not held hostage by whatever political party or elected official is holding office.

The existential magnitude of the climate change crisis is of a kind humanity has never before confronted. It requires a multigenerational form of commons governance that can continue into the indefinite future. The fear of climate change is very real, and the conditions for living on Earth are going to deteriorate far into the future and beyond our current imagination. Cities, counties, states, and the federal government will all have to be engaged in a political process without a closure date.

We have found that in the seven regional roadmap processes and subsequent deployments we have been involved in, that although governments establish peer assemblies, cabinet ministries, government bureaucracies, and special interests are often uncomfortable with and hostile to sharing their turf. They may be reluctant to say so publicly (who, in principle, wants to say they are opposed to peer assemblies?) but they often find subtle ways to undermine the process, the recommendations, and the deployments. They are far more comfortable with focus groups and stakeholder groups that are often used and abused to help bolster their executive and legislative agendas.

On the other hand, it is the executive and legislative branches of municipal, county, and state governments that initiate and oversee peer assemblies who have the ultimate responsibility of converting their recommendations, projects, initiatives, and proposals into laws, protocols, and initiatives. Peer assemblies are informal bodies that bring the voice of the public into the process and encourage elected officials and government agencies to be more responsive and integrative in their missions and assignments and to be more systemic and attentive to the multiple perspectives rising up from their communities. Peer assemblies lateralize governance by bringing the public into continuous engagement with government to advance the commonweal. Their presence requires a new generation of elected officials and government employees who are comfortable with informal sharing of governance between elections rather than exercising an exclusive territorial reign.

Climate change is going to require the ongoing engagement of the entire body politic. No single elected official or head of a government agency is going to be able to go it alone. The model that comes to mind is disaster response and relief during emergencies. The entire community comes together in these moments—local organizations, NGOs, religious bodies, schools, neighborhood associations, and the business sector. While disaster preparedness and emergencies are overseen by elected and appointed officials, disasters are often so unexpected and all-consuming that they require the full and active engagement of everyone, sometimes for weeks, months, and even years. Between disasters, civil society organizations and the business community are in continuous collaboration with public authorities, learning from past emergencies; sharing best practices; integrating new ideas, programs, and response mechanisms into their planning; and preparing for emergencies yet to come in an ongoing conversation around the mission of securing the commonweal.

Climate change now puts every community in the world in harm's way in a continuous disaster mode. This is the truth of the matter. Peer assemblies will soon become a necessity across the world if communities are to come to grips with a runaway climate. Former California governor Jerry Brown, in his last few days in office, got it right when he said that the wild changes in the weather are "the new abnormal."[25]

A final observation. Without peer assemblies, citizens everywhere in America and around the world are going to feel less listened to, more abandoned and left to their own wits, and deeply alienated from their governments. That combination of fear and isolation, if left to simmer, is potentially explosive and could easily tear apart the very fabric of civilized life. Peer assemblies are a way to channel a community's sense of powerlessness in the face of climate change into a sense of shared responsibility for the biosphere that we will need in the years ahead and centuries to come.

Let me be very clear about the timetable for ushering in a glocal Green New Deal and the transition into a smart Third Industrial Revolution. The juvenile infrastructure for the First Industrial Revolution was laid down across the United States in thirty years, between 1860 and 1890. The juvenile infrastructure for the Second Industrial Revolution was built out in twenty-five years, between 1908 and 1933. The shorter time was due, in part, to the fact that the Second Industrial Revolution infrastructure was able to build on a First Industrial Revolution infrastructure already in place. With this in mind, the Third Industrial Revolution infrastructure can likely be built out in twenty years—a single generation—by building off the two industrial revolution infrastructures that preceded it and that are still partially in place to facilitate the transition.

Please do not let anyone tell you this can't be done. By 2040, we should be there if each and every one of us pulls our own weight and carries our own load, with grit and determination, as part of a community and nationwide commitment.

■ ■ ■

The Green New Deal is not just about mobilizing the public to pressure governments to loosen the purse strings, pass legislation, and incentivize green initiatives. Rather, it's the first call for a new kind of peer political movement and commons governance that can empower entire communities to take direct charge of their futures at a very dark moment in the history of life on Earth.

Living off the fossil fuel deposits of the carboniferous era for more than two centuries gave us a false sense of an open-ended and unlimited future where everything was possible and with little price to pay. We came to believe that we are the masters of our fate and that the Earth is here for our taking. We failed to see that there is always an entropy bill for whatever takes place on this planet. We called this era the Age of Progress. Climate change is now the bill come due. We are entering a new epoch and a new journey. The Age of Resilience is now before us. How we adapt to the new planetary reality that faces us will determine our future destiny as a species. We are fast approaching a biosphere consciousness. We need to be hopeful that we can get there in time. This is the Green New Deal I believe in.

ACKNOWLEDGMENTS

I would like to express my deep gratitude and thanks to my colleagues Daniel Christensen and Claudia Salvador for their stellar contribution to the book. Their research skills, sensitivity to details, and command of the language show up on every page of the book. Their dedication to the task and commitment to tight deadlines, which often went into the evenings and on weekends, kept the project on schedule. I would also like to thank my close friend and colleague Angelo Consoli for his advice on sections of the book dealing with the history of Green New Deal–style transitions in the European Union.

I would also like to thank my editor Tim Bartlett, who quickly embraced the project and moved mountains at St. Martin's Press to spirit the book along its journey from conception to final copy. Tim's sage editorial suggestions and edits helped smooth out the wrinkles and fine-tune the text. I would also like to express my appreciation to India Cooper for the excellent copy editing that is always essential to the publishing process. Thanks also to Dante Calfayan, Katherine Jossi, and John Marino for their research assistance.

To my literary agent, Meg Thompson, thank you! Her enthusiasm and wise counsel kept all of us on mission throughout the process. Thanks also to Sandy Hodgman, my foreign rights literary agent, for engaging our publishers in markets around the world.

Finally, my deep thanks to my wife, Carol Grunewald, for suggesting I write this book. Many of the themes in the book come from countless conversations over thirty years together that have shaped our common understanding of the world we inhabit and our hopes for the future of humanity and our fellow creatures with whom we share this Earth.

NOTES

INTRODUCTION

1 Intergovernmental Panel on Climate Change, "Summary for Policy-makers," in *Global Warming of 1.5°C: An IPCC Special Report* (Geneva: World Meteorological Organization, 2018), 6.

2 Edward O. Wilson, "The 8 Million Species We Don't Know," *New York Times,* March 3, 2018, https://www.nytimes.com/2018/03/03/opinion/sunday/species-conservation-extinction.html (accessed February 4, 2019).

3 Gerta Keller et al., "Volcanism, Impacts and Mass Extinctions (Long Version)," *Geoscientist Online,* November 2012, https://www.geolsoc.org.uk/Geoscientist/Archive/November-2012/Volcanism-impacts-and-mass-extinctions-2 (accessed March 12, 2019).

4 Intergovernmental Panel on Climate Change, "Summary for Policy-makers," 14.

5 Ryan Grim and Briahna Gray, "Alexandria Ocasio-Cortez Joins Environmental Activists in Protest at Democratic Leader Nancy Pelosi's Office," *The Intercept,* November 13, 2018, https://theintercept.com/2018/11/13/alexandria-ocasio-cortez-sunrise-activists-nancy-pelosi/ (accessed February 1, 2019).

6 Sunrise Movement, "Green New Deal," updated March 26, 2019, https://www.sunrisemovement.org/gnd (accessed April 5, 2019).

7 Anthony Leiserowitz et al., *Climate Change in the American Mind: December 2018,* Yale University and George Mason University (New Haven, CT: Yale University Program on Climate Change Communication, 2018), 3.

8 Kevin E. Trenberth, "Changes in Precipitation with Climate Change," *Climate Research* 47 (March 2011): 123, doi: 10.3354/cr00953.

9 Kim Cohen et al., "The ICS International Chronostratigraphic Chart," *Episodes* 36, no. 3 (2013): 200–201.

10   Abel Gustafson et al., "The Green New Deal Has Strong Bipartisan Support," Yale Program on Climate Change Communication, December 14, 2018, http://climatecommunication.yale.edu/publications/the-green -new-deal-has-strong-bipartisan-support/ (accessed February 7, 2019).

11   Aengus Collins, *The Global Risks Report 2019* (Geneva: World Economic Forum, 2019), 6.

12   Gillian Tett, "Davos Climate Obsessions Contain Clues for Policymaking," *Financial Times*, January 17, 2019, https://www.ft.com/content /369920f2-19b4-11e9-b93e-f4351a53f1c3 (accessed January 28, 2019).

13   Leslie Hook, "Four Former Fed Chairs Call for US Carbon Tax," *Financial Times*, January 16, 2019, https://www.ft.com/content/e9fd0472-19de -11e9-9e64-d150b3105d21 (accessed January 28, 2019).

14   "Economists' Statement on Carbon Dividends," *Wall Street Journal*, January 16, 2019, https://www.wsj.com/articles/economists-statement -on-carbon-dividends-11547682910?mod=searchresults&page=1&pos =1 (accessed February 5, 2019).

15   Damian Carrington, "School Climate Strikes: 1.4 Million People Took Part, Say Campaigners," *The Guardian*, March 19, 2019, https://www .theguardian.com/environment/2019/mar/19/school-climate-strikes -more-than-1-million-took-part-say-campaigners-greta-thunberg (accessed March 20, 2019).

16   *Lazard's Levelized Cost of Energy Analysis—Version 12.0*, 2018, https:// www.lazard.com/media/450784/lazards-levelized-cost-of-energy -version-120-vfinal.pdf (accessed March 12, 2019); Naureen S. Malik, "Wind and Solar Costs Keep Falling, Squeezing Nuke, Coal Plants," Bloomberg *Quint*, November 8, 2018, https://www.bloombergquint.com /technology/wind-and-solar-costs-keep-falling-squeezing-nuke-coal -plants (accessed March 12, 2019).

17   "Cost of Electricity by Source," Wikipedia, https://en.wikipedia.org /wiki/Cost_of_electricity_by_source#Levelized_cost_of_electricity (accessed April 5, 2019).

18   *Lazard's Levelized Cost of Energy Analysis—Version 12.0*, 2018, https:// www.lazard.com/media/450784/lazards-levelized-cost-of-energy -version-120-vfinal.pdf (accessed March 12, 2019).

19   Carbon Tracker Initiative, "Fossil Fuels Will Peak in the 2020s as Renewables Supply All Growth in Energy Demand," news release, September 11, 2018, https://www.carbontracker.org/fossil-fuels-will-peak-in-the -2020s-as-renewables-supply-all-growth-in-energy-demand/ (accessed February 5, 2019).

20   Jason Channell et al., *Energy Darwinism II: Why a Low Carbon Future Doesn't Have to Cost the Earth*, report (Citi, 2015), 8.

21   Carbon Tracker Initiative, "Fossil Fuels Will Peak in the 2020s."

22   Candace Dunn and Tim Hess, "The United States Is Now the Largest Global Crude Oil Producer," US Energy Information Administration,

September 12, 2018, https://www.eia.gov/todayinenergy/detail.php?id=37053 (accessed February 5, 2019).

23 Willis Towers Watson, Thinking Ahead Institute, *Global Pension Assets Study 2018*, https://www.thinkingaheadinstitute.org/en/Library/Public/Research-and-Ideas/2018/02/Global-Pension-Asset-Survey-2018 (accessed April 5, 2019), 9.

24 "1,000+ Divestment Commitments," Fossil Free, https://gofossilfree.org/divestment/commitments/ (accessed March 15, 2019).

CHAPTER 1

1   Brian Merchant, "With a Trillion Sensors, the Internet of Things Would Be the 'Biggest Business in the History of Electronics,'" *Motherboard*, October 29, 2013, https://motherboard.vice.com/en_us/article/8qx4gz/the-internet-of-things-could-be-the-biggest-business-in-the-history-of-electronics (accessed February 6, 2019).

2   "Wikipedia.org Traffic Statistics," Alexa, https://www.alexa.com/siteinfo/wikipedia.org (accessed February 6, 2019).

3   Robert U. Ayres and Benjamin Warr, *The Economic Growth Engine: How Energy and Work Drive Material Prosperity* (Northampton, MA: Edward Elgar Publishing, 2009), 334–37; John A. "Skip" Laitner, "Linking Energy Efficiency to Economic Productivity: Recommendations for Improving the Robustness of the U.S. Economy," *WIREs Energy and Environment* 4 (May/June 2015): 235.

4   John A. "Skip" Laitner et al., *The Long-Term Energy Efficiency Potential: What the Evidence Suggests* (Washington, DC: American Council for an Energy-Efficient Economy, 2012), 65.

5   Global Covenant of Mayors for Climate & Energy, "About the Global Covenant of Mayors for Climate & Energy," https://www.globalcovenantofmayors.org/about/ (accessed February 9, 2019).

6   David E. Nye, *Electrifying America: Social Meanings of a New Technology, 1880–1940* (Cambridge, MA: MIT Press, 1991), 239–321.

7   Xavier Sala-i-Martin, chief advisor, and Klaus Schwab, ed., *The Global Competitiveness Report 2017–2018* (Geneva: World Economic Forum, 2017), 329.

8   Jonathan Woetzel et al., *Bridging Global Infrastructure Gaps: Has the World Made Progress?* McKinsey Global Institute report, 2017, 5.

9   Sala-i-Martin and Schwab, *The Global Competitiveness Report 2017–2018*, 303.

10 The White House, "Remarks by the President at a Campaign Event in Roanoke, Virginia," July 13, 2012, https://obamawhitehouse.archives.gov/the-press-office/2012/07/13/remarks-president-campaign-event-roanoke-virginia (accessed February 27, 2019), emphasis added.

11 Sterling Beard, "Republicans Take Dig at Obama with 'We Built It' Convention Theme," *The Hill*, August 21, 2012, https://thehill.com/blogs/blog

-briefing-room/news/244633-republicans-take-dig-at-obama-with-qwe
-built-itq-convention-theme (accessed May 10, 2019).

12   Joan Claybrook, "Reagan Ballooned 'Big Government,'" *New York Times*,
      November 1, 1984, https://www.nytimes.com/1984/11/01/opinion/reagan
      -ballooned-big-government.html (accessed February 8, 2019).

13   Frank Newport, "Trump Family Leave, Infrastructure Proposals Widely
      Popular," Gallup, April 7, 2017, https://news.gallup.com/poll/207905
      /trump-family-leave-infrastructure-proposals-widely-popular.aspx (ac-
      cessed February 4, 2019).

14   American Society of Civil Engineers, *The 2017 Infrastructure Report
      Card: A Comprehensive Assessment of America's Infrastructure*, https://
      www.infrastructurereportcard.org/wp-content/uploads/2017/01/2017
      -Infrastructure-Report-Card.pdf (accessed March 12, 2019), 5–7.

15   American Society of Civil Engineers, *Failure to Act: Closing the Infra-
      structure Investment Gap for America's Economic Future*, 2016, https://
      www.infrastructurereportcard.org/wp-content/uploads/2016/05/ASCE
      -Failure-to-Act-Report-for-Web-5.23.16.pdf (accessed March 12, 2019), 4–6.

16   American Society of Civil Engineers, *The 2017 Infrastructure Report
      Card*, 7–8.

17   Werling and Horst, *Catching Up*, 9.

18   Woetzel et al., *Bridging Global Infrastructure Gaps*, 2.

19   "First Telegraph Messages from the Capitol," US Senate, https://www
      .senate.gov/artandhistory/history/minute/First_Telegraph_Messages
      _from_the_Capitol.htm (accessed February 7, 2019).

20   Lee Ann Potter and Wynell Schamel, "The Homestead Act of 1862," *So-
      cial Education* 61, no. 6 (October 1997): 359–64.

21   Richard Walker and Gray Brechin, "The Living New Deal: The Unsung
      Benefits of the New Deal for the United States and California," UC
      Berkeley Institute for Research on Labor and Employment Working
      Paper 220-10, August 2010, 14.

22   Work Projects Administration, *Final Report on the WPA Program,
      1935–43* (Washington, DC: USGPO, 1947).

23   Patrick Kline and Enrico Moretti, "Local Economic Development, Ag-
      glomeration Economies, and the Big Push: 100 Years of Evidence from
      the Tennessee Valley Authority," *Quarterly Journal of Economics* 129,
      no. 1 (February 2014): 276.

24   Erica Interrante and Bingxin Yu, *Contributions and Crossroads: Our
      National Road System's Impact on the U.S. Economy and Way of Life
      (1916–2016)* (Washington, DC: US Department of Transportation, Fed-
      eral Highway Administration, 2017), 20.

25   "Servicemen's Readjustment Act (1944)," US National Archives and Rec-
      ords Administration, http://www.ourdocuments.gov/doc.php?doc=76
      (accessed February 27, 2019).

26   "GDP (Current US$)," World Bank, https://data.worldbank.org/indicator
      /NY.GDP.MKTP.CD (accessed February 26, 2019); "Fortune Global 500
      List 2018: See Who Made It," *Fortune,* May 21, 2018, http://fortune.com
      /global500/ (accessed February 14, 2019); "Labor Force, Total," World
      Bank, https://data.worldbank.org/indicator/sl.tlf.totl.in (accessed Feb-
      ruary 15, 2019).

27   World Bank Group, *Piecing Together the Poverty Puzzle* (Washington,
      DC: World Bank, 2018), 7.

28   Deborah Hardoon, *An Economy for the 99%,* Oxfam International
      Briefing Paper, January 2017, https://www-cdn.oxfam.org/s3fs-public
      /file_attachments/bp-economy-for-99-percent-160117-en.pdf (accessed
      March 12, 2019), 1.

29   "Company Info," Facebook Newsroom, https://newsroom.fb.com
      /company-info/ (accessed February 12, 2019).

30   Benny Evangelista, "Alphabet, Toronto Partner to Create Tech-Infused
      Neighborhood," *San Francisco Chronicle*, October 18, 2017, http://www
      .govtech.com/news/Alphabet-Toronto-Partner-to-Create-Tech-Infused
      -Neighborhood.html (accessed February 22, 2019).

31   North Carolina State University, "Mayday 23: World Population Be-
      comes More Urban Than Rural," *Science Daily,* May 25, 2007, https://
      www.sciencedaily.com/releases/2007/05/070525000642.htm   (accessed
      March 12, 2019).

32   Jim Balsillie, "Sidewalk Toronto Has Only One Beneficiary, and It Is Not
      Toronto," *Globe and Mail*, October 5, 2018, https://www.theglobeand
      mail.com/opinion/article-sidewalk-toronto-is-not-a-smart-city/ (accessed
      February 14, 2019).

33   Ibid.

34   Ibid.

35   Vipal Monga and Jacquie McNish, "Local Resistance Builds to Google's
      'Smart City' in Toronto," *Wall Street Journal,* August 1, 2018, https://
      www.wsj.com/articles/local-resistance-builds-to-googles-smart-city-in
      -toronto-1533135550 (accessed February 2, 2019).

36   Ibid.; Ava Kofman, "Google's 'Smart City of Surveillance' Faces New Resis-
      tance in Toronto," *The Intercept,* November 13, 2018, https://theintercept
      .com/2018/11/13/google-quayside-toronto-smart-city/ (accessed Febru-
      ary 2, 2019).

37   Jennings Brown, "Privacy Expert Resigns from Alphabet-Backed Smart
      City Project over Surveillance Concerns," *Gizmodo,* October 23, 2018,
      https://gizmodo.com/privacy-expert-resigns-from-alphabet-backed
      -smart-city-1829934748 (accessed February 14, 2019).

38   "Les Hauts-de-France envoient du rev3," Région Hauts-de-France, Octo-
      ber 18, 2018, http://www.hautsdefrance.fr/les-hauts-de-france-envoient
      -du-rev3/ (accessed February 14, 2019).

CHAPTER 2

1   "2020 Climate & Energy Package," European Commission, https://ec
.europa.eu/clima/policies/strategies/2020_en (accessed February 20, 2019).

2   "About the Group," Green New Deal Group, https://www.greennewdeal
group.org/?page_id=2 (accessed February 9, 2019).

3   New Economics Foundation, *A Green New Deal: Joined-Up Policies to
Solve the Triple Crunch of the Credit Crisis, Climate Change and High Oil
Prices,* July 20, 2008, https://neweconomics.org/2008/07/green-new-deal
(accessed March 12, 2019).

4   Katy Nicholson, ed., *Toward a Transatlantic Green New Deal: Tackling
the Climate and Economic Crises,* prepared by the Worldwatch Institute
for the Heinrich Böll Foundation (Brussels: Heinrich-Böll-Stiftung,
2009), 6 (quoted).

5   "Countdown to Copenhagen: Germany's Responsibility for Climate
Justice," Oxfam Deutschland, November 2009, https://www.oxfam.de
/system/files/20091111_Programm.pdf (accessed February 7, 2019).

6   Philipp Schepelmann et al., *A Green New Deal for Europe: Towards Green
Modernisation in the Face of Crisis,* ed. Jacki Davis and Geoff Meade,
vol. 1 (Brussels: Green European Foundation, 2009).

7   Edward B. Barbier, *Rethinking the Economic Recovery: A Global Green
New Deal,* report prepared for the United Nations Environment Programme, April 2009, https://www.cbd.int/development/doc/UNEP-global
-green-new-deal.pdf (accessed March 12, 2019).

8   Ibid., 16.

9   Enric Ruiz-Geli and Jeremy Rifkin, *A Green New Deal: From Geopolitics
to Biosphere Politics,* bilingual ed. (Barcelona, Basel, and New York: Ac-
tar, 2011).

10 New Deal 4 Europe, "Petition to the European Parliament," http://www
.newdeal4europe.eu/en/petition (accessed February 5, 2019).

11 Jill Stein and Ajamu Baraka campaign, "The Green New Deal," 2016,
https://d3n8a8pro7vhmx.cloudfront.net/jillstein/pages/27056/attach
ments/original/1478104990/green-new-deal.pdf?1478104990 (accessed
March 12, 2019).

12 Greg Carlock and Emily Mangan, *A Green New Deal: A Progressive Vi-
sion for Environmental Sustainability and Economic Stability,* Data for
Progress, September 2018, http://filesforprogress.org/pdfs/Green_New
_Deal.pdf (accessed March 12, 2019).

13 "Draft Text for Proposed Addendum to House Rules for 116th Congress of the United States," November 2018, https://docs.google.com
/document/d/1jxUzp9SZ6-VB-4wSm8sselVMsqWZrSrYpYC9slHKLzo
/edit#heading=h.z7x8pz4dydey (accessed January 3, 2019).

14 Jason Channell et al., *Energy Darwinism II: Why a Low Carbon Future
Doesn't Have to Cost the Earth,* Citi GPS report, 2015, https://cusdi.org

/wp-content/uploads/2016/02/ENERGY-DARWINISM-II-Why-a-Low
-Carbon-Future-Doesn%E2%80%99t-Have-to-Cost-the-Earth.-Citi
-GPSI.pdf (accessed March 24, 2019), 8.

15 Pilita Clark, "Mark Carney Warns Investors Face 'Huge' Climate Change
    Losses," *Financial Times*, September 29, 2015, https://www.ft.com/content
    /622de3da-66e6-11e5-97d0-1456a776a4f5 (accessed January 8, 2019).

16 Mario Pickavet et al., "Worldwide Energy Needs for ICT: The Rise of
    Power-Aware Networking," paper presented at the 2008 International
    Conference on Advanced Networks and Telecommunication Systems,
    2, doi:10.1109/ants.2008.4937762; Lotfi Belkhir and Ahmed Elmeligi,
    "Assessing ICT Global Emissions Footprint: Trends to 2040 & Recom-
    mendations," *Journal of Cleaner Production* 177 (January 2, 2018): 448,
    doi:10.1016/j.jclepro.2017.12.239.

17 Belkhir and Elmeligi, "Assessing ICT Global Emissions Footprint," 458.

18 Ibid., 458–59.

19 Apple, "Apple Now Globally Powered by 100 Percent Renewable Energy,"
    news release, April 9, 2018, https://www.apple.com/newsroom/2018/04
    /apple-now-globally-powered-by-100-percent-renewable-energy/ (accessed
    January 15, 2019).

20 Urs Hölzle, "100% Renewable Is Just the Beginning," Google news release,
    December 12, 2016, https://sustainability.google/projects/announcement
    -100 (accessed February 7, 2019).

21 Facebook, "2017 Year in Review: Data Centers," news release, Decem-
    ber 11, 2017, https://code.fb.com/data-center-engineering/2017-year-in
    -review-data-centers/ (accessed February 7, 2019).

22 "Companies," RE100, http://there100.org/companies (accessed Febru-
    ary 22, 2019).

23 "The AT&T Issue Brief on Energy Management," August 2018, https://
    about.att.com/ecms/dam/csr/issuebriefs/IssueBriefs2018/environment
    /energy-management.pdf (accessed February 22, 2019); "Intel Climate
    Change Policy Statement," December 2017, https://www.intel.com
    /content/www/us/en/corporate-responsibility/environment-climate
    -change-policy.html (accessed February 22, 2019); Cisco, "CSR Environ-
    mental Sustainability," https://www.cisco.com/c/en/us/about/csr/impact
    /environmental-sustainability.html (accessed February 22, 2019).

24 Steven Levy, "The Brief History of the ENIAC Computer: A Look Back
    at the Room-Size Government Computer That Began the Digital Era,"
    Smithsonian Magazine, November 2013, https://www.smithsonianmag
    .com/history/the-brief-history-of-the-eniac-computer-3889120/ (accessed
    March 12, 2019).

25 Simon Kemp, *Digital in 2018: Essential Insights into the Internet, Social
    Media, Mobile, and Ecommerce Use Around the World,* Hootsuite and
    We Are Social Global Digital Report, 3.

26   Peter Diamandis, "Solar Energy Revolution: A Massive Opportunity," *Forbes,* September 2, 2014, https://www.forbes.com/sites/peter diamandis/2014/09/02/solar-energy-revolution-a-massive-opportunity /#7f88662d6c90 (accessed March 12, 2019); Solarponics, *The Complete Homeowners' Guide to Going Solar,* 2016, https://solarponics.com/wp -content/uploads/2017/02/chgtgs.pdf (accessed March 24, 2019), 1.

27   LeAnne Graves, "Record Low Bids Submitted for Abu Dhabi's 350MW Solar Plant in Sweihan," *The National,* September 19, 2016, https://www .thenational.ae/business/record-low-bids-submitted-for-abu-dhabi-s -350mw-solar-plant-in-sweihan-1.213135 (accessed March 3, 2019).

28   IRENA, *Renewable Power Generation Costs in 2018,* International Renewable Energy Agency (Abu Dhabi, 2019): 18.

29   *Lazard's Levelized Cost of Energy Analysis—Version 12.0,* 2018, https:// www.lazard.com/media/450784/lazards-levelized-cost-of-energy -version-120-vfinal.pdf (accessed March 12, 2019).

30   Ramez Namm, "Smaller, Cheaper, Faster: Does Moore's Law Apply to Solar Cells?" *Scientific American* Guest Blog, March 16, 2011, https:// blogs.scientificamerican.com/guest-blog/smaller-cheaper-faster-does -moores-law-apply-to-solar-cells/ (accessed March 24, 2019).

31   Cristina L. Archer and Mark Z. Jacobson, "Evaluation of Global Wind Power," *Journal of Geophysical Research* 110 (2005): 1, doi:10.1029 /2004JD005462.

32   Mark A. Jacobson et al., "100% Clean and Renewable Wind, Water, and Sunlight All-Sector Energy Roadmaps for 139 Countries of the World," *Joule* 1 (September 6, 2017): 35.

33   Richard J. Campbell, *The Smart Grid: Status and Outlook*, Congressional Research Service, April 10, 2018, https://fas.org/sgp/crs/misc/R45156.pdf, 8.

34   Electric Power Research Institute, *Estimating the Costs and Benefits of the Smart Grid: A Preliminary Estimate of the Investment Requirements and the Resultant Benefits of a Fully Functioning Smart Grid*, March 2011, https://www.smartgrid.gov/files/Estimating_Costs_Benefits_Smart _Grid_Preliminary_Estimate_In_201103.pdf (accessed March 24, 2019), 1–2.

35   Electric Power Research Institute, *Estimating the Costs and Benefits of the Smart Grid*, 4; Electric Power Research Institute, *The Power to Reduce CO_2 Emissions: The Full Portfolio,* October 2009, https://www .smartgrid.gov/files/The_Power_to_Reduce_CO2_Emission_Full _Portfolio_Technical_R_200912.pdf (accessed March 23, 2019), 2–1.

36   Pieter Gagnon et al., *Rooftop Solar Photovoltaic Technical Potential in the United States: A Detailed Assessment,* National Renewable Energy Laboratory, January 2016, vii–viii.

37   Jürgen Weiss, J. Michael Hagerty, and María Castañer, *The Coming Electrification of the North American Economy": Why We Need a Robust Transmission Grid,* Brattle Group, 2019, 2.

38 Kerstine Appunn, Felix Bieler, and Julian Wettengel, "Germany's Energy Consumption and Power Mix in Charts," *Clean Energy Wire*, February 6, 2019; Rob Smith, "This Is How People in Europe Are Helping Lead the Energy Charge," World Economic Forum, April 25, 2018, https://www.weforum.org/agenda/2018/04/how-europe-s-energy-citizens-are-leading-the-way-to-100-renewable-power/ (accessed March 5, 2019).

39 Edith Bayer, *Report on the German Power System, Version 1.2*, ed. Mara Marthe Kleine, commissioned by Agora Energiewende, 2015, 9.

40 Appunn, Bieler, and Wettengel, "Germany's Energy Consumption and Power Mix in Charts."

41 Melissa Eddy, "Germany Lays Out a Path to Quit Coal by 2038," *New York Times*, January 26, 2019, https://www.nytimes.com/2019/01/26/world/europe/germany-quit-coal-2038.html (accessed March 4, 2019).

42 Sharan Burrow, "Climate: Towards a Just Transition, with No Stranded Workers and No Stranded Communities," OECD Insights, May 23, 2017, http://oecdinsights.org/2017/05/23/climate-towards-a-just-transition-with-no-stranded-workers-and-no-stranded-communities/ (accessed March 27, 2019).

43 Ibid.

44 Energie Baden-Württemberg, "International Committee of Experts Presents Road-Map for Climate Protection," news release, September 21, 2006, https://www.enbw.com/company/press/press-releases/press-release-details_9683.html (accessed February 7, 2019).

45 BW, *Integrated Annual Report 2017*, https://www.enbw.com/enbw_com/downloadcenter/annual-reports/enbw-integrated-annual-report-2017.pdf (accessed May 14, 2019), 3.

46 E.ON, "Separation of E.ON Business Operations Completed on January 1: Uniper Launched on Schedule," news release, January 1, 2016, https://www.eon.com/en/about-us/media/press-releases/2016/2016-01-04-separation-of-eon-business-operations-completed-on-january-1-uniper-launched-on-schedule.html (accessed February 7, 2019).

47 Vattenfall, "Fossil-Free Living Within a Generation," in German, https://fossilfreedom.vattenfall.com/de/ (accessed February 28, 2019); RWE, "Comprehensive Approach to Energy Transition Needed," news release, April 9, 2018, http://www.rwe.com/web/cms/en/3007818/press-releases/amer/ (accessed February 28, 2019).

48 International Renewable Energy Agency, *A New World: The Geopolitics of the Energy Transformation*, 2019, https://www.irena.org/publications/2019/Jan/A-New-World-The-Geopolitics-of-the-Energy-Transformation (accessed March 24, 2019), 28.

49 Jeremy Rifkin, *The Third Industrial Revolution: How Lateral Power Is Transforming Energy, the Economy, and the World* (New York: Palgrave Macmillan, 2011); Paul Panckhurst and Peter Hirschberg, eds., "China's New Leaders Burnish Image by Revealing Personal Details," *Bloomberg*

News, December 24, 2012, https://www.bloomberg.com/news/articles /2012-12-24/china-s-new-leaders-burnish-image-by-revealing-personal -details (accessed March 13, 2019).

50 Liu Zhenya, "Smart Grid Hosting and Promoting the Third Industrial Revolution," in Chinese, *Science and Technology Daily,* December 5, 2013, http://h.wokeji.com/pl/kjjy/201312/t20131205_598738.shtml (accessed February 7, 2019).

51 The White House, "U.S.–China Joint Announcement on Climate Change," news release, November 11, 2014, https://obamawhitehouse .archives.gov/the-press-office/2014/11/11/us-china-joint-announcement -climate-change (accessed February 1, 2019).

52 Seb Henbest et al., *New Energy Outlook 2018: BNEF's Annual Long-Term Economic Analysis of the World's Power Sector out to 2050,* Bloomberg-NEF, 2018, https://bnef.turtl.co/story/neo2018?teaser=true (accessed January 16, 2019).

53 Li Hejun, *China's New Energy Revolution: How the World Super Power Is Fostering Economic Development and Sustainable Growth Through Thin Film Solar Technology* (New York: McGraw Hill Education, 2015), x–16.

54 Hanergy Holding Group Limited, "Hanergy and the Climate Group Host Forum on 'The Third Industrial Revolution & China' with Dr. Jeremy Rifkin," news release, Cision PR Newswire, September 9, 2013, https://www.prnewswire.com/news-releases/hanergy-and-the-climate -group-host-forum-on-the-third-industrial-revolution—china-with-dr -jeremy-rifkin-222930411.html (accessed March 23, 2019).

55 Hanergy and APO Group–Africa Newsroom, "Running Without Charging: Hanergy Offers New Solar-Powered Express Delivery Cars to China's Top Delivery Companies," news release, December 2018, https:// www.africa-newsroom.com/press/running-without-charging-hanergy -offers-new-solarpowered-express-delivery-cars-to-chinas-top-delivery -companies?lang=en (accessed March 5, 2019).

56 "Hanergy's Alta Devices Leads the Industry, Setting New Efficiency Record for Its Solar Cell," PV Europe, November 15, 2018, https://www .pveurope.eu/Company-News/Hanergy-s-Alta-Devices-Leads-the -Industry-Setting-New-Efficiency-Record-for-Its-Solar-Cell (accessed March 5, 2019).

57 Michael Renner et al., *Renewable Energy and Jobs: Annual Review 2018,* International Renewable Energy Agency, https://www.irena.org/-/media /Files/IRENA/Agency/Publication/2018/May/IRENA_RE_Jobs _Annual_Review_2018.pdf (accessed March 13, 2019), 15.

58 CPS Energy, "Who We Are," https://www.cpsenergy.com/en/about-us /who-we-are.html (accessed February 22, 2019).

59 Greg Harman, "Jeremy Rifkin on San Antonio, the European Union, and the Lessons Learned in Our Push for a Planetary-Scale Power Shift," *San Antonio Current,* September 27, 2011, https://www.sacurrent.com

/sanantonio/jeremy-rifkin-on-san-antonio-the-european-union-and
-the-lessons-learned-in-our-push-for-a-planetary-scale-power-shift
/Content?oid=2242809 (accessed March 24, 2019).

60　Business Wire, "RC Accepts Application for Two New Nuclear Units in
Texas," news release, November 30, 2007, https://www.businesswire.com
/news/home/20071130005184/en/NRC-Accepts-Application-Nuclear
-Units-Texas (accessed March 14, 2019).

61　"NRG, CPS Energy Meet with Toshiba on Nuclear Cost," Reuters, November 12, 2009, https://www.reuters.com/article/utilities-nuclear-nrg/nrg-cps
-energy-meet-with-toshiba-on-nuclear-cost-idUSN1250181920091112
(accessed March 23, 2019).

62　Lazard, "Lazard's Levelized Cost of Energy Analysis—Version 12.0."

63　Gavin Bade, "Southern Increases Vogtle Nuke Price Tag by $1.1 Billion,"
Utility Dive, August 8, 2018, https://www.utilitydive.com/news/southern
-increases-vogtle-nuke-pricetag-by-11-billion/529682/ (accessed May 8,
2019); Grace Dobush, "The Last Nuclear Power Plant Under Construction in the U.S. Lives to See Another Day," *Fortune*, September 27, 2018,
http://fortune.com/2018/09/27/vogtle-nuclear-power-plant-construction
-deal/ (accessed March 28, 2019).

64　Rye Druzin, "Texas Wind Generation Keeps Growing, State Remains at No.
1," *Houston Chronicle,* August 23, 2018, https://www.houstonchronicle
.com/business/energy/article/Texas-wind-generation-keeps-growing
-state-13178629.php (accessed March 24, 2019).

65　Mark Reagan, "CPS Energy Sets One-Day Record for Wind Energy Powering San Antonio," *San Antonio Current*, May 31, 2016, https://www
.sacurrent.com/the-daily/archives/2016/03/31/cps-energy-sets-one-day
-record-for-wind-energy-powering-san-antonio (accessed March 24,
2019).

66　Gavin Bade, "Chicago's REV: How ComEd Is Reinventing Itself as a Smart
Energy Platform," *Utility Dive,* March 31, 2016, https://www.utilitydive
.com/news/chicagos-rev-how-comed-is-reinventing-itself-as-a-smart
-energy-platform/416623/ (accessed February 7, 2019).

67　Ibid.

68　Ben Caldecott et al., *Stranded Assets and Renewables: How the Energy
Transition Affects the Value of Energy Reserves, Buildings and Capital
Stock*, International Renewable Energy Agency, 2017, 5.

69　Ibid., 6.

70　Ibid., 7.

CHAPTER 3

1　Isabella Burch and Jock Gilchrist, *Survey of Global Activity to Phase Out
Internal Combustion Engine Vehicles,* ed. Ann Hancock and Gemma
Waaland, Center for Climate Change, September 2018 revision, https://
climateprotection.org/wp-content/uploads/2018/10/Survey-on-Global

-Activities-to-Phase-Out-ICE-Vehicles-FINAL-Oct-3-2018.pdf (accessed March 24, 2019), 2.

2 Alex Longley, "BofA Sees Oil Demand Peaking by 2030 as Electric Vehicles Boom," Bloomberg, January 22, 2018, https://www.bloomberg .com/news/articles/2018-01-22/bofa-sees-oil-demand-peaking-by-2030 -as-electric-vehicles-boom (accessed March 24, 2019); *Batteries Update: Oil Demand Could Peak by 2030,* Fitch Ratings, 2018, http://cdn.roxhill media.com/production/email/attachment/660001_670000/Fitch_Oil%20 Demand%20Could%20Peak%20by%202030.pdf (accessed March 24, 2019), 2.

3 Eric Garcetti, *L.A.'s Green New Deal: Sustainable City pLAn,* 2019, http:// plan.lamayor.org/sites/default/files/pLAn_2019_final.pdf (accessed May 9, 2019), 11.

4 Ron Bousso and Karolin Schaps, "Shell Sees Oil Demand Peaking by Late 2020s as Electric Car Sales Grow," Reuters, July 27, 2017, https:// www.reuters.com/article/us-oil-demand-shell/shell-sees-oil-demand -peaking-by-late-2020s-as-electric-car-sales-grow-idUSKBN1AC1MG (accessed March 24, 2019).

5 James Osborne, "Peak Oil Demand, a Theory with Many Doubters," *Houston Chronicle,* March 9, 2018, https://www.chron.com/business /energy/article/Peak-oil-demand-a-theory-with-many-doubters -12729734.php (accessed March 24, 2019).

6 "Daimler Trucks Is Connecting Its Trucks with the Internet," Daimler Global Media Site, March 2016, https://media.daimler.com/marsMediaSite /en/instance/ko/Daimler-Trucks-is-connecting-its-trucks-with-the -internet.xhtml?oid=9920445 (accessed February 7, 2019).

7 Ibid.

8 Steven Montgomery, "The Future of Transportation Is Driverless, Shared and Networked," Ford Social, https://social.ford.com/en_US/story/ford -community/move-freely/the-future-of-transportation-is-driverless -shared-and-networked.html (accessed March 23, 2019).

9 Barbora Bondorová and Greg Archer, *Does Sharing Cars Really Reduce Car Use?* Transport & Environment, 2017, https://www.transportenvironment .org/sites/te/files/publications/Does-sharing-cars-really-reduce-car-use -June%202017.pdf (accessed March 23, 2019), 1.

10 Lawrence D. Burns, "Sustainable Mobility: A Vision of Our Transport Future," *Nature* 497 (2013): 182, doi:10.1038/497181a.

11 Navigant Research, *Transportation Forecast: Light Duty Vehicles,* 2017, https://www.navigantresearch.com/reports/transportation-forecast -light-duty-vehicles (accessed March 24, 2019).

12 Burns, "Sustainable Mobility," 182.

13 Gunnela Hahn et al., *Framing Stranded Asset Risks in an Age of Disruption,* Stockholm Environment Institute, February 14, 2018, https://www

.sei.org/publications/framing-stranded-assets-age-disruption/ (accessed March 24, 2019), 31.

14 Colin McKerracher, *Electric Vehicles Outlook 2018*, BloombergNEF, https://about.bnef.com/electric-vehicle-outlook/ (accessed January 16, 2019).

15 Ibid.

16 Ibid.

17 Ibid.; Hahn et al., *Framing Stranded Asset Risks in an Age of Disruption*, 12.

18 Henbest et al., *New Energy Outlook 2018*.

19 Wood Mackenzie, *The Rise and Fall of Black Gold*, 2018, https://www .qualenergia.it/wp-content/uploads/2017/10/Thought_Leadership__ _Peak_Oil_Demand_LowRes.pdf (accessed March 23, 2019), 4.

20 James Arbib and Tony Seba, *Rethinking Transportation 2020–2030: The Disruption of Transportation and the Collapse of the Internal-Combustion Vehicle and Oil Industries*, a RethinkX Sector Disruption Report, May 2017, https://static1.squarespace.com/static/585c3439be65942f022bbf9b/t /591a2e4be6f2e1c13df930c5/1494888038959/RethinkX+Report_051517 .pdf (accessed March 23, 2019), 7.

21 Ibid., 7.

22 Ibid.

23 INRIX, "Los Angeles Tops INRIX Global Congestion Ranking," news release, 2017, http://inrix.com/press-releases/scorecard-2017/ (accessed March 23, 2019).

24 Arbib and Seba, *Rethinking Transportation 2020–2030,* 8.

25 Ibid., 15, 32.

26 Longley, "BofA Sees Oil Demand Peaking by 2030 as Electric Vehicles Boom"; Bousso and Schaps, "Shell Sees Oil Demand Peaking by Late 2020s."

27 Tom DiChristopher, "Big Oil Is Sowing the Seeds for a 'Super-Spike' in Crude Prices Above $150, Bernstein Warns," CNBC, July 6, 2018, https://www.cnbc.com/2018/07/06/big-oil-sowing-the-seeds-for-crude -prices-above-150-bernstein-warns.html (accessed May 10, 2019).

28 Ibid.

29 Assembly Bill No. 3232, Chapter 373 (Cal. 2018), https://leginfo.legislature .ca.gov/faces/billTextClient.xhtml?bill_id=201720180AB3232 (accessed March 23, 2019).

30 "Zero Net Energy," California Public Utilities Commission, http://www .cpuc.ca.gov/zne/ (accessed February 8, 2019).

31 Yolande Barnes, Paul Tostevin, and Vladimir Tikhnenko, *Around the World in Dollars and Cents,* Savills World Research, 2016, http://pdf .savills.asia/selected-international-research/1601-around-the-world-in -dollars-and-cents-2016-en.pdf (accessed March 23, 2019), 5.

32 Mike Betts et al., *Global Construction 2030: A Global Forecast for the Construction Industry to 2030,* Global Construction Perspectives and

Oxford Economics, 2015, https://www.globalconstruction2030.com/ (accessed March 23, 2019), 6.

33 Heidi Garrett-Peltier, *Employment Estimates for Energy Efficiency Retrofits of Commercial Buildings,* University of Massachusetts Political Economy Research Institute, 2011, https://www.peri.umass.edu/publication /item/426-employment-estimates-for-energy-efficiency-retrofits-of -commercial-buildings (accessed March 24, 2019), 2.

34 "Questions and Answers: Energy Efficiency Tips for Buildings and Heating," Federal Ministry for the Environment, Nature Conservation and Nuclear Safety (Germany), https://www.bmu.de/en/topics/climate -energy/energy-efficiency/buildings/questions-and-answers-energy -efficiency-tips-for-buildings-and-heating/ (accessed February 1, 2019); John Calvert and Kaylin Woods, "Climate Change, Construction and Labour in Europe: A Study of the Contribution of Building Workers and Their Unions to 'Greening' the Built Environment in Germany, the United Kingdom and Denmark," paper presented at the Work in a Warming World (W3) Researchers' Workshop "Greening Work in a Chilly Climate," Toronto, November 2011, http://warming.apps01.yorku.ca/wp-content /uploads/WP_2011-04_Calvert_Climate-Change-Construction-Labour -in-Europe.pdf (accessed March 23, 2019), 15.

35 *The Internet of Things Business Index: A Quiet Revolution Gathers Pace,* Economist Intelligence Unit, 2013, http://fliphtml5.com/atss/gzeh/basic (accessed May 9, 2019), 10.

36 Jeremy Rifkin, *The Zero Marginal Cost Society: The Internet of Things, the Collaborative Commons, and the Eclipse of Capitalism* (New York: Palgrave Macmillan, 2014).

37 Haier, "Haier Group Announces Phase 2.0 of Its Cornerstone 'Rendan-heyi' Business Model," Cision PR Newswire, September 21, 2015, https:// www.prnewswire.com/news-releases/haier-group-announces-phase -20-of-its-cornerstone-rendanheyi-business-model-300146135.html (accessed March 5, 2019).

38 Jim Stengel, "Wisdom from the Oracle of Qingdao," *Forbes,* November 13, 2012, https://www.forbes.com/sites/jimstengel/2012/11/13/wisdom-from -the-oracle-of-qingdao/#3439fecd624f (accessed March 5, 2019); Haier, "Zhang Ruimin: Nine Years' Exploration of Haier's Business Models for the Internet Age," February 25, 2015, http://www.haier.net/en/about _haier/news/201502/t20150225_262109.shtml (accessed March 5, 2019).

39 Garrett-Peltier, *Employment Estimates for Energy Efficiency Retrofits of Commercial Buildings,* 2.

40 Kevin Muldoon-Smith and Paul Greenhalgh, "Understanding Climate-related Stranded Assets in the Global Real Estate Sector," in *Stranded Assets and the Environment: Risk, Resilience and Opportunity,* ed. Ben Caldecott (London: Routledge, 2018), 154; Kevin Muldoon-Smith and Paul Greenhalgh, "Suspect Foundations: Developing an Understanding

of Climate-Related Stranded Assets in the Global Real Estate Sector," *Energy Research & Social Science* 54 (August 2019): 62.

41 M. J. Kelly, *Britain's Building Stock—A Carbon Challenge* (London: DCLG, 2008).

42 Ben Caldecott, "Introduction: Stranded Assets and the Environment," in Caldecott, *Stranded Assets and the Environment*, 6.

43 "More Than 250 US Mayors Aim at 100% Renewable Energy by 2035," United Nations, June 28, 2017, https://unfccc.int/news/more-than-250-us -mayors-aim-at-100-renewable-energy-by-2035 (accessed March 24, 2019).

44 Muldoon-Smith and Greenhalgh, "Understanding Climate-related Stranded Assets in the Global Real Estate Sector," 157.

45 Ibid., 158.

46 Ibid., 159.

47 Lara Ettenson, "U.S. Clean Energy Jobs Surpass Fossil Fuel Employ- ment," NRDC, February 1, 2017, https://www.nrdc.org/experts/lara -ettenson/us-clean-energy-jobs-surpass-fossil-fuel-employment (ac- cessed February 25, 2019); US Department of Energy, *2017 U.S. Energy and Employment Report*, https://www.energy.gov/downloads/2017-us -energy-and-employment-report (accessed March 24, 2019).

48 Ettenson, "U.S. Clean Energy Jobs Surpass Fossil Fuel Employment."

49 Brookings Institution, *Advancing Inclusion Through Clean Energy Jobs*, April 2019, https://www.brookings.edu/wp-content/uploads/2019/04 /2019.04_metro_Clean-Energy-Jobs_Report_Muro-Tomer-Shivaran -Kane.pdf#page=14.

50 Ibid.

51 "Mayor Bowser Opens the DC Infrastructure Academy," press re- lease, March 12, 2018, https://dc.gov/release/mayor-bowser-opens-dc -infrastructure-academy.

52 Fabio Monforti-Ferrario et al., *Energy Use in the EU Food Sector: State of Play and Opportunities for Improvement*, ed. Fabio Monforti-Ferrario and Irene Pinedo Pascua, European Commission Joint Research Cen- tre, 2015, http://publications.jrc.ec.europa.eu/repository/bitstream /JRC96121/ldna27247enn.pdf (accessed March 23, 2019), 7.

53 Pierre J. Gerber et al., *Tackling Climate Change Through Livestock: A Global Assessment of Emissions and Mitigation Opportunities* (Rome: Food and Agriculture Organization of the United Nations, 2013), xii.

54 Food and Agricultural Organization of the United Nations, *Livestock and Landscapes*, 2012, http://www.fao.org/3/ar591e/ar591e.pdf (accessed March 23, 2019), 1.

55 Timothy P. Robinson et al., "Mapping the Global Distribution of Live- stock," *PLoS ONE* 9, no. 5 (2014): 1, doi:10.1371/journal.pone.0096084; Susan Solomon et al., *AR4 Climate Change 2007: The Physical Science Basis*, Intergovernmental Panel on Climate Change, https://www.ipcc .ch/report/ar4/wg1/ (accessed March 24, 2019), 33.

56   H. Steinfeld et al., *Livestock's Long Shadow* (Rome: FAO, 2006), xxi.

57   Emily S. Cassidy et al., "Redefining Agricultural Yields: From Tonnes to People Nourished per Hectare," *Environmental Research Letters* 8, no. 3 (2013): 4, doi:10.1088/1748-9326/8/3/034015.

58   Janet Ranganathan et al., "Shifting Diets for a Sustainable Food Future," World Resources Institute Working Paper, 2016, https://www.wri.org /sites/default/files/Shifting_Diets_for_a_Sustainable_Food_Future_0 .pdf (accessed March 23, 2019), 21.

59   Alyssa Newcomb, "From Taco Bell to Carl's Jr., Grab-and-Go Vegetarian Options Are on the Rise," NBC News, February 6, 2019, https://www .nbcnews.com/business/consumer/taco-bell-mcdonald-s-vegetarian -options-are-rise-n966986 (accessed March 6, 2019); Danielle Wiener-Bronner, "Burger King Plans to Roll Out Impossible Whopper Across the United States," CNN, April 29, 2019, https://www.cnn.com/2019 /04/29/business/burger-king-impossible-rollout/index.html (accessed May 9, 2019).

60   Monforti-Ferrario et al., *Energy Use in the EU Food Sector,* 7.

61   Helga Willer and Julia Lernoud, eds., *The World of Organic Agriculture: Statistics and Emerging Trends 2018,* FiBL and IFOAM–Organics International, https://shop.fibl.org/CHde/mwdownloads/download/link/id /1093/?ref=1 (accessed March 24, 2019).

62   Organic Trade Association, "Maturing U.S. Organic Sector Sees Steady Growth of 6.4 Percent in 2017," news release, May 18, 2018, https://ota .com/news/press-releases/20236 (accessed February 14, 2019).

63   Karlee Weinmann, "Thanks to Co-op, Small Iowa Town Goes Big on Solar," Institute for Local Self-Reliance, February 3, 2017, https://ilsr.org /thanks-to-co-op-small-iowa-town-goes-big-on-solar (accessed February 14, 2019).

64   Debbie Barker and Michael Pollan, "A Secret Weapon to Fight Climate Change: Dirt," *Washington Post*, December 4, 2015, https://www .washingtonpost.com/opinions/2015/12/04/fe22879e-990b-11e5-8917 -653b65c809eb_story.html?utm_term=.b2aa65cc4e76 (accessed March 7, 2019).

65   Jeff Stein, "Congress Just Passed an $867 Billion Farm Bill. Here's What's in It," *Washington Post*, December 12, 2018, https://www.washingtonpost .com/business/2018/12/11/congresss-billion-farm-bill-is-out-heres-whats -it/?utm_term=.042ac7ab46fa (accessed March 6, 2019).

66   April Reese, "Public Lands Are Critical to Any Green New Deal," *Outside*, April 8, 2019, https://www.outsideonline.com/2393257/green-new -deal-public-lands-clean-energy (accessed April 8, 2019).

67   Matthew D. Merrill et al., *Federal Lands Greenhouse Gas Emissions and Sequestration in the United States: Estimates for 2005–14*, US Geological Survey, 2018, https://pubs.usgs.gov/sir/2018/5131/sir20185131.pdf (accessed May 9, 2019).

68 Ibid.

69 Ibid.

70 Marie-Jean-Antoine-Nicolas Caritat, Marquis de Condorcet, *Outlines of an Historical View of the Progress of the Human Mind* (Philadelphia: M. Carey, 1796) https://oll.libertyfund.org/titles/1669 (accessed May 11, 2019).

CHAPTER 4

1   J.-F. Mercure et al., "Macroeconomic Impact of Stranded Fossil Fuel Assets," *Nature Climate Change* 8, no. 7 (2018): 588–93, doi:10.1038/s41558-018-0182-1.

2   "Declaration of the European Parliament on Establishing a Green Hydrogen Economy and a Third Industrial Revolution in Europe Through a Partnership with Committed Regions and Cities, SMEs and Civil Society Organisations," 2007, https://eur-lex.europa.eu/legal-content/EN/TXT/?uri=CELEX%3A52007IP0197 (accessed March 23, 2019).

3   "Directive 2009/28/EC of the European Parliament and of the Council on the Promotion of the Use of Energy from Renewable Sources," *Official Journal of the European Union* (2009): L 140/17.

4   "Renewable Energy: Are Feed-in Tariffs Going out of Style?" *Power-Technology*, January 18, 2017, https://www.power-technology.com/features/featurerenewable-energy-are-feed-in-tariffs-going-out-of-style-5718419/ (accessed March 24, 2019).

5   David Coady et al., "How Large Are Global Fossil Fuel Subsidies?" *World Development* 91 (March 2017): 11, doi:10.1016/j.worlddev.2016.10.004.

6   Kingsmill Bond, *2020 Vision: Why You Should See the Fossil Fuel Peak Coming,* Carbon Tracker, September 2018, https://www.carbontracker.org/reports/2020-vision-why-you-should-see-the-fossil-fuel-peak-coming/ (accessed March 23, 2019), 31.

7   Kingsmill Bond, *Myths of the Energy Transition: Renewables Are Too Small to Matter,* Carbon Tracker, October 30, 2018, https://www.carbontracker.org/myths-of-the-transition-renewables-are-too-small/ (accessed March 23, 2019), 1.

8   Roger Fouquet, *Heat, Power and Light: Revolutions in Energy Services* (New York: Edward Elgar, 2008).

9   Bond, *Myths of the Energy Transition,* 3–4.

10 Bond, *2020 Vision,* 4.

11 Ibid., 5.

12 Ibid., 32.

13 Bobby Magill, "2019 Outlook: Solar, Wind Could Hit 10 Percent of U.S. Electricity," Bloomberg Environment, December 26, 2018, https://news.bloombergenvironment.com/environment-and-energy/2019-outlook-solar-wind-could-hit-10-percent-of-us-electricity (accessed March 23, 2019); Bond, *2020 Vision,* 18, 22.

14   Bond, *2020 Vision*, 31.

15   Ibid.

16   Ibid., 32.

17   Magill, "2019 Outlook."

18   Megan Mahajan, "Plunging Prices Mean Building New Renewable Energy Is Cheaper Than Running Existing Coal," *Forbes,* December 3, 2018, https://www.forbes.com/sites/energyinnovation/2018/12/03/plunging -prices-mean-building-new-renewable-energy-is-cheaper-than-running -existing-coal/#3918a07731f3 (accessed March 24, 2019).

19   Justin Wilkes, Jacopo Moccia, and Mihaela Dragan, *Wind in Power: 2011 European Statistics,* European Wind Energy Association, February 2011, https://windeurope.org/about-wind/statistics/european/wind -in-power-2011/ (accessed March 23, 2019), 6.

20   T. W. Brown et al., "Response to 'Burden of Proof: A Comprehensive Review of the Feasibility of 100% Renewable-Electricity Systems," *Renewable and Sustainable Energy Reviews* 92 (2018): 834–47; Ben Elliston, Iain MacGill, and Mark Diesendorf, "Least Cost 100% Renewable Electricity Scenarios in the Australian National Electricity Market," *Energy Policy* 59 (August 2013): 270–82.

21   Kathryn Hopkins, "Fuel Prices: Iran Missile Launches Send Oil to $147 a Barrel Record," *The Guardian,* July 11, 2008, https://www.theguardian .com/business/2008/jul/12/oil.commodities (accessed March 23, 2019).

22   Gebisa Ejeta, "Revitalizing Agricultural Research for Global Food Security," *Food Security* 1, no. 4 (2018): 395, doi:10.1007/s12571-009-0045-8.

23   Jad Mouawad, "Exxon Mobil Profit Sets Record Again," *New York Times,* February 1, 2008, https://www.nytimes.com/2008/02/01/business/01cnd -exxon.html (accessed March 24, 2019).

24   Gunnela Hahn et al., *Framing Stranded Asset Risks in an Age of Disruption,* Stockholm Environment Institute, March 2018, https://f88973py3 n24eoxbq1o3o0fz-wpengine.netdna-ssl.com/wp-content/uploads /2018/03/stranded-assets-age-disruption.pdf (accessed March 23, 2019), 14.

25   Ibid., 12, 15.

26   US Energy Information Administration, *Annual Energy Outlook 2019,* January 2019, https://www.eia.gov/outlooks/aeo/ (accessed March 24, 2019), 72.

27   Christopher Arcus, "Wind & Solar + Storage Prices Smash Records," CleanTechnica, January 11, 2018, https://cleantechnica.com/2018/01/11 /wind-solar-storage-prices-smash-records/ (accessed March 23, 2019).

28   "Tumbling Costs for Wind, Solar, Batteries Are Squeezing Fossil Fuels," BloombergNEF, March 28, 2018, https://about.bnef.com/blog/tumbling -costs-wind-solar-batteries-squeezing-fossil-fuels (accessed March 23, 2019).

29   Gavin Bade, "'Eyes Wide Open': Despite Climate Risks, Utilities Bet

Big on Natural Gas," *Utility Dive,* September 27, 2016, https://www
.utilitydive.com/news/eyes-wide-open-despite-climate-risks-utilities
-bet-big-on-natural-gas/426869/ (accessed March 24, 2019).

30 International Renewable Energy Agency, *A New World: The Geopolitics of the Energy Transition,* January 2019, https://www.irena.org
/publications/2019/Jan/A-New-World-The-Geopolitics-of-the-Energy
-Transformation (accessed March 23, 2019), 40.

31 Enerdata, "Natural Gas Production," *Global Energy Statistical Yearbook 2018,* https://yearbook.enerdata.net/natural-gas/world-natural-gas
-production-statistics.html (accessed February 19, 2019).

32 Mark Dyson, Alexander Engel, and Jamil Farbes, *The Economics of Clean
Energy Portfolios: How Renewables and Distributed Energy Resources
Are Outcompeting and Can Strand Investment in Natural Gas–Fired
Generation,* Rocky Mountain Institute, May 2018, https://www.rmi.org
/wp-content/uploads/2018/05/RMI_Executive_Summary_Economics
_of_Clean_Energy_Portfolios.pdf (accessed March 23, 2019), 6.

33 Ibid.

34 Ibid., 8–9.

35 Ibid., 10.

36 Enerdata, "Crude Oil Production," *Global Energy Statistical Yearbook 2018,*
https://yearbook.enerdata.net/crude-oil/world-production-statitistics
.html [*sic*] (accessed February 19, 2019).

37 Julie Gordon and Jessica Jaganathan, "UPDATE 5—Massive Canada
LNG Project Gets Green Light as Asia Demand for Fuel Booms," CNBC,
October 2, 2018, https://www.cnbc.com/2018/10/02/reuters-america
-update-5-massive-canada-lng-project-gets-green-light-as-asia-demand
-for-fuel-booms.html (accessed March 22, 2019).

38 "Coastal GasLink," TransCanada Operations, https://www.transcanada
.com/en/operations/natural-gas/coastal-gaslink/ (accessed February 19,
2019).

39 Gordon and Jaganathan, "UPDATE 5."

40 Jurgen Weiss et al., *LNG and Renewable Power: Risk and Opportunity in
a Changing World,* Brattle Group, January 15, 2016, https://brattlefiles
.blob.core.windows.net/files/7222_lng_and_renewable_power_-_risk
_and_opportunity_in_a_changing_world.pdf (accessed March 22,
2019), iii.

41 International Renewable Energy Agency, *A New World,* 40.

42 Weiss et al., *LNG and Renewable Power,* v.

43 Ibid., vi–viii.

44 Akshat Rathi, "The EU has spent nearly $500 million on technol-
ogy to fight climate change—with little to show for it," *Quartz,* October
23, 2018, https://qz.com/1431655/the-eu-spent-e424-million-on-carbon
-capture-with-little-to-show-for-it/ (accessed April 9, 2019); European
Court of Auditors, *Demonstrating Carbon Capture and Storage and*

Innovative Renewables at Commercial Scale in the EU: Intended Progress Not Achieved in the Past Decade, October 23, 2018, https://www.eca .europa.eu/Lists/ECADocuments/SR18_24/SR_CCS_EN.pdf (accessed May 10, 2019).

45 Vaclav Smil, "Global Energy: The Latest Infatuations," *American Scientist* 99 (May–June 2011): 212, doi: 10.1511/2011.90.212.

46 Joe Room, "Mississippi Realizes How to Make a Clean Coal Plant Work: Run It on Natural Gas," *ThinkProgress*, June 22, 2017, https:// thinkprogress.org/clean-coal-natural-gas-kemper-24e5e6db64fd/ (accessed April 5, 2019).

47 "Why Aren't All Commercial Flights Powered by Sustainable Fuel?" *The Economist*, March 15, 2018, https://www.economist.com/the-economist -explains/2018/03/15/why-arent-all-commercial-flights-powered-by -sustainable-fuel (accessed May 2, 2019).

48 Bioways, *D2.1 Bio-based products and applications potential*, May 31, 2017, http://www.bioways.eu/download.php?f=150&l=en&key=441a4e6 a27f83a8e828b802c37adc6e1, 8–9.

49 Glenn-Marie Lange, Quentin Wodon, and Kevin Carey, eds., *The Changing Wealth of Nations 2018: Building a Sustainable Future* (Washington, DC: World Bank, 2018), 103, http://hdl.handle.net/10986/29001.

50 Ibid., 14.

51 Lange, Wodon, and Carey, *The Changing Wealth of Nations*, 111.

52 Lazard, "Lazard Releases Annual Levelized Cost of Energy and Levelized Cost of Storage Analyses," news release, November 8, 2018, https:// www.lazard.com/media/450781/11-18-lcoelcos-press-release-2018_final .pdf (accessed March 22, 2019).

53 Ibid.

54 Bank of England, "PRA Review Finds That 70% of Banks Recognise That Climate Change Poses Financial Risks," news release, September 26, 2018, https://www.bankofengland.co.uk/news/2018/september/transition-in -thinking-the-impact-of-climate-change-on-the-uk-banking-sector (accessed March 19, 2019).

55 Task Force on Climate-Related Financial Disclosures, *Recommendations of the Task Force on Climate-Related Financial Disclosures*, June 2017, https://www.fsb-tcfd.org/wp-content/uploads/2017/06/FINAL-TCFD -Report-062817.pdf (accessed March 24, 2019), iii.

56 Ibid., ii, citing Economist Intelligence Unit, *The Cost of Inaction: Recognising the Value at Risk from Climate Change*, 2015, 41.

57 Task Force on Climate-Related Financial Disclosures, *Recommendations*, ii, citing International Energy Agency, "Chapter 2: Energy Sector Investment to Meet Climate Goals," in *Perspectives for the Energy Transition: Investment Needs for a Low-Carbon Energy System*, OECD/IEA and IRENA, 2017, 51.

58 Economist Intelligence Unit, *The Cost of Inaction: Recognising the Value*

at Risk from Climate Change, 2015, https://eiuperspectives.economist .com/sites/default/files/The%20cost%20of%20inaction_0.pdf (accessed April 10, 2019), 17.

59 Task Force on Climate-Related Financial Disclosures, *2018 Status Report*, September 2018, https://www.fsb-tcfd.org/wp-content/uploads/2018/09 /FINAL-2018-TCFD-Status-Report-092618.pdf (accessed April 23, 2019), 2.

60 Bloomberg Philanthropies, "TCFD Publishes First Status Report While Industry Support Continues to Grow," news release, September 26, 2019, https://www.bloomberg.org/press/releases/tcfd-publishes-first-status -report-industry-support-continues-grow/ (accessed March 24, 2019).

CHAPTER 5

1 Tom Harrison et al., *Not Long Now: Survey of Fund Managers' Responses to Climate-Related Risks Facing Fossil Fuel Companies,* Climate Change Collaboration and UK Sustainable Investment and Finance Association, April 2018, http://uksif.org/wp-content/uploads/2018/04/UPDATED -UKSIF-Not-Long-Now-Survey-report-2018-ilovepdf-compressed.pdf (accessed March 24, 2019), 3, 5; Felicia Jackson, "Three Risks That Are Haunting Big Oil," *Forbes,* April 26, 2018, https://www.forbes.com /sites/feliciajackson/2018/04/26/three-risks-that-are-haunting-big-oil /#335c06212739 (accessed March 29, 2019).

2 Thinking Ahead Institute, *Global Pension Assets Study 2018,* Willis Towers Watson, February 5, 2018, https://www.thinkingaheadinstitute.org /en/Library/Public/Research-and-Ideas/2018/02/Global-Pension-Asset -Survey-2018 (accessed March 23, 2019), 3, 5, 11.

3 International Trade Union Confederation, "Just Transition Centre," https://www.ituc-csi.org/just-transition-centre (accessed February 19, 2019).

4 Pension Rights Center, "How Many American Workers Participate in Workplace Retirement Plans?" January 18, 2018, http://www.pensionrights .org/publications/statistic/how-many-american-workers-participate -workplace-retirement-plans (accessed March 24, 2019).

5 *Congressional Record,* May 13, 1946, 4891–911.

6 Personal interview with William Winpisinger, July 18, 1977.

7 Nicholas Lemann, *The Promised Land: The Great Black Migration and How It Changed America* (New York: Vintage Books, 1992), 5.

8 Willis Peterson and Yoav Kislev, "The Cotton Harvester in Retrospect: Labor Displacement or Replacement?" University of Minnesota, Department of Agricultural and Applied Economics, Staff Paper P81-25, September 1991, 1–2.

9 Lemann, *The Promised Land,* 6.

10 Marcus Jones, *Black Migration in the United States: With Emphasis on Selected Central Cities* (Saratoga, CA: Century 21 Publishing, 1980), 46.

11   William Julius Wilson, *The Declining Significance of Race* (Chicago: University of Chicago Press, 1978), 93; Thomas J. Sugrue, "The Structures of Urban Poverty: The Reorganization of Space and Work in Three Periods of American History," in *The Underclass Debate: Views from History,* ed. Michael Katz (Princeton: Princeton University Press, 1993), 102.

12   UAW data submitted to *Hearings Before the United States Commission on Civil Rights,* held in Detroit, December 14–15, 1960 (Washington, DC: USGPO, 1961), 63–65.

13   John Judis, "The Jobless Recovery," *New Republic,* March 15, 1993, 20.

14   Will Barnes, "The Second Industrialization of the American South," 2007, posted by IDP August 1, 2013, https://libcom.org/library/second-industrialization-american-south (accessed April 16, 2019).

15   Jeremy Rifkin and Randy Barber, *The North Will Rise Again: Pensions, Politics and Power in the 1980s* (Boston: Beacon Press, 1978), 7.

16   Ibid., 10–11.

17   Ibid., 13.

18   Ibid.

19   Michael Decourcy Hinds, "Public Pension Funds Tempt States in Need," *New York Times,* December 2, 1989, https://www.nytimes.com/1989/12/02/us/public-pension-funds-tempt-states-in-need.html (accessed February 28, 2019); Jeffery Kaye, "Unions Map Investment Guidelines," *Washington Post,* March 9, 1980, https://www.washingtonpost.com/archive/business/1980/03/09/unions-map-investment-guidelines/2008e77d-5e0a-42bf-99fb-6980854f0b77/?utm_term=.a04a4b604fbf (accessed April 10, 2019).

20   Owen Davis, "All Roads Lead to Wall Street," *Dissent Magazine,* October 16, 2018, https://www.dissentmagazine.org/online_articles/working-class-shareholder-labor-activism-finance (accessed February 19, 2019).

21   Richard Marens, "Waiting for the North to Rise: Revisiting Barber and Rifkin After a Generation of Union Financial Activism in the U.S.," *Journal of Business Ethics* 52, no. 1 (2004): 109.

22   Ibid.

23   Richard Marens, "Extending Frames and Breaking Windows: Labor Activists as Shareholder Advocates," *Ephemera* 7, no. 3 (2007): 457, http://www.ephemerajournal.org/sites/default/files/7-3marens.pdf (accessed March 23, 2019).

24   "1,000+ Divestment Commitments," Fossil Free, https://gofossilfree.org/divestment/commitments/ (accessed March 15, 2019).

25   ICLEI, *New York City Moves to Divest Pension Funds from Billions of Dollars in Fossil Fuel Reserves,* 2018, http://icleiusa.org/wp-content/uploads/2018/09/NYC-Divestment-Case-Study-ICLEI-USA.pdf (accessed March 23, 2019), 9.

26   Oliver Milman, "New York City Plans to Divest $5bn from Fossil Fuels and Sue Oil Companies," *The Guardian,* January 10, 2018, https://www

.theguardian.com/us-news/2018/jan/10/new-york-city-plans-to-divest
-5bn-from-fossil-fuels-and-sue-oil-companies (accessed February 4,
2019).

27 City of New York, Community Development Block Grant Disaster Recovery, "Impact of Hurricane Sandy," https://www1.nyc.gov/site/cdbgdr
/about/About%20Hurricane%20Sandy.page (accessed February 26, 2019).

28 Emily Cassidy, "5 Major Cities Threatened by Climate Change and Sea
Level Rise," *City Fix*, October 15, 2018, https://thecityfix.com/blog/5
-major-cities-threatened-climate-change-sea-level-rise-emily-cassidy/
(accessed March 23, 2019).

29 ICLEI, *New York City Moves to Divest*, 13.

30 City of New York, *One New York: The Plan for a Strong and Just City*,
2015, http://www.nyc.gov/html/onenyc/downloads/pdf/publications
/OneNYC.pdf (accessed March 23, 2019), 166.

31 Bill de Blasio and Sadiq Khan, "As New York and London Mayors, We
Call on All Cities to Divest from Fossil Fuels," *The Guardian*, September 10, 2018, https://www.theguardian.com/commentisfree/2018/sep/10
/london-new-york-cities-divest-fossil-fuels-bill-de-blasio-sadiq-khan
(accessed March 24, 2019).

32 Ibid.

33 Gail Moss, "Biggest US Pension Funds 'Must Consider Climate-Related
Risks,'" *Investments & Pensions Europe*, September 3, 2018, https://www
.ipe.com/news/esg/biggest-us-pension-funds-must-consider-climate
-related-risks-updated/10026446.article (accessed March 23, 2019).

34 California State Legislature, "Bill Information," SB-964, Public Employees' Retirement Fund and Teachers' Retirement Fund: Investments:
Climate-Related Financial Risk (2017–18), https://leginfo.legislature.ca
.gov/faces/billStatusClient.xhtml?bill_id=201720180SB964   (accessed
March 23, 2019).

35 Ibid.

36 California State Teachers' Retirement System, "CalSTRS at a Glance,"
fact sheet, January 2019, https://www.calstrs.com/sites/main/files/file
-attachments/calstrsataglance.pdf (accessed February 26, 2019).

37 CalPERS, "CalPERS Board Elects Henry Jones as President, Theresa
Taylor as Vice President," news release, January 22, 2019, https://
www.calpers.ca.gov/page/newsroom/calpers-news/2019/board-elects
-president-vice-president (accessed March 24, 2019).

38 Ivan Penn and Peter Eavis, "PG&E Is Cleared in Deadly Tubbs Fire of
2017," *New York Times*, January 24, 2019, https://www.nytimes.com
/2019/01/24/business/energy-environment/pge-tubbs-fire.html (accessed
March 4, 2019).

39 Rob Smith, "The World's Biggest Economies in 2018," World Economic
Forum, April 18, 2018, https://www.weforum.org/agenda/2018/04/the
-worlds-biggest-economies-in-2018/ (accessed March 23, 2019).

40   Patrick Collinson and Julia Kollewe, "UK Pension Funds Get Green Light to Dump Fossil Fuel Investments," *The Guardian*, June 18, 2018, https://www.theguardian.com/business/2018/jun/18/uk-pension-funds-get-green-light-to-dump-fossil-fuel-investments (accessed February 26, 2019).

41   Ibid.

42   Department for Work and Pensions, United Kingdom, *Consultation on Clarifying and Strengthening Trustees' Investment Duties: The Occupational Pension Schemes (Investment and Disclosure) (Amendment) Regulations 2018*, June 2018, https://assets.publishing.service.gov.uk/government/uploads/system/uploads/attachment_data/file/716949/consultation-clarifying-and-strengthening-trustees-investment-duties.pdf (accessed April 10, 2019), 19.

43   UNISON, *Local Government Pension Funds—Divest from Carbon Campaign: A UNISON Guide*, January 2018, https://www.unison.org.uk/content/uploads/2018/01/Divest-from-carbon-campaign.pdf (accessed March 23, 2019), 2.

44   Nina Chestney, "Ireland Commits to Divesting Public Funds from Fossil Fuel Companies," Reuters, July 12, 2018, https://www.reuters.com/article/us-ireland-fossilfuels-divestment/ireland-commits-to-divesting-public-funds-from-fossil-fuel-companies-idUSKBN1K22AA (accessed February 19, 2019).

45   Richard Milne and David Sheppard, "Norway's $1tn Wealth Fund Set to Cut Oil and Gas Stocks," *Financial Times*, March 8, 2019, https://www.ft.com/content/d32142a8-418f-11e9-b896-fe36ec32aece (accessed March 8, 2019).

46   Douglas Appell, "South Korean Pension Funds Declare War on Coal," *Pensions & Investments*, October 5, 2018, https://www.pionline.com/article/20181005/ONLINE/181009888/south-korean-pension-funds-declare-war-on-coal (accessed February 19, 2019).

47   Korea Sustainability Investing Forum, "Two Korean Pension Funds Worth US$22 Billion Exit Coal Finance," 350.org, October 4, 2018, http://world.350.org/east-asia/two-korean-pension-funds-worth-us22-billion-exit-coal-finance/ (accessed February 19, 2019).

48   Peter Bosshard, *Insuring Coal No More: The 2018 Scorecard on Insurance, Coal, and Climate Change*, Unfriend Coal, December 2018, https://unfriendcoal.com/2018scorecard/ (accessed March 23, 2019), 4–6.

49   Consumer Watchdog, "Top Ten U.S. Insurance Companies' Investment in Climate Change," https://www.consumerwatchdog.org/top-ten-us-insurance-companies-investment-climate-change (accessed March 18, 2019); Aon Benfield, *Weather, Climate & Catastrophic Insight: 2017 Annual Report*, http://thoughtleadership.aonbenfield.com/Documents/20180124-ab-if-annual-report-weather-climate-2017.pdf (accessed March 23, 2019), 30.

50 Vitality Katsenelson, "Stocks Are Somewhere Between Tremendously and Enormously Overvalued," *Advisor Perspectives,* October 30, 2018, https://www.advisorperspectives.com/articles/2018/10/30/stocks-are -somewhere-between-tremendously-and-enormously-overvalued (accessed February 19, 2019).

51 Pew Charitable Trusts, "The State Pension Funding Gap: 2015," April 20, 2017, https://www.pewtrusts.org/en/research-and-analysis/issue-briefs /2017/04/the-state-pension-funding-gap-2015 (accessed February 19, 2019).

52 Tom Sanzillo, "IEEFA Update: 2018 Ends with Energy Sector in Last Place in the S&P 500," Institute for Energy Economics and Financial Analysis, January 2, 2019, http://ieefa.org/ieefa-update-2018-ends-with -energy-sector-in-last-place-in-the-sp-500/ (accessed April 8, 2019).

53 Alison Moodie, "New York Pension Fund Could Have Made Billions by Divesting from Fossil Fuels—Report," *The Guardian,* March 4, 2016, https://www.theguardian.com/sustainable-business/2016/mar/04/fossil -fuel-divestment-new-york-state-pension-fund-hurricane-sandy-ftse (accessed February 19, 2019).

CHAPTER 6

1 Morgan Stanley Institute for Sustainable Investing, *Sustainable Signals: New Data from the Individual Investor,* 2017, https://www.morganstanley .com/pub/content/dam/msdotcom/ideas/sustainable-signals/pdf /Sustainable_Signals_Whitepaper.pdf (accessed March 23, 2019), 1.

2 Forum for Sustainable and Responsible Investment, "Sustainable Investing Assets Reach $12 Trillion as Reported by the US SIF Foundation's Biennial Report on US Sustainable, Responsible and Impact Investing Trends," news release, October 31, 2018, https://www.ussif.org/files /US%20SIF%20Trends%20Report%202018%20Release.pdf (accessed February 19, 2019).

3 George Serafeim, *Public Sentiment and the Price of Corporate Sustainability,* Harvard Business School Working Paper 19-044, 2018, https:// www.hbs.edu/faculty/Publication%20Files/19-044_a9bbfba2-55e1 -4540-bda5-8411776a42ae.pdf (accessed March 4, 2019); Nadja Guenster et al., "The Economic Value of Corporate Eco-Efficiency," *European Financial Management* 17, no. 4 (September 2011): 679–704, doi:10.1111/ j.1468-036X.2009.00532.x; Gordon Clark, Andreas Finer, and Michael Viehs, *From the Stockholder to the Stakeholder: How Sustainability Can Drive Financial Outperformance,* University of Oxford and Arabesque Partners, March 2015, https://arabesque.com/research/From_the _stockholder_to_the_stakeholder_web.pdf (accessed March 24, 2019).

4 Jessica Taylor, Alex Lake, and Christina Weimann, *The Carbon Scorecard,* S&P Dow Jones Indices, May 2018, https://us.spindices.com /documents/research/research-the-carbon-scorecard-may-2018.pdf (accessed March 23, 2019), 1.

5   Ibid.

6   Jonathan Woetzel et al., *Bridging Infrastructure Gaps: Has the World Made Progress?* McKinsey & Company, October 2017, https://www.mckinsey.com/industries/capital-projects-and-infrastructure/our-insights/bridging-infrastructure-gaps-has-the-world-made-progress (accessed March 24, 2019), 5; Jeffery Stupak, *Economic Impact of Infrastructure Investment,* Congressional Research Service, https://fas.org/sgp/crs/misc/R44896.pdf (accessed March 24, 2019), 1.

7   Ipsos, "Global Infrastructure Index—Public Satisfaction and Priorities 2018," 2018, https://www.ipsos.com/en/global-infrastructure-index-public-satisfaction-and-priorities-2018 (accessed February 27, 2019), 5.

8   Lydia DePillis, "Trump Unveils Infrastructure Plan," CNN, February 12, 2018, https://money.cnn.com/2018/02/11/news/economy/trump-infrastructure-plan-details/index.html (accessed February 27, 2019).

9   Ed O'Keefe and Steven Mufson, "Senate Democrats Unveil a Trump-Size Infrastructure Plan," *Washington Post,* January 24, 2017, https://www.washingtonpost.com/politics/democrats-set-to-unveil-a-trump-style-infrastructure-plan/2017/01/23/332be2dc-e1b3-11e6-a547-5fb9411d332c_story.html?utm_term=.0c4ac52f5d8c (accessed February 27, 2019).

10 "America's Splurge," *The Economist,* February 14, 2008, https://www.economist.com/briefing/2008/02/14/americas-splurge (accessed February 27, 2019).

11 "The Interstate Highway System," History (TV network), May 27, 2010, https://www.history.com/topics/us-states/interstate-highway-system (accessed February 27, 2019).

12 KEMA, *The U.S. Smart Grid Revolution: KEMA's Perspectives for Job Creation,* January 13, 2009, https://www.smartgrid.gov/files/The_US_Smart_Grid_Revolution_KEMA_Perspectives_for_Job_Cre_200907.pdf (accessed April 3, 2019), 1.

13 U.S. Department of Transportation Federal Highway Administration, "Why President Dwight D. Eisenhower Understood We Needed the Interstate System," updated July 24, 2017, https://www.fhwa.dot.gov/interstate/brainiacs/eisenhowerinterstate.cfm (accessed April 3, 2019).

14 Electric Power Research Institute, Estimating the Costs and Benefits of the Smart Grid: A Preliminary Estimate of the Investment Requirements and the Resultant Benefits of a Fully Functioning Smart Grid, March 2011, https://www.smartgrid.gov/files/Estimating_Costs_Benefits_Smart_Grid_Preliminary_Estimate_In_201103.pdf (accessed March 24, 2019), 1–4.

15 Terry Dinan, *Federal Support for Developing, Producing, and Using Fuels and Energy Technologies,* Congressional Budget Office, March 29, 2017, https://www.cbo.gov/system/files/115th-congress-2017-2018/reports/52521-energytestimony.pdf (accessed April 10, 2019), 3; David Funkhouser, "How Much Do Renewables Actually Depend on Tax

Breaks?" Earth Institute, Columbia University, March 16, 2018, https:// blogs.ei.columbia.edu/2018/03/16/how-much-do-renewables-actually -depend-on-tax-breaks/ (accessed March 28, 2019).

16   *The Plug-In Electric Vehicle Tax Credit*, Congressional Research Service, November 6, 2018, https://fas.org/sgp/crs/misc/IF11017.pdf (accessed April 10, 2019).

17   *United States Building Energy Efficiency Retrofits: Market Sizing and Financing Models*, Rockefeller Foundation and Deutsche Bank Group, March 2012, http://web.mit.edu/cron/project/EESP-Cambridge/Articles /Finance/Rockefeller%20and%20DB%20-%20March%202012%20-%20 Energy%20Efficiency%20Market%20Size%20and%20Finance%20Models .pdf (accessed April 10, 2019), 3.

18   Jürgen Weiss, J. Michael Hagerty, and María Castañer, *The Coming Electrification of the North American Economy: Why We Need a Robust Transmission Grid*, Brattle Group, March 1, 2019, https://manitobaenergy council.ca/information/the-coming-electrification-of-the-north-american -economy (accessed April 10, 2019).

19   Elizabeth McNichol, *It's Time for States to Invest in Infrastructure*, Center on Budget and Policy Priorities, 2017, https://www.cbpp.org/sites /default/files/atoms/files/2-23-16sfp.pdf (accessed March 23, 2019), 5.

20   Woetzel et al., *Bridging Infrastructure Gaps*, 5.

21   Jeffery Werling and Ronald Horst, *Catching Up: Greater Focus Needed to Achieve a More Competitive Infrastructure*, report to the National Association of Manufacturers, September 2014, https://www.nam.org/Issues /Infrastructure/Surface-Infrastructure/Infrastructure-Full-Report -2014.pdf (accessed March 12, 2019), 9.

22   Jeff Stein, "Ocasio-Cortez Wants Higher Taxes on Very Rich Americans. Here's How Much Money That Could Raise," *Washington Post*, January 5, 2019, https://www.washingtonpost.com/business/2019/01/05/ocasio -cortez-wants-higher-taxes-very-rich-americans-heres-how-much -money-could-that-raise/?utm_term=.bcc9d21df1ca (accessed March 28, 2019).

23   "The World's Billionaires, 2018 Ranking," *Forbes*, https://www.forbes .com/billionaires/list/ (accessed March 5, 2019).

24   Kathleen Elkins, "Bill Gates Suggests Higher Taxes on the Rich—The Current System Is 'Not Progressive Enough,' He Says," CNBC, February 14, 2019, https://www.cnbc.com/2019/02/13/bill-gates-suggests-higher-taxes -on-those-with-great-wealth.html (accessed March 1, 2019).

25   Emmie Martin, "Warren Buffett and Bill Gates Agree That the Rich Should Pay Higher Taxes—Here's What They Suggest," CNBC, February 26, 2019, https://www.cnbc.com/2019/02/25/warren-buffett-and-bill -gates-the-rich-should-pay-higher-taxes.html (accessed March 1, 2019).

26   American Society of Civil Engineers, *The 2017 Infrastructure Report Card: A Comprehensive Assessment of America's Infrastructure*, https://

www.infrastructurereportcard.org/wp-content/uploads/2017/01/2017
-Infrastructure-Report-Card.pdf (accessed March 12, 2019), 7.

27   Adam B. Smith, "2017 U.S. Billion-Dollar Weather and Climate Disasters: A Historic Year in Context," NOAA, January 8, 2018, https://www.climate.gov/news-features/blogs/beyond-data/2017-us-billion-dollar-weather-and-climate-disasters-historic-year (accessed February 27, 2019).

28   Jeff Stein, "U.S. Military Budget Inches Closer to $1 Trillion Mark, as Concerns over Federal Deficit Grow," *Washington Post,* June 19, 2018, https://www.washingtonpost.com/news/wonk/wp/2018/06/19/u-s-military-budget-inches-closer-to-1-trillion-mark-as-concerns-over-federal-deficit-grow/?utm_term=.1f2b242af129 (accessed February 27, 2019).

29   Congressional Budget Office, "Weapon Systems," https://www.cbo.gov/topics/defense-and-national-security/weapon-systems (accessed February 27, 2019).

30   "U.S. Defense Spending Compared to Other Countries," Peter G. Peterson Foundation, May 7, 2018, https://www.pgpf.org/chart-archive/0053_defense-comparison (accessed March 27, 2019).

31   Dana Nuccitelli, "America Spends over $20bn per Year on Fossil Fuel Subsidies. Abolish Them," *The Guardian,* July 30, 2018, https://www.theguardian.com/environment/climate-consensus-97-per-cent/2018/jul/30/america-spends-over-20bn-per-year-on-fossil-fuel-subsidies-abolish-them (accessed May 13, 2019); Janet Redman, *Dirty Energy Dominance: Dependent on Denial,* Oil Change International, October 2017, http://priceofoil.org/content/uploads/2017/10/OCI_US-Fossil-Fuel-Subs-2015-16_Final_Oct2017.pdf (accessed May 14, 2019), 5.

32   Ingo Walter and Clive Lipshitz, "Public Pensions and Infrastructure: A Match Made in Heaven," *The Hill,* February 14, 2019, https://thehill.com/opinion/finance/430061-public-pensions-and-infrastructure-a-match-made-in-heaven (accessed March 27, 2019).

33   Green Bank Network, "Green Bank Network Impact Through July 2018," https://greenbanknetwork.org/gbn-impact/ (accessed April 19, 2019).

34   International Trade Union Confederation, *What Role for Pension Funds in Financing Climate Change Policies?* May 23, 2012, https://www.ituc-csi.org/what-role-for-pension-funds-in,12358 (accessed April 19, 2019).

35   Devashree Saha and Mark Muro, "Green Bank Bill Nods to States," Brookings blog *The Avenue,* May 20, 2014, https://www.brookings.edu/blog/the-avenue/2014/05/20/green-bank-bill-nods-to-states/ (accessed April 19, 2019). The text of the bill is at https://www.congress.gov/bill/113th-congress/house-bill/4522/text.

36   Coalition for Green Capital, "Example Green Banks," http://coalitionforgreencapital.com/green-banks/ (accessed April 19, 2019).

37   Chijioke Onyekwelu, "Will a National Green Bank Act Win Support?"

Clean Energy Finance Forum, July 18, 2017, https://www.cleanenergyf inanceforum.com/2017/07/18/will-national-green-bank-act-win-support (accessed April 19, 2019).

38 James Murray, "Green Bank Design Summit: Developing Nations Join Forces to Explore Green Bank Plans," *BusinessGreen*, March 18, 2019, https://www.businessgreen.com/bg/news/3072689/green-bank-design -summit-developing-nations-join-forces-to-explore-green-bank-plans (accessed April 19, 2019).

39 United Nations Industrial Development Organization (UNIDO), published November 29, 2011, YouTube video, https://www.youtube.com /watch?feature=player_embedded&v=wJYuMTKG8bc (accessed May 6, 2019).

40 PwC and GIAA, *Global Infrastructure Investment: The Role of Private Capital in the Delivery of Essential Assets and Services,* 2017, https:// www.pwc.com/gx/en/industries/assets/pwc-giia-global-infrastructure -investment-2017-web.pdf (accessed March 23, 2019), 5.

41 Caisse de dépôt et placement du Québec, "Construction of the Réseau express métropolitain Has Officially Started," news release, April 12, 2018, https://www.cdpq.com/en/news/pressreleases/construction-of-the -reseau-express-metropolitain-has-officially-started (accessed May 10, 2019).

42 Ingo Walter and Clive Lipshitz, "Public Pensions and Infrastructure: A Match Made in Heaven," *The Hill,* February 14, 2019, https://thehill.com /opinion/finance/430061-public-pensions-and-infrastructure-a-match -made-in-heaven (accessed May 13, 2019).

43 Attracta Mooney, "Pension Funds Crave More Infrastructure Projects," *Financial Times,* October 21, 2016, https://www.ft.com/content/a05fe960 -95ec-11e6-a1dc-bdf38d484582 (accessed February 27, 2019).

44 Ibid.

45 David Seltzer, "Potential New Federal Policy Tools to Encourage Pension Fund Investment in Public Infrastructure," lecture, National Conference on Public Employee Retirement Systems, San Francisco, September 11, 2017.

46 Maryland Energy Administration, *Guide to Energy Performance Contracting for Local Governments,* July 2014, https://energy.maryland.gov /Documents/FINALEPCAPLocalGovernmentEPCGuide071014.pdf (accessed March 22, 2019).

47 Hawaii State Energy Office, "Pros & Cons of Guaranteed Energy Savings vs. Shared Savings Performance Contracts," fact sheet, February 2013, https://energy.hawaii.gov/wp-content/uploads/2012/06/Pros-and-Cons -of-guaranteed-vs.-shared-energy-savings-2013.pdf (accessed March 23, 2019).

48 "Study: Climate Change Damages U.S. Economy, Increases Inequality," *Rutgers Today,* June 29, 2017, https://news.rutgers.edu/news/study

-climate-change-damages-us-economy-increases-inequality/20170628#
.XNxoVbh7l-U (accessed May 15, 2019).

49 Tom Machinchick and Benjamin Freas, *Navigant Research Leaderboard: ESCOs: Assessment of Strategy and Execution for 14 Energy Service Companies*, Navigant Research, 2017, 11.

CHAPTER 7

1   European Commission, *Communication from the Commission to the European Parliament, the European Council, the Council, the European Economic and Social Committee, the Committee of the Regions, and the European Investment Bank: A Clean Planet for All—A European Strategic Long-Term Vision for a Prosperous, Modern, Competitive, and Climate Neutral Economy*, November 28, 2018, 5.

2   "7th European Summit of Regions and Cities," European Committee of the Regions, July 8–9, 2016, https://cor.europa.eu/en/events/Pages /7th-European-Summit-of-Regions-and-Cities.aspx (accessed April 4, 2019).

3   Jeremy Rifkin, "A History of the Future—The World in 2025," lecture, European Central Bank, Frankfurt, January 31, 2019, https://www .youtube.com/watch?v=TUVeg-x9Za4&t=1s (accessed March 24, 2019).

4   "Investing in Europe: Building a Coalition of Smart Cities & Regions," European Committee of the Regions, https://cor.europa.eu/de/events /Pages/Investing-in-Europe-building-a-coalition-of-smart-cities -regions.aspx (accessed March 1, 2019).

5   European Commission, "The Commission Calls for a Climate Neutral Europe by 2050," news release, November 28, 2018, https://ec.europa.eu /clima/news/commission-calls-climate-neutral-europe-2050_en (accessed February 27, 2019).

6   European Commission, *Communication from the Commission*, 4.

7   Ibid., 5.

8   Ibid.

9   Jeremy Rifkin, *The Empathic Civilization* (New York: Tarcher/Penguin, 2009).

10 European Commission Directorate-General for Trade, "Countries and Regions: China," last modified April 16, 2018, http://ec.europa.eu/trade /policy/countries-and-regions/countries/china/ (accessed February 27, 2019).

11 State Council of the People's Republic of China, "Chronology of China's Belt and Road Initiative," http://english.gov.cn/news/top_news/2015/04 /20/content_281475092566326.htm (accessed March 1, 2019).

12 Pan Xiang-chao, "Research on Xi Jinping's Thought of Ecological Civilization and Environment Sustainable Development," *IOP Conf. Series: Earth and Environmental Science* 153, no. 5 (2018), doi:10.1088/1755-1315/153/6/062067.

13 European Commission, *Joint Communication to the European Parliament, the Council of the European Economic and Social Committee, the Committee of the Regions and the European Investment Bank: Connecting Europe and Asia—Building Blocks for an EU Strategy*, September 19, 2018.

14 "MEP Issues the Guidance on Promoting Green Belt and Road with Three Line Ministries," Belt and Road Portal, May 8, 2017, accessed February 27, 2019, https://eng.yidaiyilu.gov.cn/qwyw/rdxw/12484.htm; Belt and Road Portal, "Guidance on Promoting Green Belt and Road," May 8, 2017, http://eng.yidaiyilu.gov.cn/zchj/qwfb/12479.htm (accessed February 27, 2019).

15 Long Yongtu, *Digital Silk Road: The Opportunities and Challenges to Develop a Digital Economy Along the Belt and Road* (Beijing: Post & Telecom Press, 2017), 1–8; Morgan Stanley, "Inside China's Plan to Create a Modern Silk Road," March 14, 2018, https://www.morganstanley.com/ideas/china-belt-and-road (accessed March 1, 2019).

16 Arman Aghahosseini et al., "Analysing the Feasibility of Powering the Americas with Renewable Energy and Inter-Regional Grid Interconnections by 2030," *Renewable and Sustainable Energy Reviews* 105 (2019): 187–204, doi:10.1016/j.rser.2019.01.046.

17 Arturs Purvin et al., "Submarine Power Cable Between Europe and North America: A Techno-economic Analysis," *Journal of Cleaner Production* 186 (2018): 131–45, doi:10.1016/j.jclepro.2018.03.095.

18 Kerstine Appun, Felix Bieler, and Julian Wettengel, "Germany's Energy Consumption and Power Mix in Charts," *Clean Energy Wire*, February 6, 2019; Rob Smith, "This Is How People in Europe Are Helping Lead the Energy Charge," World Economic Forum, April 25, 2018, https://www.weforum.org/agenda/2018/04/how-europe-s-energy-citizens-are-leading-the-way-to-100-renewable-power/ (accessed March 5, 2019).

19 Edith Bayer, *Report on the German Power System, Version 1.2*, ed. Mara Marthe Kleine, commissioned by Agora Energiewende, 2015, 9.

20 "State Renewable Portfolio Standards and Goals," National Conference of State Legislatures, February 1, 2019, http://www.ncsl.org/research/energy/renewable-portfolio-standards.aspx (accessed March 27, 2019).

21 Brad Plummer, "A 'Green New Deal' Is Far from Reality, but Climate Action Is Picking Up in the States," *New York Times*, February 8, 2019, https://www.nytimes.com/2019/02/08/climate/states-global-warming.html (accessed March 27, 2019).

22 Ibid.

23 Tom Machinchick and Benjamin Freas, *Navigant Research Leaderboard: ESCOs: Assessment of Strategy and Execution for 14 Energy Services Companies*, Navigant Research, 2017, 7.

24 TIR Consulting Group, "Office of Jeremy Rifkin," https://www.foet.org
    /about/tir-consulting-group/ (accessed February 19, 2019).
25 "'The New Abnormal': Gov. Brown Warns of 'Changed World' as Fires
    Ravage California," CBS Los Angeles, November 11, 2018, https://
    losangeles.cbslocal.com/2018/11/11/gov-brown-abnormal-fire/ (accessed
    February 19, 2019).

INDEX

JEREMY RIFKIN, one of the most popular social thinkers of our time, is the bestselling author of twenty books, including *The Zero Marginal Cost Society* and *The Third Industrial Revolution*. His books have been translated into more than thirty-five languages. Rifkin is an advisor to the European Union, the People's Republic of China, and heads of state around the world. He has taught at the Wharton School's Executive Education Program at the University of Pennsylvania since 1995 and is the president of the Foundation on Economic Trends in Washington, DC.